The Magic Presence

THE MAGIC PRESENCE

"I AM" RELIGIOUS ACTIVITY
OF THE
SAINT GERMAIN FOUNDATION

The "I AM" Religious Activity represents the Original, Permanent, and Highest Source of the Ascended Masters' Instruction on the Great Laws of Life, as first offered to the Western World by the Ascended Master Saint Germain through His Accredited Messengers, Mr. and Mrs. Guy W. Ballard.

In the early 1930's, the Ballards established the Saint Germain Foundation and Saint Germain Press, Inc., which under Saint Germain's Guidance have expanded into worldwide organizations that offer to mankind the True Ascended Master Teachings on the Great Cosmic Words, "I AM"! The Saint Germain Foundation strives to keep this "I AM" Ascended Master Instruction in Its pure, unadulterated form, free from any human interpretation, personal monetary gain, or any proselytizing, as It is a Gift from the Great Ascended Masters and Cosmic Beings to bring Illumination and Perfection to mankind.

Hundreds of "I AM" Sanctuaries and "I AM" Temples exist throughout the world, where the Teachings are applied in "I AM" Decree Groups. The Books of the Saint Germain Series are available through the Saint Germain Press, Inc., and in many libraries and bookstores. For further information please contact:

SAINT GERMAIN FOUNDATION
SAINT GERMAIN PRESS, INC.
1120 Stonehedge Drive
Schaumburg, Illinois 60194

(708) 882-7400   (800) 662-2800

THE MAGIC PRESENCE

BY
GODFRE RAY KING

SAINT GERMAIN PRESS, INC.

• • •

TRADEMARKS AND SERVICE MARKS OF THE SAINT GERMAIN FOUN-
DATION INCLUDE THE FOLLOWING:

Ascended Masters' Instruction of the "Mighty I AM Presence,"ᴿᴹ The Ascended
Masters' Instruction,ˢᴹ "Beloved Mighty I AM Presence,"® Daughters of Light,®
Honor Cross,™ Honor Cross Design,ˢᴹ "I AM"ˢᴹ "I AM" Activity,®
"I AM" Angels of Light,® "I AM" Ascended Master Youth,ˢᴹ "I AM"
COME!® "I AM" Emblem,® "I AM" Music of the Spheres,® "I AM" Reading
Room,ˢᴹ "I AM" Religious Activity,ˢᴹ "I AM" Religious Broadcast,ˢᴹ "I AM"
Sanctuary,ˢᴹ "I AM" School,ˢᴹ "I AM" Student Body,® "I AM" Study
Groups,ˢᴹ "I AM" Temple,ˢᴹ "I AM," Violet Flame,ˢᴹ The Magic Presence,®
"Mighty I AM Presence," ® Minute Men of Saint Germain,® Music of the
Spheres,® Saint Germain,ˢᴹ Saint Germain Foundation,® Saint Germain Pan-
try,ˢᴹ Saint Germain Press, Inc.® Saint Germain Restaurant,ˢᴹ Shasta
Springs,® Unfed Flame Design,® Violet Consuming Flame,® Violet Flame,® "Voice
of the I AM" ®

Library of Congress Cataloging-in-Publication Data
King, Godfré Ray, 1878-1939.
    The magic presence / by Godfré Ray King. — 5th ed.
        p. cm. — (Saint Germain series : v. 2)
    1. I AM Religious Activity.   I. Title   II. Series.
BP605.Il8K56   1982
299' .93 — dc19   84-50382

ISBN 1-878891-07-3

DEDICATION

THIS Series of Books is dedicated in Deepest Eternal Love and Gratitude to our Beloved Ascended Masters, Saint Germain, Jesus, Nada, the Great Divine Director, our Beloved Ascended Messenger Guy W. Ballard, The Great White Brotherhood, The Brotherhood of the Royal Teton, The Brotherhood of Mount Shasta, the Great Ascended Masters from Venus, the Great Cosmic Beings, the Great Angelic Host, the Great Cosmic Light, and those other Ascended Masters whose Loving Help has been direct and without limit.

TRIBUTE

THE hour is at hand when the humanity of this Earth must give more recognition to the Activity of the Great Ascended Masters and Angelic Host who are constantly pouring out Their Transcendent Light and Assistance to mankind. There must come more conscious cooperation between the outer physical life of humanity and these Great Beings who are the Protectors and Teachers of the human beings in this world.

There is a Special Group of these Great Ones working at the present time with America to stabilize and protect Her. Among Them, the Ascended Masters Saint Germain, Jesus, Nada, Cha Ara, Lanto, Cyclopea, the Great Master from Venus, Arcturus, the Lords of the Flame from Venus, and one known as the Great Divine Director are working here very definitely by establishing Tremendous Pillars and Rays of Light in America. They are also focusing Great Outpourings of Light at certain other points on the Earth.

They pour out Their Rays of Light through the consciousness of all individuals who will accept Them, harmonize their feeling, and turn their attention unto the "Mighty I AM Presence." If the people will acknowledge this Great Host of Perfected Beings and call Their Ascended Master Consciousness into the Hearts and minds of mankind, They can give Assistance and Protection without limit to those who make the Call, and through them, reach the rest of humanity.

Only the Ascended Master Consciousness, which is the "Mighty I AM Presence," can ever reestablish order and security upon this Earth. Only Its Consuming Flame of Divine Love can ever dissolve the fear in the feeling of the people. Only as the individual turns his attention to these Great Ascended Masters and asks Their Blessing upon the rest of mankind is the connection made and the Door opened by which Their Help can come through, releasing Its Perfection unto humanity and the Earth itself.

The Ascended Master always points each one to two things: first, the individual must look unto his own Divinity, God, the "Mighty I AM Presence," for all good, keeping his attention upon It and giving It his *first and greatest Love;* second, he must harmonize his feeling by pouring out Divine Love as a FORCE to bless everywhere. To the person who will do so, these Great Beings will give Assistance without limit, for They work only and always through the Divine Self of the individual.

The Beloved Ascended Master Saint Germain is the Emissary from The Great White Brotherhood who of His own Volition and Great Love is doing certain Protective Work and bringing certain Illumination into America at the present time. He speaks of Her often as "The Jewel of My Heart—for whom I have labored for centuries." Beloved Jesus has offered to give a Special Service in connection with Beloved Saint Germain and has said: "These Rays of Light which We pour out are very Real, Tangible Currents of Energy, containing within Them all good things, and blessing you according to your acceptance."

As in the days of old and in all Golden Ages, these Great Perfected Beings who have attained the "Victory" through human embodiment, will walk and talk face to face with mankind upon Earth. They will explain the Original Divine Way of Life once again, that human concepts may be cleared and Eternal Truth be revealed.

This Book carries the definite Radiation of the Ascended Masters who are working for America at this time, and is charged with Beloved Saint Germain's Ascended Master Consciousness of Freedom and Victory in the Light.

Human fears and limitations shall be cut away; the Earth shall be set into Divine Order once again, and filled full to overflowing with "The Light of God that never fails."

GODFRE RAY KING

FOREWORD

THIS Book contains the second group of Experiences which I was privileged to have through the Love and Assistance of the Beloved Ascended Master Saint Germain.

In the first Book, *Unveiled Mysteries,* He revealed many, many things which have been held in secret and sacredly guarded for many centuries.

In *The Magic Presence* my Experiences were the results of applying the Knowledge He had previously revealed.

In the various Retreats of The Great White Brotherhood which we visited, I was shown the Tremendous Work They do for mankind through Their Messengers who are sent into the outer world. The good They constantly pour out to this Earth and its humanity is beyond any power of words to describe.

All They accomplish is done through Divine Love, for They never use a destructive force at any time and never intrude upon the Free Will of the individual. Those who are Their representatives give everything as a glad free service of Love, and know no such thing as failure.

The purpose of this Book is to reveal to the individual the whereabouts of his own Divine Self,

God, the "Mighty I AM Presence," that all who
desire may return to their Source, receive their
Eternal Inheritance, and feel once again their Divine
Self Respect.

If the student or reader of this Book will feel
himself going through these same experiences, asking the Ascended Masters to illumine his consciousness by the Light of the Cosmic Christ, he will receive
that Outpouring of Love which is the Open Door to
all good things, and which sets mankind free.

America is blest beyond any other part of the Earth,
and because of Her Great Blessing, She must pour out
Great Light. She is the "Cup" through which The
Great White Brotherhood can ever expand the Great
Divine Love of the Universe and set mankind Free.
For that reason, Their Work in America is of *very
great importance;* and if it be necessary for Her Protection, then "that 'Light as of a Thousand Suns' shall
descend and consume all selfishness from the Earth."

The Truth, Explanation of Law, and my Experiences given in this Book are real, true, and eternal.
The Retreats, people, and instruments I saw and
associated with while with the Ascended Masters are
real, physical places and things, and Tangible, Living, Breathing Beings. They were not imaginary nor
symbolic and are not to be interpreted in any such
way.

The Truth of everything in this Book is for the

reader to accept or reject as he chooses. If he does not accept or agree with it, that does not remove the Truth or Its Activity from the Universe; but if he can accept the Truth herein contained, he can only be blest thereby, and his world will be a greater and more wonderful place in which to live.

The Great Ascended Master Saint Germain has told us that the Books of the Saint Germain Series in the Ascended Masters' Octave of Light are bound in Covers of Jewels. May we also value and obey the Words of the Ascended Masters contained herein, and become Their Great Love, Victory, Perfection, Illumination and Freedom to all Life forever.

If the student or reader can feel the Great Rays of Light and Love poured out by these Ascended Masters, and can live constantly in adoration to his own "Mighty I AM Presence, " he will positively become the Full Manifestation of Perfection, and will have his Eternal Freedom from the limitations of Earth.

May the Great Love, Light and Happiness of the Ascended Masters flood the Being and world of everyone who reads this Book! May It forever be a Blazing Golden Sun illumining the way to Peace, Prosperity and Freedom, until everyone becomes a Great Heart of ever-expanding Perfection, and experiences the Full Victory of his Ascension. In the Eternal Service of "The Light of God that never fails,"

GODFRE RAY KING

THE MAGIC PRESENCE
BY CHANERA

"I AM" the Presence, the Eternal One,
"I AM" the God-Source—the Great Central Sun;
"I AM" the Love-Breath, the Heartbeat of Light,
"I AM" the Power in Wisdom and Might.
"I AM" the Seer, the All-Seeing Eye,
"I AM" the sunlight, the earth, and the sky;
"I AM" the mountain, the ocean, the stream,
"I AM" the quiver in morning's bright gleam.
"I AM" the Blessing in Angels and Love,
"I AM" the Life, flowing in, 'round, above;
"I AM" the Glory all had once in Me,
"I AM" the Light Rays that set mankind Free!
"I AM" the One Heart that hears every Call,
"I AM" the Legion of Light answering all;
"I AM" the Scepter of Light's Loving Power,
"I AM" the Master, each moment, each hour.
"I AM" the Spheres, every song that they sing,
"I AM" the Heart of Creation—Its swing;
"I AM" all forms, never two quite the same,
"I AM" the Essence, the Will, and the Flame!
"I AM" Myself, all Beings, and You;
"I AM"—"The Magic Presence"—the God-Self
    come through!

CONTENTS

THE MAGIC PRESENCE

BY GODFRE RAY KING

CHAPTER I

A Strange Occurrence

I LEFT you, my reader, at the end of *Unveiled Mysteries,* with the Great Ascended Master Lanto sending forth His Blessing to America and mankind from the Retreat in the Royal Teton. In this book I shall describe another group of important and wonderful experiences which I was privileged to have during those months of association with our Beloved Ascended Master Saint Germain.

I received a Message from Him one morning, enclosing a letter of introduction to a Mr. Daniel Rayborn at the Brown Palace Hotel in Denver. The next day as I entered the hotel to inquire for him, I met an old friend, Mr. Gaylord, whom I had known for years. He was accompanied by an elderly gentleman whom he presented at once, and who, to my surprise, proved to be Mr. Rayborn. I gave him the letter of introduction, and after a few moments chat, we agreed to have dinner together that evening. The next day found us all en route to the Diamond K Ranch in Wyoming, one of the Rayborn mining properties where the Experiences described in this Book began. Little did I realize that day what my association with him would mean, and to what it would lead later. Such Experiences make one realize how Perfect the Great, Wise, All-Pervading Intelligence is that directs us unerringly to persons, places, and conditions when and where they are most needed.

My impression of Rayborn was very pleasant, for his whole attitude was one of harmony and kindliness, and at the same time I felt that he was a man of strong character with a keen sense of honor. He had a finely-shaped head, classic features, iron gray hair, and clear, piercing blue-gray eyes. He stood very erect and was fully six feet two inches in height. He had a son eighteen and a daughter sixteen years old who had just returned from school in the East.

We reached our destination, where the children met us at the train. After chatting a moment, we entered the Rayborn car and were driven to the ranch, a distance of about twenty miles. The son, Rex, was a tall, splendid, good-looking young chap with the same classic features as his father whom he resembled strongly. He was at least six feet one inch in height with abundant, light brown, wavy hair, and piercing violet-blue eyes. The daughter, Nada, was strikingly beautiful with a strange sort of old-world dignity and grace. She was about five feet seven, slight of build, with hair like her brother's, and deep blue eyes. There was a certain charm about all three Rayborns which everyone felt immediately.

The wonderful location and beauty of the house and grounds enchanted us, for it lay at the entrance to a narrow valley extending westward into the embrace of the Great Rockies. To the north, a towering peak rose to a height of over eight thousand feet. The house, facing south, was built of blue-gray granite, making one think of the turreted castles of medieval times in Europe and the ancient buildings of the Far East. The grounds immediately surrounding it were beautifully laid out and perfectly maintained. The building itself was large and rectangular in shape with a tower on each corner— the one at the southwest, facing the mountains, forming a large circular room on the third floor. The rest of the structure was only two stories high and had evidently been built for many, many years. Daniel Rayborn, at the time he was twenty, had inherited the entire estate from an uncle who traveled extensively, was deeply interested in Higher

Research Work, and had lived for many years in India and Arabia.

We entered the house, Rex showing me to a suite of rooms on the second floor at the southeast corner of the building. Dinner was soon announced, and we enjoyed a delicious meal and the beautifully appointed table. While dining we entered into the discussion of our plans.

During the course of our meal Mr. Rayborn spoke of expecting John Grey, the superintendent from his mines, to join us that evening. We had scarcely mentioned his name when he was announced. He stepped into the room, greeted the family pleasantly, and I was presented to him. As we shook hands, a cold chill passed over my body, accompanied by a feeling of repulsion. He was a fine-looking man of about forty, almost six feet tall, with piercing dark eyes which I noticed were never still. I saw his eyes follow the daughter very often with a peculiar look which the others did not seem to notice. Mr. Rayborn excused himself, and with the superintendent went into the library. The rest of us went into the music room and enjoyed two hours of delightful music, for both children had remarkable voices. It was during the discussion of their musical training that a shade of sadness passed over Nada's face. She remarked:

"We both inherited our voices from Mother, who

sang a great deal in opera, where Father first met her. My mother, in speaking of it, often said: 'We recognized in each other an Inner something that grew stronger and stronger as time went on. Later we learned we were "Twin Rays," which of course accounts for the many wonderful things that have happened to us since. We both have said many times that it seemed as if each had been searching for the other through the centuries; and of course, there has always been that very great Love and Perfect Understanding between us.'

"Mother's father was an Englishman, and her mother, who was educated in England, was the daughter of an Arab sheik. Two years ago Mother was taken ill and passed on within a few weeks— although everything possible was done to save her life. During the last four weeks she received Transcendent Revelations which have explained many things to us. Shortly after I was born, our Beloved Master Saint Germain came to her. He explained she had Work to do on the Higher Planes of Life, and that He would always hold Rex and me in His Great Loving, Protecting Care. He is so wonderful and loving to us that I wish we might share our Joy with the whole world. The East and Far East—that is, India, China, Arabia, Egypt, and Persia—give much greater recognition to and understand much more clearly what the Great Ascended Masters have done for humanity and how much the entire race of our Earth owes to Their Transcendent Love and far-reaching Care.

"He has taught us so plainly the Way by which these Great Ones have been able to raise and illumine the physical body by purifying it through the use of the Consuming Flame of Their own Divinity, which He calls the 'Mighty I AM Presence.' He tells us this can only be accomplished by Adoration to that 'Presence' and *complete obedience* of the personality, or outer consciousness, *to Its every Direction!* He says the secret is to keep in constant Inner Communion with the 'I AM Presence' at all times (through the feeling), so the Perfection which It is ever pouring forth can come through the outer consciousness without being distorted by our own inharmony or that of the physical world around us.

"It is in this way, Beloved Saint Germain explained, the Ascended Masters have reached Complete Dominion over all manifestation and have finished the work in human embodiment which Beloved Jesus said everyone must sometime do. They express—forever—Full Mastery over all conditions on this physical Earth; for all substance and energy are Their willing and obedient servants, even to the Elements and Powers of Nature, because They have become the Fullness of Divine Love.

Their entire Work with mankind is to lead everyone eventually to this same Mastery, but It can only come through the Self-effort of the individual and the fullness of enough Love.

"Mother had many strange experiences in her childhood, and my grandmother told her of others still stranger, for her grandfather had seen many of the remarkable things which these Great Ones do. One whom he knew quite well was from my grandmother's own land of Arabia. He was greatly adored by all He contacted, as His entire Life was a constant Blessing and Service to mankind.

"Beloved Saint Germain first came to Mother one night at the beginning of her career in grand opera. She had been singing only a few months when one evening she became almost speechless with stage-fright. She was in her dressing room shortly before the performance when a frantic fear seized her, making her forget everything. Beloved Saint Germain stepped through in His Tangible Body, introduced Himself, and touched her forehead with the fingers of His right hand. Instantly all nervousness left, the memory of her part returned, and she was calm and at ease. That night her success was tremendous, and it continued to increase, becoming brilliant beyond her fondest dreams.

"He told her she had earned the right to the Protecting Presence of the Ascended Masters, and from that time on, It would be permanent. He described the man she was to marry—also the son and daughter who were to come to her. After this He came at regular intervals and taught her many Inner Laws, which she was able to comprehend and apply with astonishing results—astonishing at least to those who are unable to use the Higher Law, but perfectly natural always to those who understand and manipulate those Laws through Love.

"Father, Beloved Saint Germain said, was not sufficiently awakened to be told of such Activities until about a year ago, when because of danger that threatened, Saint Germain came to him in the Tangible Body and explained that Father would come very near death at the hands of one whom he trusted as a friend, but to remain at peace, for the Ascended Masters would give the needed Protection."

We were all so engrossed in this conversation that I felt almost disappointed when Mr. Rayborn and the superintendent joined us. After listening to Nada and Rex sing an Arabian love song for their father, we all parted for the night and went to our rooms. I was so thrilled because Beloved Saint Germain had come to Mrs. Rayborn that I had no desire for sleep. I began to feel there was a greater reason for my being in their home than I was outwardly aware of. I sat down in a comfortable chair and gave myself up to the contemplation of the Ascended Masters with deep gratitude to Them for the gracious welcome with which these blessed people had received me.

I must have dropped off to sleep, for I awakened with a start and thought I had heard someone calling me. I felt such an urge to get up and go out into the open air that I could not resist it. I was thoroughly awake and keenly expectant of something, but what, I knew not. I went downstairs, out of the house, and down a path near a large barn. In a moment, there was a movement among the shadows, and following a sudden impulse, I stepped behind a tree. At the same instant, a man came out of the barn. I saw another movement among the trees and, looking closer, discerned a man standing with a rifle to his shoulder, dimly visible in the darkness. As he took aim at the man coming out of the barn, I wanted to call out a warning, but I could not make a sound. Before I could think, a blinding flash of light struck the man with the rifle full in the face, revealing his features as he fell face forward as if struck by lightning—yet the sky was crystal clear. Still I was unable to move from my position, and the man from the barn came steadily on, totally unaware of his escape. I saw it was Mr. Rayborn, though he did not see me, so I remained where I was until he had passed into the house, and I hurried to the spot where I had seen the man fall—but he had fled. I searched around for some distance but found no trace of him, so I returned to my rooms. It was then almost one o'clock. I got into bed quickly and by a strong effort was able to go to sleep.

When I went down to breakfast the next morning, all were radiantly happy except Grey, the superintendent, who seemed nervous and extremely pale. The Rayborns, Gaylord, and I had a most enjoyable time planning our day, which ended with the children suggesting that we go to Table Mountain, one of their favorite haunts in the Wyoming Rockies.

Meanwhile, Grey was almost sullenly silent, refusing to meet the eyes of anyone. He finished breakfast, excused himself, and drove to the station. When he was gone, my first impulse was to tell Rayborn of the previous night's experience, but upon second thought decided to wait until I could see him alone.

I excused myself, prepared for our trip up the mountain, and returned just in time to see the groom bringing out our horses. One of them was a beautiful Arabian steed, cream in color, with white mane and tail—the most wonderful animal I have ever seen. He came directly up to Nada, to whom he belonged, and with a look in his eyes that was almost of human intelligence, stood proudly before her waiting for the lumps of sugar she held out. She loved him and he knew it. "This is Pegasus," she said, patting him. He reached out, put his nose against my face, went over to Rex, and then back to Nada as if giving consent to my being a member of the party.

"He approves of you and accepts you as a trusted friend," Nada commented after watching his expression a moment. "That is a new behavior for him, as he has never made friends with anyone but Rex, the groom, and myself."

"Where did you get him?" I asked.

"He was given to Mother," she replied, "by an Arab sheik in appreciation for a concert she gave in Cairo. He was sent here to the ranch as a surprise when she returned from her last tour. It was really the last concert of her career, and her success was tremendous. The old sheik loved music, and enjoyed that concert especially.

"Pegasus is handsome, isn't he?" she continued. The Love in Nada's voice was unmistakable and justifiable, for no one could help but admire the beautiful creature. We mounted our horses, waved good-by to Rayborn, cantered off across the valley and soon entered the mountain trail. It wound steadily upward through the beautiful timber.

Occasionally we came into a clearing and stopped to enjoy the magnificent view. We followed the mountain stream for quite a distance. The song of the birds, the fragrance of the flowers, and the exhilaration of the rarefied air made us feel radiantly strong and glad to be alive.

We reached the top of the mountain near noon, and there before us lay a level space covering at least twenty acres, a veritable plateau suspended in the midst of those towering giants. A cozy little cabin and a shelter for the horses had been built. It was made of stone with a built-in stove—very unique and serviceable. We enjoyed the beauty of the surrounding country for a while and then sat down to a delightful lunch.

"You know," Rex commented, "I feel as if we had all known each other for ages"; and Nada and I admitted we felt the same. "Let's go to the cave by the other trail as soon as we finish lunch," he suggested, and we agreed. By crossing over to the opposite side of the mountain, we found a good trail leading down where the scenery was more wild and rugged. In some places the rocks looked as if they had been stained green, blue, and black by some marvelous mineral coloring. The sunlight and shadow played upon them as we changed our position, producing the effect of a beautiful, inspiring panorama. We continued down the trail about four thousand feet, turned sharply, and came to the eastern face of the mountain.

Thousands of years ago a portion of it had evidently split away, making the whole side a sheer cliff at least a thousand feet above us. The trail we were on wound around the south side, turning toward the eastern wall and running along a shelf-like projection that brought us to the entrance of the cave. The trail was strewn with great boulders that made it rough and difficult of access. A wing of rock hid the entrance as if Nature jealously guarded Her secrets from curious eyes. We left the horses tied safely nearby, and Rex took three powerful flashlights from his saddlebag.

"Prepare for a surprise," he exclaimed, turning to me, and then led the way into the cave. About fifty feet from the opening we entered a medium-sized cavern. As soon as my eyes became adjusted to the change of light, I saw the entire ceiling was covered with a pink and white crystalline substance. We crossed the first space, a distance of about thirty feet, and passed through an archway leading into an immense vaulted chamber at least two hundred feet across.

The ceiling was covered with rainbow-colored stalactites in the most amazing forms I have ever seen. There were crosses, circles, crosses within circles, triangles, and many, many occult symbols that have been in use on this Earth since its very beginning. It looked as if these symbols had been suspended from the ceiling ages ago and Nature had covered them with a carbonate of lime formation, highly colored and most artistically decorated by Her pigments. The beauty of it made one speechless, fascinated with wonder and admiration. It gave one the feeling of eyes watching every moment.

Rex called to us to come to the far side of the chamber where he stood. We crossed the intervening space and stood before a wall upon which there were three arches about twenty feet apart. Within each was a highly polished surface. The first one to my left was a Chinese red, the second a glittering white, and the third a cobalt blue. Immediately I felt they were significant of something concerning America. The feeling grew so great I could hardly stand it.

"This is the Work of a Mighty Intelligence in ages past," I said, "and I feel these arches close entrances to other chambers or passages beyond." Nada and Rex looked at me very steadily and their faces were white with the intensity of something they saw.

"What is the matter?" I asked.

"Don't you feel it—don't you see it?" they asked in return.

"What?" I replied. They then realized that I was

unaware of what they saw, and explained:

"You are evidently being overshadowed," said Nada, "by an etheric form you wore ages ago, for the garments are unlike anything of which I have ever seen or heard. The body is at least six feet eight inches tall, the hair is golden, coming almost to your shoulders, and the skin is fair and clear. I am sure some ancient memory is trying to come forth into the outer consciousness.

"Let's tell him of our experience the last time we were here," she suggested to Rex.

"Just a year ago," Rex explained, "we came to this Cave, and as I stood before the blue arch, I was so fascinated that I put out my hand and was running it over the surface when a Voice right out of the atmosphere said: 'Stop!' The Voice was not one of anger, but rather that of Supreme Authority. We left the Cave immediately and have never returned until now."

"Before I have ended my visit with you dear people, I feel certain some amazing explanation of it all will be given," I replied. We returned to our horses and found the beautiful Arabian Pegasus in a state of great agitation, for he was highly sensitive to the Spiritual Power focused within this mountain and it made him restless because of the intensity of the energy. Only by very great gentleness could Nada quiet him and prevent him from racing madly home. She said there seemed to be no limit to his speed when he became excited.

We continued on our way homeward, winding around the foot of the mountain until we came to the end of our descent; then we gave the horses free rein, and in half an hour reached the ranch just before sunset. Daniel Rayborn came out to meet us and said dinner would soon be ready. During the meal we related the experiences of the day, Rex telling his father of the overshadowing form seen above my head in the Cave. As he finished speaking, without giving any explanation, his father said he wanted to talk to all three of us in the library after dinner, and to meet him there at eight o'clock.

In the meantime we went to the music room, while Nada went to her mother's room and brought back an Arabian instrument something like an Hawaiian guitar. It was given to her by Beloved Saint Germain who taught her to play a certain melody upon it just before her meditation hour. Nada and Rex both sang and took turns playing the accompaniments on the instrument. It formed a most wonderful background for their voices, for there was something in the quality of the tone which seemed like a living thing that penetrated to the very Center of Existence.

CHAPTER II

Revelations

P ROMPTLY at eight o'clock we entered the library and found Daniel Rayborn had preceded us. He went straight to the matter in hand.

"At two o'clock today," he began, "I received information the men had made a rich strike at the mine in Colorado, and I have sent Grey on ahead. Day after tomorrow, I must join him. I would like all of you to come with me. Nada will be comfortable in the bungalow at the camp, and you two can stay with me in the mine.

"I have something else to tell you that is both grave and strange. At four o'clock this morning, I was awakened by a 'Presence' in my room, and when I became fully aroused, I saw it was our Beloved Saint Germain. He talked to me for at least two hours and, among other things, said that Grey had attempted to take my life last night. He saw the intent, and at the moment Grey tried to fire, Beloved Saint Germain directed a flash of Electronic Force which knocked him senseless for the time being. He has been warned that if he makes another such attempt, his own destructive motive will be permitted to react instantly and his own body will pay the penalty."

Then I told them of my experience the night of my arrival, and how I had witnessed the whole affair. Rayborn was deeply moved, and rising to his feet, he extended his hand to me saying: "You are surely one of us, and I am deeply, deeply grateful. Beloved Saint Germain said you had been brought into our home because you were greatly needed, and from now on you would act in the capacity of elder brother to Nada and Rex. It seems we have known each other in a number of previous embodiments. He also told me none of us was to be concerned in the least about danger of any kind, for we have lived clean lives and held close to High Ideals. This, it seems—from the Ascended Masters' standpoint—makes it possible to wield a Mighty Force for the Protection of all.

Beloved Saint Germain also instructed me regarding other things of importance. He explained to me the Activity one experiences after he has made the Ascension. Beloved Jesus gave the public an Example of This and sought to teach mankind Its Meaning, pointing everyone to that same Attainment. I am, before long, to enter this Great Freedom. Our Beloved Master made it very clear, one is sometimes raised into this

Condition previous to or near the change called death, but all must accomplish It from the physical side of life. If the Silver Cord of Light flowing into the body has been withdrawn, it is impossible to illumine and raise that body; and the one thus striving must re-embody once more in order to attain the Final Freedom from the physical side of human experience. All Ascensions must take place consciously, for this Ascended Master Attainment is the Complete Victory over all outer experiences through the personal self. I shall read you His own Words which I took down at His Direction." Turning to a portfolio which lay upon his desk, he opened it and read:

" 'So-called death is but an opportunity for rest and reattunement of the faculties of the personal consciousness. This is to free them from the turmoil and discords of Earth long enough to receive an Inflow of Light and Strength which will enable the outer activity of the mind to take up the work of physical experience again. Physical embodiment is for the purpose of preparing, perfecting, and illumining a body whose vibratory action can be raised to *blend with* the Body of the "Mighty I AM Presence." We call It "The Magic Presence." Beloved Jesus referred to It as the Seamless Garment.

" 'In this Body, which is made of Pure Electronic Substance, the individual has complete Freedom from all limitation, and through intense devotion to the "Mighty I AM Presence," anyone can release Its Power to the point where he can see this Blazing Body of Substance—so Dazzling that at first one can only gaze upon It for an instant because of the Intensity of Its Light. Through such devotion one begins to manifest more and more of his own individual Conscious Dominion over all manifestation. This is everyone's Eternal Birthright and the purpose for which all decreed the journey through human experience.

" 'When the one striving for such Freedom has reached the point where he releases any amount of Light he desires from his Electronic Body instantly by his own conscious command, then he can control all manifestation, no matter in what sphere he may choose to express. One has but to observe the world at large to see what discord in thought and feeling does to the beautiful bodies that Nature provides for our experience in the physical part of Life. In childhood and youth, the flesh structure of the physical body is beautiful, strong, and responsive to the demands made upon it; but when discordant thoughts and feeling are allowed to express in the personal self over the years, as one goes through Life, the body becomes incapacitated and the Temple falls into ruins—because the outer waking consciousness does not obey the *One Law of Life*—

Love, Harmony, Peace!

" 'Call it what you will, the Eternal Truth remains that discord is another name for disintegration—a synonym for death. When mankind learns to live its Life by the *One Eternal Law of Love,* it will find that such obedience will have released it from the wheel of birth and rebirth, and hence the problems of human existence will have disappeared. In their place will come the Joy of ever expanding the Perfection which forever abides within Love. Constant new creation will ever go on, for *Life is Perpetual Motion* and neither slumbers nor sleeps, but is ever and forever a Self-Sustained Stream of Expanding Perfection in Joy, in Ecstasy, and Eternally New Design. This Perfect Activity and Joy of Life are all contained within Obedience to the *Law of Love.*

" 'The last enemy, death, will have disappeared, for it is but a means of release from a garment which no longer has anything of value to give for the use of the Perfection of Life. When the physical body is so incapacitated that the personality occupying it can no longer make Self-Conscious effort to express Perfection, then Nature herself takes a hand in things and dissolves the limitation, that the individual may have a new chance to make effort which is of benefit.

" 'Grief for the death of a loved one is selfishness

and but retards the greater good the loved one should be enjoying. Grief from a sense of loss is really rebellion against the Action of a Law that has seen fit to give another greater opportunity for rest and growth, because nothing in the Universe goes backward, and all—no matter what the temporary appearance—is moving forward to greater and greater Joy and Perfection. The God Consciousness in us cannot and does not grieve, and the human part should know that as no one can ever get out of this Universe, he must be somewhere better than the place he left. If there be Real, True Divine Love, It can never cease to exist, and *must* sometime, somewhere, draw us to that which we love. In True Divine Love there is no such thing as separation, and that which feels a sense of separation is not Love. The sense of separation is merely one of the mistakes of the personal self which it continues to dwell in because it does not understand the nature of Consciousness. Where the Consciousness is, there the individual is functioning, for the individual is his Consciousness.

" 'When one thinks of a loved one who has passed on, he is really with that loved one in his Higher Mental Body the moment his Consciousness is upon the other person. If the Western World could understand this Truth, it would lift the chains which cause such useless suffering. Such grief is all due to the fact that the personality—especially in the feeling—accepts the body as being the individual instead of knowing the body is only a garment which the individual wears. Over it everyone should have *complete* and *Eternal* Dominion and should exact Perfect Obedience at all times.

" 'If one really loves another, he wants that other one to be happy and harmonious. If, through so-called death, an individual chooses to accept a better opportunity for future expression—if there be the slightest spark of Love, one should have no grief nor desire to hold that loved one in a state of incapacity when he might go on to greater Ease and Freedom.

" 'It is the ignorance of this Truth which enables such selfishness to keep humanity bound in its self-created chains of limitation. This sort of igno-rance binds the Life Expression of the whole race and is a stubborn refusal to understand Life. It drags thousands of human beings every year into the depths of despair—wholly unnecessary and avoidable—when they could and should be enjoying happiness and living the way the "Mighty I AM Presence" intended them to live. Such an attitude toward Life not only prevents the accomplishment of everything worthwhile, but incapacitates the indi-vidual and fills him with self-pity—one of the most subtle and insidious ways by which the sinister force breaks down his resistance and makes him negative. The individual must remain positive if he is to attain his Victory and express Mastery. The sinister force which humanity on this Earth has generated uses this method to keep aspiring, marvelous individuals from gaining their Freedom and using the Full Power of Divinity which has been theirs from the beginning—the Gift of the Father to His children.

" 'Of all the faults humanity has generated, self-pity is the most inexcusable, because it is the apex of human selfishness. Through self-pity the attention of the personal consciousness, or outer self, is entirely absorbed by the petty, puny, human, useless desires of the physical body—and the Great, Glorious, Adorable, All-Wise, All-Powerful Light of the "Beloved Mighty I AM Presence" always abiding above the physical body, is entirely ignored; yet Its Energy is being used for this destructive purpose.

" 'Humanity cannot have anything better than it is experiencing today until it looks away from the little self long enough to acknowledge and feel the Presence of God, the "Mighty I AM Presence," the Source of every individual's Life and of all Perfect Manifestation.

" 'Grief is colossal selfishness—not Love! Discord is selfishness—not Love! Lethargy is selfishness

—not Love and not Life! These sink the race into slavery because they break down the resistance of the individual by wasting the Energy of Life which should be used for the creation of Beauty, Love and Perfection. This slavery continues because the outer activity of the personal consciousness does not make the necessary determined effort to free itself from the domination of the psychic world.

The psychic stratum contains only those creations of humanity generated by the discordant thoughts, feeling and words of the outer activity or personal consciousness. This means the daily activities of the mind, body and feeling with which the personality continues to entangle the creative expression of Life. The entire race has become so bound by its own discord that Great, Glorious, Transcendent Ascended Masters—out of sheer Compassion for the slowness of mankind's growth and the misery of its degradation—*offer to cut away the barnacles of the psychic plane and give humanity a new start!*

" 'People are entertained, fascinated, and self-hypnotized by the various conditions of the psychic world, but I tell you—and I know both the Inner and outer activities of Life from the Ascended Masters' standpoint—that there is nothing good nor permanent within the psychic stratum! It is as dangerous as quicksand, and just as undependable!

The psychic plane and the outer activity of the mental and emotional world, unless they report Perfection to you, are one and the same thing. It is entirely the creation of the human sense consciousness and is but the accumulation of human thoughts and forms energized by human feeling. It contains nothing whatsoever of Christ—the "Cosmic Light."

" 'The desire for and fascination of psychic phenomena is a feeling—a very subtle feeling—by which it holds the attention of the personality away from the acknowledgment, the constant adoration, the continual communion and the Permanent Acceptance of the individual's "Mighty I AM Presence." Attention to the activities of the psychic plane depletes the personal self of the energy and the ability required to reach to the God Source and anchor there permanently!

" 'I tell you Eternal Truth when I say that nothing of the Christ comes from the psychic realm, regardless of any seeming evidence to the contrary, because the psychic or outer activity of the mentality is forever changing its qualities, while the Christ, which is the Eternal Light, is Ever-Expanding Perfection—the One—Changelessly Supreme, Imperishable Quality.

" 'It is because of the attention to and the subtle fascination of the psychic plane that mankind is today as a mass of children needing much Help and the Wisdom of the Ascended Masters to raise it once more into the Understanding of the Light— which is the only means of Release from the darkness of Earth's present chaos.

" 'World Saviors have come at regular intervals to give this kind of Help throughout the centuries ever since the end of the Second Golden Age upon this Earth. Following that Activity, humanity became fascinated by the world of form and the creation of things. The individual's attention was held most of the time in the outer activities, and the Conscious Recognition of his own Individualized God Self was *forgotten.* Hence, the "Mighty I AM Presence" abiding in his Electronic Body was completely ignored. *Thus he has only been able to express part of his Life Plan.'*

"Beloved Saint Germain asked that you, my Brother," continued Mr. Rayborn, turning to me, "watch your feeling and impressions very closely while you are in and at the mine, for work of a certain nature is to be done there—now or never! He wishes to utilize a certain Cosmic Activity occurring at this time for reasons He did not give me. He said He would come again very soon and speak with us all. He will then endeavor to give further Light on the Cave of Symbols you visited recently and to which we shall all go with Him on His next Visit.

Grey will pass on very shortly from natural causes, and I am not to let him suspect that I know anything of his attempt on my Life."

The *Tales of the Arabian Nights* were hardly stranger than the Truths we were receiving and the wonderful things we were experiencing. It seemed as if we had entered another world where the activity of the mind became instantly manifest in physical form. Beloved Saint Germain had shown such conclusive evidence that He knew every incident and activity of our lives when He desired to do so, and even saw the innermost thoughts and intents of each of us. I felt a tremendous Uplift and a Happiness unspeakable.

At first Nada and Rex were inclined to be sad when they realized the parting with their father was to come so soon; but I knew positively they would be sustained by the One Great Presence of the "I AM" when the time came. I asked Nada and Rex as we passed out of the library if they would sing a song or two for their new brother, and they laughingly agreed. They sang "Love's Light Eternal," for which Nada had written the music and Rex the lyrics. The melody and power of it seemed to linger and continue to lift one's consciousness to the Great Creator of all things, the "Mighty I AM Presence." As we stood together when they had finished singing, I put my arms around both the children, led them over to their father, and we formed a circle about him.

"Beloved Brother," I said, "we encircle you with Hearts of Love, and may the Pathway of each be that of Supreme Happiness through the Radiant Power of Divine Love within us all." I told them how words failed utterly to express my joy and gratitude for their Love, friendship, and hospitality.

"My Brother," said Daniel Rayborn, "it is I who wish to express my gratitude to Beloved Saint Germain and you for the privilege of your friendship, that my beloved children may have you as a companion when I am elsewhere serving in my humble way. Let us rejoice in the happiness we can give each other. I think we had better get all the rest we can tonight and tomorrow, as we are driving to the mine in Colorado and we ought to leave early the following morning."

The next morning at breakfast, after a wonderful night's rest, Daniel Rayborn greeted us by saying that he had found a Message from Beloved Saint Germain on the table as he awakened, asking the four of us to meet in the Tower Room at eight o'clock that evening. Needless to say, we were all interest in a moment and joyous with the anticipation of His Coming.

At twenty minutes to eight, Daniel Rayborn announced it was time to go to the Tower Room for

our meeting, but somehow I felt temporarily restrained from doing it. When we came to the door,
he stood still before it a few moments as though in
meditation. Presently the door slowly opened without anyone touching it, and as we entered I saw it
was richly carpeted and handsomely furnished. In
the center of the gorgeous blue carpet was woven
the Secret, Sacred Symbol of Life where our Beloved Saint Germain produced the Life-giving and
Consuming Flame.

The walls were covered with a glistening white
material that looked like frosted silk. The chairs
were unlike anything I have ever seen. They were
made of some kind of white metal resembling
frosted silver, upholstered in silk plush of the same
rich blue as the carpet and so perfectly designed as
to give the body ease, poise and balance when
seated in them. There was a chair placed at each of
the four points of the compass, forming a square
within the circle of the room. The two windows and
the door locked from the inside. When all were
in readiness, Daniel Rayborn asked each of us
to close our eyes and remain perfectly calm and
silent until Beloved Saint Germain appeared
and spoke. In a few moments a deep, rich Voice
said:

"I bring you Greetings, My Beloved Students."

I opened my eyes and there was the Blessed,

Wonderful Presence of our Beloved Master. He stood fully six feet one inch in height, slender, royal and real. His hair was dark brown, wavy and abundant. His face portrayed a Beauty, Majesty and Power no words can describe—a face revealing Eternal Youth, with eyes of the deepest violet one can imagine through which the Wisdom of the Ages poured out upon the world expressing the Love and Mastery that are His.

He stepped across the room to where Nada sat, bowed, and touched her forehead with the thumb of His right hand, the fingers extending over the top of her head. He did the same thing to Rex, myself, and Daniel Rayborn. It is in this way that an Ascended Master can give a Radiation which does for the individual what nothing else can do. It is a tremendous aid in clearing the mind, for It releases certain Higher Activities from within the student's Inner Bodies while he is within the Master's Aura.

"Beloved Ones," He began, "this evening I have come to explain certain Laws that will enable you to manifest Dominion over human limitation, once you know and fully understand the Life Principle within your human body. Then you will know and feel It truly is All-Wise and All-Powerful. When you really comprehend this, you will see it is not only natural and possible, but eventually compulsory that you transcend all outer activity—its laws and its

limitations! These come into existence through ignorance and express in the outer activity because
the intellect is allowed to act without the Light from
within the Heart illumining it. Discord and limitation are imposed upon the outer activity by man and
man alone; for an All-Wise, All-Perfect, All-
Powerful, Supreme Creator does not and cannot
create a limitation, a lack or a discord.

"The concept that it is possible for All-Perfection
to create imperfection or anything unlike Itself is
absurd, vicious, and entirely untrue. The Supreme
Creator gives to the individual with Free Will the
Use of the Attributes of the Creator with which to
manipulate manifestation at his particular point in
the Universe. The individual is endowed with the
capacity to form conclusions through using the
intellect alone, which are the results of fragmentary
information. It comes about from using only a part
of the Creative Powers with which the individual is
endowed.

"Conclusions drawn from partial instead of complete information must of necessity bring about
unsatisfactory results. The individual must have
Free Will or he could not be a Creator. If he
chooses to experiment with the spoke instead of the
entire wheel, there is naught to say him nay in his
desire to experience those results.

"His wheel of manifestation cannot and is not

complete until he recognizes his 'Beloved Mighty I AM Presence,' for It is the *only* Source which knows all required to build any pattern of manifestation that produces Perfection for him.

"All Patterns of Perfection are stored within the All-Knowing, Fathomless, Dazzling Mind of the 'Beloved Mighty I AM Presence' and can never be made manifest in the physical world of mankind until the outer activity of the mind, which is the intellectual consciousness, is illumined by the Ray of Golden Light within the Heart. This Ray comes always and only from the Electronic Body of the individual. This is 'The Magic Presence'—'I AM.'

"This 'Beloved Mighty I AM Presence' of mankind's Being does not cognize and never can create the maze of confusion, chaos and destruction that exists in the outer mentality and world of humanity—any more than the Sun creates a cloud. It is the Birthright and Privilege of every individual to express the Fullness of this Glorious Inner Presence and Power of Perfection, but if the personal self will not call the Power of the 'Presence' into action through the Higher Mentality into the outer activity at all times, then all outer experience merely remains the ever-changing condition or dumping ground of the thoughts and feeling of other human beings surrounding it.

"The 'Presence of the Mighty I AM' abides

within the Electronic Body of every individual, resting from twelve to fifty feet or more above the physical body, and is occupied only with creating, expanding, and forever pouring out Perfection. It lives in Its own Realm, doing Creative Work at Cosmic Levels.

"Only in the outer activity of the human personality, which is but a fragmentary part of each one's individuality, can imperfection be generated and experienced. It is through the Higher Mentality that the Discriminative and Selective Intelligence acts. In this Body, the Individualized Intelligence can look upon the discord of human creation and observe the conditions by which the personality is surrounded and those it is passing through, but does not accept them into Its Consciousness or World. It sees what is required to produce Perfection in the physical experience and can reach into the Electronic Body—the individual's 'Beloved Mighty I AM Presence'—and draws forth that which produces Perfection in the outer activity.

"In transcending all earthly laws, We but claim our God-given Authority to live and act in Perfect Accord with the 'Beloved Mighty I AM Presence' of man and Infinity. This 'Presence' is Eternal, Changeless Perfection, yet forever expanding Itself through the individual. As you see, I come into your presence in a locked room with walls of solid stone. These seemingly impassable walls are no barrier nor obstruction to the 'Beloved Mighty I AM Presence,' anymore than they are to an electrical impulse. This 'Presence' is the Mighty Master Within, the God Self of every individual. When one acknowledges, accepts, understands, and feels this 'Beloved Mighty I AM Presence,' Its Limitless Powers are released into his use.

"This home and room were dedicated to the Ascended Masters of Love, Light and Wisdom at the time the tower was built, and it will continue to be a Focus for Their Activity as long as They desire to use it.

"When the shell, which means the discord of the outer self, is dissolved—not by passing through the change called death, but by consciously raising and illumining the body and its every activity by the 'Light' of the 'Beloved Mighty I AM Presence'—Its Power is released into the outer world through the individual, and he manifests *complete Mastery*, the Dominion as given him in the beginning by the Father.

"Through his consciousness, every human being can release the Limitless Power of the 'Beloved Mighty I AM Presence.' When one disciplines his outer faculties and makes them obedient to his Conscious Command of Perfection, he is then able to let this Tremendous Power flow through him unobstructed and to use It constructively. Within each of you is the same Mighty Power I am using! You can use It as I do when you acknowledge, accept, and admit at all times that the 'Beloved Mighty I AM Presence' is always in action. This is the Cosmic Christ, and the only Consciousness in the Universe which can say 'I AM.'

"The Thinking Flame of God is the only Activity of Life anywhere in manifestation which can acknowledge Its own Individualization, use the 'Creative Word of God,' and send It forth into the Universe to cause manifestation. Only the Son of God, which means the individual with Free Will, can decree as God decrees and say 'I AM.' Whatever quality follows that sound spoken into the ethers becomes a manifestation in the world of substance, and thus becomes a form.

"When the individual says 'I AM,' he is using the Creative Attribute of the Godhead and announcing Creation at his particular point in the Universe. The vibratory action of the Word 'I AM,' either in thought or spoken word, is the Release of the Power of Creation; and whatever quality follows that Decree is instantly imposed upon the electronic substance in the ethers. This being the only substance and energy in existence whose nature is to be qualified in some manner, it must outpicture the pattern within the Decree. If the Decree be always for Perfection, then the experiences in the individual's world express the Fullness of the Plan of Life; but if the individual does not send forth that Decree, it is impossible for that Perfection to outpicture in his experiences until the Decree is released into the ethers in which he lives.

"Every individual can think Perfection at every instant, if he only will, and it takes no more substance and energy to build Beautiful, Perfect Forms and Experiences than it does the imperfect; but if the individual wants this Perfection expressed in his own world, he *must* use his own energy to utter the Decree which will release that Perfection unto him. Such is the *Law of his Being,* and nothing can change It!

"Life is the only Presence, Intelligence, and Power that can act or ever did act. These three Activities within Life are coexistent everywhere! The Pure Electronic Light which fills Infinity is the Self-Luminous, Intelligent Substance of the 'Mighty I AM Presence,' existing at all points and of which all forms are composed. Discord and limitation can build a film, so to speak, around this Substance, shutting off at least to some degree the Radiance of its Light; but imperfection of any kind can never enter into the Electronic Substance itself. The discords and limitations that humanity has wound around itself are due to the activities of the intellect and the emotions, which have not been trained to look within the Light of the individual's own 'Mighty I AM Presence' for the Plan of Perfection upon which each one should construct all his outer activities.

"This Perfect Plan does not exist anywhere except within the 'Mighty I AM Presence.' When the intellect and emotions are purified and illumined by the Light of this Great 'Presence,' then the Perfect Ideas and Activities within It can flow through the personality without becoming distorted by the fragmentary information in the outer activity of the consciousness. The reports of the human sense consciousness are merely unillumined activities, for when Light is directed into them from the 'Mighty I AM Presence,' they melt into Its Glorious Perfection at once.

"Love, Peace, Balance, Order, and Perfect Activity, or the coordination of all outer activities with the Patterns of Perfection from the 'Presence,' can only be brought about by the One Great Light, the 'I AM.' There, and only There, does the Design of Perfection ever exist. If the student or individual will fix his attention with determined tenacity and hold it upon the 'Mighty I AM Presence,' he can release such Divine Love, Light, Wisdom, Power, Courage, and Activity as he cannot possibly comprehend at present.

"Divine Love contains the Perfect Activity of *every* Attribute of the Godhead. When the individual enters the *conscious path* of Self-Mastery, he should fully understand and realize that from then on, he is obligated to accomplish everything he attempts by the Power of Divine Love from within his own 'I AM Presence'! He must know unmistakably and remember at all times that Divine Love contains within It the Complete Wisdom and Almighty Power of the 'Beloved Mighty I AM Presence.'

"When an individual generates enough Divine Love and sends It forth into all outer activities, he may command what he will through the 'Mighty I AM Presence,' and his request is always fulfilled. He may go among the wild beasts of the jungle and no harm can come to him. Divine Love, when consciously generated within the individual, is an Invisible, Invincible, and Invulnerable Armor of Protection against all disturbing activity. There is only one thing that can bring about Perfection anywhere in the Universe, and that is enough Divine Love. Therefore, love your own 'Mighty I AM Presence' *intensely,* and nothing else can enter your Being or world!

"You four Beloved Ones have come to the point where the 'I AM Presence' commands the Assistance of the Ascended Masters. Therefore it will be My Great Pleasure to be of any help to you that may be required. Before I proceed further, I wish to convey the Great Love and Blessing from your beloved mother and companion. Soon you will have the Joy of seeing and greeting Her face to face, and never again will you be disturbed by the thought or change called death. It gives Me Great Joy to feel and see such wonderful harmony within your mental and emotional bodies.

"My Brother," He said, turning to me, "I welcome and bless you for so noble a nature, a sincere Heart, and such Great Love. You will soon become aware that you have much to do besides your writing." Turning to Nada and Rex, He addressed them:

"My Beloved Nada and Rex, I feel like both Father and Mother to you, although I cannot take the place of your earthly father who is so noble—so fine—and whose earthly pilgrimage is nearing its close. He may be with you many months yet. Please forget entirely that which you regard as separation and enter fully into the activities before you."

"I am more than pleased," He continued, turning to me, "to see in your Heart a great willingness to serve wherever that service is most needed. That attribute will bring you *Very Great Light.*" Including all, He continued:

"After your trip to the mine, I will impart to each of you certain Private Instructions that will greatly assist and hasten the awakening of certain Faculties whose use you will soon need, and through which I will be able to reach you much more easily. This will bring to you a clearness that bars all doubt.

"The superintendent at your mine," He said, speaking to Rayborn, "will retain his physical body only until He can say a few parting words to you. North of the tunnel where the last strike was made, which has been considered very good, there is a deposit immensely richer that has been passed. I will indicate the place when you reach the exact spot in the tunnel. You are to mark it," He directed, glancing toward me.

"There are those in touch with Grey which make it unwise to open this up until he is out of their reach. It will be much greater wisdom in the future to forbid any report going out of strikes made in the mine. This body of ore which shall be indicated to you contains over twenty million dollars in gold, clear and above all operating expenses.

"Little do those of humanity who are in great need realize how easily and quickly they could and would be given their *financial freedom* if they would but turn their attention to the 'Beloved Mighty I AM Presence,' *and hold it there with determined tenacity.* Great would be their reward for such effort.

"I will be present while you are in the mine, but not visible to your outer sight. This is the reestablishing of our former wonderful association. You will realize how beautiful it is when you become consciously aware of the Tremendous Power of the 'Mighty I AM Presence' within and above each of you. This Almighty Power you will draw forth and use without limit." He gave each a hearty handclasp and asked us to take the same position as before He came, saying we were all to meet again soon. When we opened our eyes a few moments later, He had disappeared—as quickly as He had come.

Nada and Rex said the experience was the most glorious of their lives and the happiest two hours they had ever spent thus far. Only a small part of such Transcendent Work can be conveyed in words to those who have not experienced these things; but all humanity may have the same opportunity when the individual is earnest, sincere, humble and unselfish enough in his desire for the Light, and really loves his own 'Mighty I AM Presence.'

It was so remarkable and uplifting to see the room brilliantly lighted by the Radiant Presence of Beloved Saint Germain, and it was conclusive proof that His 'Presence' was Its own Light. Each of us experienced such Peace and Love as we never dreamed were in existence. We could not refrain from embracing each other, and there were tears of joy in our eyes out of deep gratitude for such a Divine Privilege. We said good-night and went to our rooms, as we were to leave early the following morning for the mine. We left very early, driving nearly five hundred miles over a highway that was in splendid condition. The day was calm, bright and lovely—the scenic beauty gorgeous. We took turns at the wheel so no one was in the least tired, and at exactly seven o'clock in the evening we drove into camp. We noticed a great deal of activity and excitement. As soon as the men saw us, one of them came running to the car, saying excitedly, "Come! Come! Grey has been badly hurt in the mine. It happened while we were changing shifts."

Daniel Rayborn hurried away while Rex and I took Nada to the bungalow. The men took care of the luggage, and we hurried to the superintendent's quarters to which Grey had been carried. As we arrived, the room was being cleared of the men, as Grey wished to speak to Rayborn alone. We stepped in, greeted him, gave what encouragement we could, and then left the two alone.

Thirty minutes later, Rayborn came out. He was deeply moved because, as he afterward told us, the man had made a full confession, asked forgiveness, and passed on immediately. Beloved Saint Germain, referring to it later said: "The Soul withdrew from its temple of flesh when it realized that the human self could not withstand the temptation."

"In shooting the holes drilled by the day shift," Rayborn explained, "a large piece of rock became loosened; and as Grey was inspecting and sampling the day's work, the rock fell, striking him on the head. He dropped unconscious, and another piece fell upon his chest, crushing him so badly there was no hope of recovery.

"He remained conscious until I reached his side, and made a full confession concerning his attempt upon my life because he knew he could not live. I gladly and freely forgave all, that he might pass on in Freedom. His Soul can thus have its greatest opportunity for growth. His gratitude was unspeakable for the opportunity to free his conscience and be forgiven. His passing was really in very great peace."

We were all rather stunned by the suddenness and accuracy with which Beloved Saint Germain's statements were being fulfilled. At eleven o'clock the next morning a short service was held in camp, and the body then taken to the railway station, some three miles away. Bob Singleton accompanied it to San Francisco, where Grey's mother and brother lived. Mr. Rayborn sent them a check for twenty-five thousand dollars and paid all expenses.

In all my mining experience, I have never seen so

marvelous a camp of men as Rayborn employed. Everything possible had been done for their comfort and convenience, no intoxicating drinks of any kind ever being allowed. The location of the mine was deep in the heart of very rugged mountains, and all possible was done to maintain the utmost Harmony.

Nada and Rex used every opportunity to make me acquainted with the camp, and everywhere it was plainly evident that Rayborn was much loved by his men. The entire atmosphere was one of harmonious cooperation, and there was a total absence of all coarse or undesirable elements.

It was Rayborn's custom to pay every man a bonus of one dollar a day as long as any rich strike lasted. He made Bob Singleton superintendent, for he was a fine, noble, upright, honest chap with splendid ability. We spent a wonderful day going through the concentrating plant—from which only the concentrates were shipped to the smelter. Most of the richer gold was free milling, being run into bullion and shipped direct to the mint in Denver.

That night at dinner Daniel Rayborn, in speaking of Bob Singleton said, "I have long wanted to make Singleton our superintendent, for I feel that he is a man that can be absolutely trusted. I think we had better not go into the mine until he returns from San Francisco, which will probably be the second day after tomorrow. In the meantime we can trace the surface outcropping and surveys.

"I want both of you boys to become familiar with the boundaries and all departments of the mine. I will show you the principal veins of ore at the surface. While we have had this mine for about twelve years, yet you will see as you go over it that we have really only explored a small part, although we have taken out millions of dollars in value."

Singleton returned late in the afternoon of the fourth day, and plans were made to go carefully through the underground workings the day following. During that evening I felt as if I were being tremendously charged with a Dynamic Electrical Current. Nada had brought her Arabic musical instrument, and she and Rex entertained us royally after dinner.

At nine o'clock the next morning, we went to the shaft-house and met Singleton, who was waiting there ready to take us into the mine. We entered the cage and descended to the four hundred foot level. Here we went through various tunnels and cross-cuts. As we were going through one tunnel that led to the southwest, I suddenly felt an Electrical Current pass through me. I stopped, and turning to Singleton, said, "What does this formation contain toward the north at this point?"

"There is only country rock," he replied,

"between these two veins. They are about four
hundred feet apart at the surface, with apparently
very little dip."

We started to pass on, but without the others
seeing me, I marked the place with blue chalk. We
then went to the six hundred foot level and continued to go through the various workings. We came to
a tunnel leading to the southwest; and almost under
the spot where I had felt the current two hundred
feet above, I felt it again, but more powerful than
before. I looked to my right and saw an intense blue
light with a center of molten gold. This stood out
clear and bright upon the wall of the tunnel. I
marked the spot quickly, and at the same moment
my Inner Sight was greatly quickened. I saw clearly
through the rock what seemed to be a great cavity
between the two main veins at least two hundred
feet apart. The opening was fully two hundred
feet high and nearly the same in circumference. A stringer—or crack in the formation—led
into the top, just about the four hundred foot
level.

During an ancient volcanic activity the ore had
been forced to this point forming very rich veins,
but this crevice had allowed it to pour through,
filling the cavity. It was one of those strange things
that happen in Nature, very seldom of course, but
nevertheless, they do occur.

The whole activity had been flashed on my consciousness in a moment, as all truly Cosmic Flashes do occur. I marked the spot, then went on with the others to examine the new strike. It was tremendously interesting. The two walls of the vein had suddenly widened in their formation, and at that point the large body of ore had been created—but it was not more than a tenth as large as the one I had marked. Just at this time Bob Singleton was called away by one of his men, and I had a chance to explain to Rex and his father what I had been shown by Beloved Saint Germain. I knew positively it was by His Power that I had been enabled to see within the formation and mark its location. Rayborn decided immediately to have a cross-cut tunnel run in from the spot I had marked to contact the ore-body that had been revealed to me. When Singleton returned, Rayborn gave the order to have the men start work at once on this cross-cut.

The superintendent looked at him in perfect amazement. However, none of his men ever thought of questioning anything he suggested, and Bob began making arrangements at once to carry out the order. Rayborn did give him a little explanation by saying,

"Bob! I know you do not understand why I am having this done, but when this special work is accomplished, I will explain."

"Mr. Rayborn," said Singleton with a gentle, humble dignity, "it will always be my pleasure to carry out your orders without question."

"I wish," continued Rayborn, "you would put the most rapid and trustworthy men on this part of the work. Use three shifts, and finish it as quickly as possible."

"How many feet can the men break down in twenty-four hours?" I asked the superintendent.

"I think at least ten feet," he replied, "more or less, according to the hardness of the rock." At that rate, I felt they would be able to reach the ore-body in about ten days, and I could have almost shouted for joy because I knew there was no uncertainty about what they would find when they reached it.

Rex and I liked Bob Singleton very much, for he seemed a man of fine, strong character, though very young for the type of position he held. He left us as soon as we came out of the mine, for there was a shipment of ore to be sent out that afternoon.

"I have wired the foreman at the ranch," Rayborn explained, "that we will not return for two weeks unless something vitally important demands it, because I wish to stay here and watch the progress of the new cross-cut tunnel." The days passed quickly, the work went steadily ahead, and we occupied our time writing, hiking, and enjoying the music that Nada and Rex gave us on the

Arabian instrument—Bob Singleton joining us at dinner several times.

The work on the tunnel cut through forty-eight feet the first five days. Each of the men received a bonus of one dollar a foot, and Singleton fifty dollars for the good work accomplished. Bob asked Nada and Rex if they would sing for the men one evening while at the camp. They both agreed, and Nada, as a surprise for everybody, wired to Denver for Arabic costumes—and when they appeared for their first number, the men almost went wild with joy. The program closed, and one of the men arose and asked if they might all shake hands with the children in gratitude for the evening's wonderful entertainment. The children agreed and said afterwards that they had never felt such inspiration or such power in their voices. Both felt the Master Saint Germain had been present and used the opportunity to pour His Radiation through the music to the men, thus raising their consciousness and loyalty to a still greater height. This was His Way of neutralizing the influence that had attempted to enter through Grey, which had been unable to accomplish its nefarious purpose.

At twelve o'clock on the eleventh day, I was in the office of the mine with Bob Singleton when a man came rushing in, greatly excited, saying they had struck rich ore in the new cross-cut. The superintendent looked at me utterly speechless, so plainly did he show his surprise. It was then I realized that he had really never dreamed of finding ore in the new workings.

Merely by the use of ordinary geological observations, this ore-body never would have been located, for geologists seldom take into consideration the freakish formations that sometimes occur in Nature, and that She does occasionally extraordinary things. This deposit would never have been found except by the Superhuman Power of our Beloved Master.

Singleton asked me to find Rex and his father and tell them the news. I hurried to the camp quarters and found them awaiting me at lunch. When I told of what had happened, we all silently gave praise and thanks to the "Beloved Mighty I AM Presence" and our Blessed Saint Germain for making this rich strike possible.

Rayborn sent word to Bob that we would be ready to go with him and examine the new discovery at half-past one. Nada decided to await our report. When we reached the spot, I saw the last shots had broken well into the ore-body, as the entire face of the tunnel was in ore.

"Bob," instructed Daniel Rayborn, "sample this strike and push the work as fast as possible, that we may determine its extent."

"I will," Bob replied, and went on to explain: "The formation in the ore deposit itself is much more easily drilled and broken than the ordinary rock." As we returned to the surface, he could stand it no longer and burst forth:

"Mr. Rayborn, this is the most remarkable thing I have ever read or heard of in all my life. How did you know the ore was there? No outer signs indicated it."

"Bob, my boy," he replied, "have patience. You will soon know. We shall prolong our stay another ten days, and if I am not mistaken, they will make twice the speed in the ore-body itself as they did getting to it. Keep this ore entirely separate from all the rest in the mine. I will explain the reason why later."

That evening at dinner, Mr. Rayborn asked Nada, Rex, and myself to meet with him at eight o'clock.

"I suggest," he began, as soon as we were all seated, "that we take Bob Singleton into partnership with us as general manager of the entire mine— including what in the future will be known as the 'Master Discovery.' I think he had better select an assistant of whom we all approve. I feel certain he can be trusted as one of us. We have every evidence before us that all our Beloved Master said of the ore-body is physically true. However, let us say nothing to Bob of this until the tunnel-drift is through."

The following days were filled with great activity and tremendous interest as the work progressed. Almost every evening, Bob was invited to dine with us that all might become better acquainted. Twenty days after the ore-body was reached, the tunnel-drift was through to the opposite side, a distance of fully two hundred feet, and Rayborn was more than happy that we had waited to learn the extent of it.

The evening the tunnel was finished, he announced at dinner that Bob was to be taken in as one of the partners; and while the "Master Discovery" really belonged to Nada and Rex, they wanted him to share a certain specified interest in the mine also, in addition to his salary. Then he explained how the ore-body came to be discovered. He gave a short description of our Beloved Master, Saint Germain, telling of the Protection he and his family had been given for years, of the recent attempt upon his Life, and his escape. Tears of gratitude and joy streamed down Bob's cheeks as he tried to express his appreciation.

"Your deep feeling" said Rayborn, "proves your sincerity to me beyond question. We shall all feel a Great Love for you Bob, and I am certain you can be trusted as one of us."

"I thank each of you," said Bob with sincerity,

"and I will do my best to prove worthy and true to the trust you place in me, and for your very great kindness." It was then we learned that Bob had a sister, Pearl, of whom he was very fond, and who was his only living relative, with the exception of an aunt with whom she lived.

"I expect Pearl," he continued, "to reach here tomorrow, as she is coming on to visit me for a time." He was very enthusiastic in his praise of her and drew forth her picture from his pocket.

She was about eighteen, remarkably good looking, and yet one felt she had tremendous strength of character with a natural sense of poise and command. He told Daniel Rayborn of the desire he always had to provide the means for her university training, and with his recent good fortune of sharing in the mine, this became possible of accomplishment.

The following day, Nada, Rex, Bob and I drove to the station to meet Pearl. As the train stopped and the passengers were alighting, we saw someone rush into Bob's arms. It made us realize how dearly they loved each other. That evening Bob told her of his new interest in the mine and the good fortune that had come to him. Later, when she met Daniel Rayborn, she threw her arms about him and kissed him in deep gratitude for his kindness to Bob. She tried to thank him, but he said:

"My Child, it gives me still greater happiness to know you are to share the joy with your brother whom we all have learned to love." That evening we spent listening to Nada and Rex sing, and I think Pearl was without question the happiest, most grateful person I have ever seen.

The next day came a message from the ranch saying Daniel Rayborn was needed there, so we made preparations to leave the second morning following. The assistant superintendent whom Bob had chosen to help him was to arrive at the camp ten days later, and Nada persuaded Bob to let Pearl go back to the ranch with her until he had time to visit with her. Rayborn planned to stay at the ranch only two or three weeks and then return to the mine again.

At six o'clock on the day of our departure, all the men who were off duty came to see us off, and as Bob said good-by, he held Pearl in his strong, fond embrace and expressed his gratitude that she had found so wonderful a friend in Nada. Rex and I took turns in driving, that Daniel Rayborn might have a chance to become better acquainted with Nada's newly-found friend. We noticed Pearl was a very close observer, and her appreciation of the beautiful scenery we drove through was very deep.

Time passes rapidly when all is joy and harmony, and this is one of the Great Laws of Life. If humanity would but comprehend the imperative need for its operation in their lives and understand the vital factor it becomes in their conscious use, we would be living in a most marvelous world more quickly than we can possibly realize now.

We made a long detour while returning, but arrived home at eight o'clock, ready for the splendid dinner that awaited us. We all seemed a little tired by the long drive except Pearl. The newness of the scenes kept her interest so aroused she seemed not to feel anything but the great happiness of the experience. We retired early, deeply grateful to the "Mighty I AM Presence" for the wonderful Blessings It had bestowed upon us.

CHAPTER III

Subterranean Marvels

THE next day, Nada, Pearl, Rex and I went to our favorite mountain lake. Pearl had gone for a walk while the rest of us were sitting very quietly on the bank. We had been there almost an hour when the strangest feeling passed over me as if Pearl were in danger. I called to Rex; we discussed my feeling and then hurried in search of her. We passed around a high rock that projected across the trail and saw her standing motionless. Fortunately we did not call, but walked rapidly forward. As we came nearer we beheld a huge rattlesnake coiled, waiting its opportunity to strike.

Rex always carried a rope around his waist. Without a word and quicker than it takes to tell it, he made a lasso, and with a quick, deft movement, sent it forward, catching the snake just below its head. He killed it instantly and turned to Pearl, expecting to find her greatly frightened. Imagine our surprise when she faced us calm and serene, and smiling curiously, said:

"I came upon that snake unexpectedly, but I knew it could not harm me so long as I kept my eyes on its eyes. Somehow I knew you would come." By that time Nada had come up to us, and we explained the incident.

"My dear sister," she said, turning to Pearl, "you certainly have wonderful courage and poise." Pearl looked at her with a peculiar expression we had never seen before.

"Nada my dear," she replied, "you know the Great Master would not allow any of us to be harmed." Finally I found my voice and asked:

"What Master?" She looked at me steadily for a moment and remarked:

"What a foolish question. The same Master each of you knows." Nada threw her arms around Pearl's neck and exclaimed:

"God bless you, my dear, how did you know Him?"

"When I was not quite ten years old," she continued, "shortly after my mother passed on, a Blessed Being appeared to me whom I afterwards came to know as the Master Saint Germain. After His first appearance He continued to visit and instruct me, but I was forbidden to tell anyone, not even my brother, until I was granted permission to do so.

"He told me to come out here to see Bob at this time, and I noticed an unusual twinkle in His eye at the time He said it, but I did not understand why He was so amused. Now it is all clear. Little did

I dream I was going to meet those who knew my Beloved Angel-Master, as I have always called Him."

From that time on, it seemed as though Pearl were a long-lost sister who had returned. That night we sprang our great surprise on Daniel Rayborn, and he was overjoyed when he learned that Pearl was a pupil of our Blessed Saint Germain.

The next morning we all had a real surprise awaiting us when we went down to breakfast; for Daniel Rayborn, as he awoke, had received a Message from our Master—for Saint Germain had asked that all of us meet at the "Cave of Symbols" in Table Mountain by eight o'clock, the morning of the third day following. That was Thursday morning. Pearl was very anxious to know something about the Cave, and after hearing some description of it, remarked, "You will find some very great Revelation concerning it is about to take place."

At six o'clock on the morning indicated, we appeared at breakfast in our hiking outfits, bubbling over with joy and the happy anticipation of seeing our Blessed Saint Germain again, for we all felt tremendous things were in store for us. We drove by auto as far as the road went, which left only a distance of about two miles for us to hike.

The day was glorious, and the very air seemed charged with a magical fragrance, a powerful highly attenuated Spiritual Energy. The drive was delightful. We found a safe, secluded spot for the automobile, taking our flashlights with extra batteries, and reached the entrance to the Cave at exactly ten minutes to eight.

We entered the first chamber and were immediately conscious of a Powerful Vibration, almost like that produced by the throbbing of great machinery. As we came to the arched entrance of the great Inner Room, there stood our Beloved Master. He was clothed in spotless white that contrasted strangely with the hiking clothes we wore. Enfolding each in His Divine Embrace, He said:

"Beloved Ones, I greet you in the Name of the 'Mighty I AM Presence.' This Great 'Presence' within you will become as familiar to you ere long as you are with each other, as Real, as Tangible and as Vital. I see it is unnecessary to introduce my faithful pupil, Pearl, whose name symbolizes her great purity of soul.

"I rejoice exceedingly that it has been possible for Me to bring together in the physical expression such beautiful souls as you all are. It is a most unusual thing, I assure you, as you will see later. If you will kindly follow me, we shall proceed."

He moved toward the archway of white described in the first chapter and stopped about three feet in front of it. He extended His right hand, and in a moment, a Dazzling White Light like a dense vapor enveloped the entire place. The entrance to a tunnel filled with a Soft White Light opened.

We entered, followed Saint Germain for a distance of several hundred feet, and at last came to another door on which in raised figures were the ancient symbols of Life. Presently the door opened, and we were admitted into a chamber of extraordinary shape and remarkable beauty, having twelve sides of equal dimensions, a beautiful dome forming its ceiling.

Each side was made of a different kind of substance. Four of these panels were dazzling white, each different, yet giving off a soft, glowing, Sparkling Light, and making a square within the twelve-pointed figures. The others were of varying colors of most delicate, beautiful shades. The room was at least sixty feet in diameter, and on the east side stood an instrument in a transparent case that looked like a radio as far as I could tell. On each side of this case, forming a circle around the entire room about three feet from the wall, were twelve chairs made of the same transparent metal as the case, one in front of each panel. Saint Germain seated us and stepped to the instrument.

"Beloved Students," He began, "your surmise is correct. Within this case is the most remarkable radio yet produced on Earth. The case, as you see, is perfectly transparent, yet the material of which it is made is as tough and strong or stronger than steel—so hard you cannot make an impression on it with a hammer. The inventor of this super-radio will be here tonight, when you shall meet Her.

"I wish you to be my guests here for three days. I will see that a written message is delivered to your home by a visible messenger tonight, and that your automobile is guarded. Now if you will come with me, we shall proceed, as we have much to do before evening." He went to the opposite side of the room from which we had entered and pressed His hand against the wall. A panel slid back and revealed an opening into a large oblong room.

"This is a chemists' laboratory," He explained, "in which the Great Master Chemists have been working for the past fifty years—perfecting formulas for the protection of America in the next and final crisis of Her experience. After this crisis Her people will be taught the use of the Universal Energy for Light, Heat and Power. This will come forth in still greater Perfection than has ever been known in any previous age."

We went to the far end of the laboratory and passed into another room fully three times as large where electrical experiments were being carried on. This entire room was lined with the same transparent material as had been used in the case of the radio.

"Many discoveries and inventions," He continued, "are being brought forth here by awakening the past memory within those who are doing the experimental work. By calling into the outer activity of the mind that which has been attained in previous lives and adding to this the *greater and simpler Perfection* of the future, those doing this work are preparing Wonders and Blessings untold for America, Her people, and through Her, for the world. During the next seventy years America and Her people will scarcely recognize themselves as they look back upon their limited activities of today.

"These Wonderful Beings who have become so clearly aware of their 'Mighty I AM Presence' are perfecting and preparing for actual use many wonderful things for the great benefit and enlightenment of humanity, as people ascend in *conscious understanding* to the point where such things can be accepted and used. Many of these formulas and inventions have been and are being taken from cities hermetically sealed that lie at the bed of the Atlantic Ocean, having sunk beneath its waters when the last cataclysm destroyed Atlantis.

"These Great Ones have drawn such formulas from within these sealed cities and are testing and improving upon them. This is how the Greater Perfection comes forth for the use and upliftment of the race in the coming Golden Age. The Great

Ascended Masters guard, watch, and direct this work. Their students who have been trained to come and go from the physical body consciously are the ones who carry out the experiments in the laboratory.

"The Ascended Masters are the Guardians of humanity and have worked through the centuries from the invisible as well as the physical to awaken, to bless, to enlighten and lift mankind out of its self-created degradation and selfishness. We have conquered death by Complete and Eternal Dominion over the atomic substance of the physical body and world. All things obey Our Commands! The Laws of Nature and the Universe are Our willing, obedient servants. In these wonderful, secret Chambers of Nature, the work goes on quietly, unknown to the outer world; and wherever the individual seeks the Light for the Light Itself, then truly all things are added."

Saint Germain called our attention to one thing after another that had already been perfected, and others that were under construction. I can never put in words the feeling of Joy and Exhilaration this gave every one of us. One thing in particular attracted the attention of all, and we asked its purpose.

"It is a mechanical way of quickening the atomic vibration of the human body," He replied, "and assisting to raise it into the Pure Electronic Body which Beloved Jesus referred to as the Seamless Robe or the Bridal Garment of the Spirit. It is composed of Pure Electronic Light, for in and upon It no imperfection can ever be recorded.

"Light, you see," He emphasized, "is Substance, Energy, and Luminosity—all three in one. This Pure Electronic Light of which the Eternal Spiritual Body is composed, is condensed—as it were—by your 'Mighty I AM Presence' into a Self-luminous Substance, which is for you a Self-sustained, Immortal, Ever-expanding, Ever-Perfect Form and Reservoir of Divine Love, Light, Wisdom and Power from the very Heart of God. It is your Eternal, Individualized Temple of Life and the Heart Center of your world of manifested form. It is sometimes referred to as the White Fire Body because the Dazzling White Light It sends forth is so blazing, so intense and so All-powerful that to the human eye It looks like White Fire. The ordinary person can only gaze upon It for the fraction of a second.

"This is the Body in which Beloved Jesus made the Ascension! As the Light within It increased into that Higher Octave of Life, being a more rapid vibratory action, It became invisible to the watching, adoring multitude that witnessed His Ascension. The human eye only records within certain octaves of vibration. As the human, through

Self-purification, increases its vibratory rate, the Light within every electron of the physical body glows brighter. It expands Its Radiation to such a degree that the physical form becomes first, Self-luminous; next, transcends the gravity pull of Earth, and then is able to express consciously and at will in any octave of vibration the individual desires. He can come and go freely anywhere within Infinity; for the Pure Electronic Light exists everywhere throughout Creation. As soon as the atomic structure of anyone's physical body becomes all Light, it has entered into the One Eternal Element—the *Great Universal Sea of Blazing White Essence* from which God created all forms. Only in this Condition of Life is Complete Freedom, Mastery and Attainment possible. This is the Reality and Ultimate of human existence! Then the human becomes raised until it is all Divinity, which is forever Free, Omnipresent, Omnipotent, Omniscient, going everywhere and doing all It desires, still knowing Itself as an individual, Self-Conscious Focus of the 'Mighty I AM Presence.'

"In almost every secret society that stands for constructive activity, or in other words that recognizes the 'Light' as the Source of all good, there is always used in the initiations the word 'raised.' That 'raising' is literally, figuratively, eternally and physically true; for the vibratory action of the physical atom is 'raised' until it all becomes the Pure, Electronic, Self-expanding Essence or Spirit— the Pure God Substance—LIGHT—LIGHT— LIGHT!

"We call this device an Atomic Accelerator, and It will be used a great deal in the future to assist in raising the physical flesh atom into its Divine Purity and Structure—the Electronic Body. This Perfect Body remains forever Eternally Youthful, Beautiful, Strong, Perfect, and Free from every conceivable limitation. In this Body, individuals can and do function wherever they choose in the Universe, for in It there are no barriers of time, place, space, or condition.

"The desire for this Perfect condition of existence is an innate Idea and Ideal within the entire race of mankind, and has been always. In the legends, myths, and fairy tales of every race and nation that has ever existed on this Earth, there are stories of Perfected Beings—Immortal, All-Wise, Eternally Youthful and Transcendently Beautiful. These stories have a Cause, an Original Idea from which they sprang, and It is this Eternal Truth of Being which they carry forward from age to age, that the Ideal may always be held before the mind of mankind. *This is the master record upon which humanity was modeled in the beginning—the image the image and likeness of God, 'The Mighty I AM Presence.'*

"If one be a Real Student of Life, he will dig deep into the thoughts and feeling of those Beings who express the Superhuman Conditions, Qualities, and Transcendent Ideals. These, the ordinary personality considers impossible because of the Greatness of the Power required to bring Them into outer expression. The effort needed to attain and express these Divine Qualities is more than the ordinary person cares to make. The effort this kind of Attainment requires is a sincere, strict discipline of the human sense-consciousness until it learns Obedience to the Pattern of 'Perfection' instead of its own selfish temporary whims and appetites. The Real Student of Life knows that whatever God Quality the Consciousness of the individual can think about, he can bring into existence through the Creative Power of his own thought and his feeling of Divine Love.

"Divine Thoughts, Divine Feeling, Divine Qualities, Divine Ideals, can only be found by thinking upon *Divinity,* for they do not exist nor abide anywhere else, and like produces like throughout Infinity. Divinity is the *Light* and the *Perfection* of Life.

"You shall see this Atomic Accelerator in operation while here for your Instruction and Enlightenment. The Ascended Masters have permitted It to come forth that more of humanity may know of this possibility and make the needed effort for its Attainment at the present time.

"The Ascended Masters are Masters of Love, Light and Wisdom. Only through Them can humanity understand Life and reach Attainment, for They know all, have experienced the activity of this Earth, are now wholly Divine and Master of its forces. They have trod every foot of the path the human being now treads and know every step of the way. Because of this, They can and do show the student its pitfalls if he cares to listen and be protected from them; but They will not and never do intrude upon the Free Will of the individual, for that is his Divine Birthright, and they respect It."

Saint Germain then led the way to the entrance of a shaft in which there was a metal cage—or elevator. We entered and began moving downward. We descended about a hundred feet, and the cage stopped in the center of a circular room. It was about twenty feet in diameter and facing us was a stone door. He pulled a lever at the right of the entrance. The massive door swung open and disclosed an immense chamber that contained marvelous, complete equipment for making every kind of material that was used in constructing the various devices in both the chemical and electrical laboratories. In this great room there were large electrical furnaces and huge rollers for changing the various metals into thin sheets. Everything was electrically operated.

"This is the place," remarked Saint Germain, "from which you felt the throbbing vibration within the mountain as you entered the Cave. The machinery is seldom operated during the day. Today it is necessary to do so in order to be ready for the Work that we are to accomplish tonight, and for which you have been invited here.

"Every kind of material we wish to use is produced right here in this chamber. Of course We do not need great quantities for the experimental work We are doing, but this work is to bring into practical use for the future the Great Genius and Marvelous Ideals of highly illumined Individuals who are fully awakened to the Conscious Recognition of the 'Mighty I AM Presence' and the use of Its Limitless Wisdom and Power.

"It is my desire to explain everything in as simple language as possible so the Essence and Principle of it may be most easily and permanently comprehended. It is necessary in the present age to simplify the technical terminology, that the average person may be enabled to understand these Truths easily and quickly.

"The time has come when great numbers among the mass of humanity will awaken to the Truth and

realize they have a Divine Master within them—
'The Magic Presence' of the 'Mighty I AM.' There
are many who from an Inner Standpoint are far
along the Path of Enlightenment due to previous
Self-effort and attainment. Yet in this present embodiment they are outwardly unaware of it and have
not had academic training. Something must be done
to give such souls the Freedom which they crave and
for which they are really ready. These shall have
help, and to this end do We work here to give it."
Beloved Saint Germain then turned to Nada and
Pearl, and remarked:

"Are you weary after so many hours of this kind
of observation in what is generally supposed to be
man's domain?" They quickly assured Him they
were not, and judging from the intense sparkle of
their eyes, no one doubted it.

"I have never been so vitally interested in anything in my entire life," Pearl replied.

"You do me great honor," He responded, "by
your intense interest, and it gives me real happiness
to know you enjoy it also. Now if you will honor My
humble quarters with your presence, we shall refresh the outer form. Let us return to the electrical
laboratory."

We returned by the cage; and crossing the room,
Saint Germain stepped to a door leading to the
heart of the mountain. It opened at His touch, and

we entered an oblong sort of reception hall having a dome-like ceiling. The walls and ceiling were all of a most beautiful, delicate milk-white color, the floor being covered with a creamy, soft wool-like material at least an inch and a half thick. There were five chairs made of semi-opaque substance in a similar cream color and upholstered in the same soft blue plush as the chairs in the Tower Room of the Rayborn home. Four of the chairs were exactly alike, but the fifth one had a high carved back. Each chair was placed near a door—the largest one being in the center.

Saint Germain escorted Nada and Pearl to the first door at the left as we came in. He requested them to enter, bathe, and clothe themselves in the Raiment they found provided, then return to this room and await the summons to dine.

Turning to Rex and me, he led us to the far door at the right, with a similar request to prepare for dinner. We entered the room He had indicated and both of us were speechless with surprise, for it was most magnificent, fit for a prince or a king's palace. It was circular in shape, a domed ceiling, finished in white and gold, furnished with two beautiful couches, a chair placed beside each with a long bevelled mirror set into the wall between them. There was a curious chest of drawers built into the wall itself so they could not be distinguished from it except for the handles. The chairs and frames of the couches were both of the same semi-opaque substance that seemed like a metal.

Rex crossed to a small opening at our left and asked me to look. I stepped to where he was and saw an exquisite Roman bath, also circular in form. It was filled with water that sparkled and moved incessantly, as though charged with the "Essence of Life." We could not find any means of ventilation, yet in every room we visited the air was clean, fresh, invigorating, and filled with the scent of roses.

We bathed, and our bodies felt all aglow with a sense of health we had never before experienced. Lying on the couches were the Robes we were to wear. They were seamless, and made of a fabric I have never seen or heard of, something like a rich, thick silk, but very, very soft, and extremely light in weight. The one for Rex was a wonderful sapphire blue, embroidered in gold. The embroidery formed a girdle around the waist and wide bands around the neck, loose sleeves, and bottom of the Robe. Mine was white, embroidered in gold. There were also beautiful sandals to match, which fitted perfectly.

Our preparation finished, we returned to the reception room. A few moments later the girls entered dressed in Robes like ours, and they were visions of loveliness. The Robes of Pearl and Rex were alike, and Nada's was like mine. Their room was evidently a duplicate of ours except that it was decorated in a soft pink shade. We were very much occupied comparing notes when the most heavenly chimes sounded through the room, and instantly, the middle door opened. We entered and were thrilled at the beauty upon which we gazed.

Here again, the room was in the same soft, milk-white and gold combination. The dome-like ceiling was colored sky blue, and on it were clouds that gave one the impression of really looking at the sky. The walls were draped with the most marvelous cloth that looked like diamond dust, for something in the composition of the fabric gave it an indescribable Radiance.

This audience chamber was perhaps forty by eighty feet, and in its center stood a large golden table with a crystal top. At the far end of the room there was a duplicate of this table about one-third its size, and around it were placed chairs for six persons. In one corner was a beautiful organ, and opposite in another corner stood a beautiful piano, the case being made of the same metal-like substance as the other furniture. All were so absorbed in admiration and enjoyment of this beauty that we did not notice Beloved Saint Germain and Daniel Rayborn enter until we felt Them close behind us.

Our Beloved Master led the way to the small table

where He seated Rayborn at one end and took the head Himself. Pearl was placed at His right, and then Rex; Nada at His left, and then myself. He said:

"May I have the pleasure of ordering the food for each one? You see my culinary department is in the invisible to you, but it is very real and tangible to me." We acquiesced very happily, and He continued:

"Let us bow our heads in adoration and praise of the 'Mighty I AM Presence' within each of us."

In just a moment, and without another spoken word, a Crystal Goblet filled with a Golden Sparkling Liquid appeared at the right hand of each one.

"To the enlightenment and happiness of each of you and of all humanity," He said, raising His glass, and as we drank this Marvelous Nectar everyone felt the quickening power of Its Life-giving Essence rush through the body. Next there appeared what looked like a vegetable loaf, with a piece of honey cake that was only slightly sweet. These were most delicious, and all agreed it was the most perfect thing we had ever eaten. A fruit salad followed, or at least that was what it most nearly resembled, and Saint Germain said it was most nourishing.

For dessert we ate something that resembled ice cream, refreshingly cool, not ice cold, and with it a kind of angel-food cake, but much more delicious than anything we know of in the outer world. Lastly there appeared Crystal Goblets filled with a Creamy Liquid, and as we drank it, a force rushed through our bodies like Living Light.

As each course was finished, the empty service simply disappeared. None of us had ever before partaken of anything half so delicious, nourishing and satisfying as this marvelous dinner our Blessed Saint Germain had produced for us direct from the Omnipresent Universal Substance. As we finished, Rayborn turned to Him and said:

"This Experience that is so amazing, so wonderful to us, is all quite natural and normal to You. We feel that we have never been so honored, so pleased in our lives, as we are tonight."

"My Beloved Children," Saint Germain replied, "each one of you has this same 'Mighty I AM Presence,' the Master God Self and Almighty God Power within you with which to do these things. You can produce everything you require direct from the Universal Supply. I have acquired the Understanding of how to use this Mighty Power and how to direct Its Limitless Energy to do My bidding. If you so desire, you too can soon be directing this Mighty Energy—which is God Energy—to do what you now call great miracles. All mankind may learn to do this also, if it only will.

"There is naught in the Universe to say nay to whatever you desire, so long as it does not harm another of God's children.

"It requires much less energy and is much easier to produce everything you wish to use directly from the ever Pure, Universal Substance, than it is to go through the process of nature to grow it—once you know how." Turning to Nada and Rex, He said:

"Will you two beloved ones do me the honor to sing two of your own compositions for our enjoyment?" "Gladly," they replied. Nada seated herself at the piano and ran over a phrase of the melody they were going to sing. She stopped, astonished by the tone of the instrument, for it was unlike anything ever produced on Earth in musical tone. They sang a favorite, "The Arabic Love Song." Their voices and this marvelous piano produced an effect of indescribable beauty. When they had finished, Beloved Saint Germain, with all the grace and courtesy of a courtier, bowed low before them in recognition of the "Mighty I AM Presence" which had been allowed to come through so perfectly.

"I bow before thy gracious throne of song," He complimented them, "and never have I heard anything more Divine. Now let us go to the radio chamber. Friends are awaiting us there."

When we reached it, we were presented to three

ladies and three gentlemen who had arrived ahead of us. They wore the same sort of Robes as ours, only of different color. Among them was an elderly gentleman with white hair and beard who seemed almost feeble. One of the three ladies, whom we shall call Leonora, stepped to the radio and said:

"This Perfected Radio is the result of my work during seven different embodiments. In four of these I used a masculine body. I carried the memory of it over with me each time, and at last it has reached the Perfection intended. This radio possesses three fields of operation: that which I term high, medium, and low.

"In high, it reaches other planets of our Solar System. In medium, it reaches anywhere on our own planet Earth, including its Etheric Belts; and in low it reaches the interior of our Earth. Let us first connect with some of our cities."

In a few moments we heard clearly and distinctly a lecture being broadcast by one of the most prominent stations in New York. Afterwards we picked up an orchestra broadcast from another New York station. Then She got connections with London, Paris, Vienna, Cairo, Calcutta, Hong Kong, Melbourne and Tokyo. Distance seemed to make no difference in clear reception, and at no time was there ever the slightest indication of static.

"Now let us reach into the first Etheric Belt

around the Earth," She said. Immediately we heard the most majestic soul-stirring Music, and then a wonderful Voice was heard, saying:

"This is from the Golden Etheric City over the Sahara Desert. We always know when an Earth connection is made, but We have a still Higher Means of communication. It is the operation of the Sound Ray to speak over and the Light Ray to see through. When these two are combined, it becomes the highest form of television. However, the mechanical television will reach a very high state of perfection, and in a few years it will be as prevalent in the outer world as your telephone of today. Oh, that more of humanity might raise its consciousness and become attuned highly enough to have the marvelous use of these Rays!

"You see, the 'Mighty I AM Presence' within the individual does not recognize time, place, space or condition. It is only in the outer activity of the mind, or human sense consciousness, that such conceptions of limitation occur." Leonora adjusted the radio into high, and in a moment, we heard a Voice saying:

"Leonora, this is Venus. We know You because Yours is the only mechanical instrument that reaches Us from Earth. Your usual communication with Us is over the Light and Sound Rays, so We judge this is for the benefit of others than yourself.

Our instruments here indicate the planet with which We are connected by the sound and color of the vibration. The day is fast approaching when your mechanical television will be able to reach Us also. Your scientists will not reach this success until they understand that there are Etheric Rays. They must be made aware of Them and taught to use Them. This will make all kinds of communication within Cosmic Space a very simple matter, and it will then become a daily occurrence to keep in communication with Us.

"Within the next ten years, or perhaps twenty— depending entirely upon the Harmony maintained among the inhabitants of Earth—a number of Our Great Inventions will be given to those of your people who are attuned to receive them. These will be of very great benefit to your humanity, as is the wonderful Atomic Accelerator which is near you. That Instrument will one day bless your people tremendously. Call Us whenever We can be of service to You. Our Love, Light and Wisdom enfold You and all the Earth."

Leonora then changed from high to low, and in about three minutes a deep Voice was heard, saying, "I recognize your call, and I am answering in person. This is Pelleur. It is interesting and encouraging to know there are those on the Earth's surface who have some idea of the possibility that God

Beings can and do exist within the interior of the Earth. We think We have less to contend with than you, for We do not have extremes of temperature or seasons of heat and cold. We have the 'Eternal White Light' which is soft and restful. Our climate is very delightful, like that of the semi-tropics on Earth. Your America will one day have something quite similar, and yet there will always be some slight change of seasons. They will be much less severe than those you have at present. We have what might be called the 'Eternal Sun of Even Pressure.' This produces an Atmosphere that is always of equal pressure and harmonious to all who live within It.

"The 'Mighty I AM Presence' provides Perfect Conditions in every phase of Its expression. If all the world could but realize and understand this, the terrible agony that fear produces would drop away entirely from the humanity on Earth's surface. You see, I am cognizant of many of Earth's conditions outside of My own Activity here, for when We, as you, reach into God's Mind, *all knowledge* can be obtained, because Our Motive is pure and unselfish."

"We may not continue these observations further," Leonora explained. "At this time other things demand Our Attention and Service." Saint Germain saw and felt the unanswered questions in our minds, as to why there were inhabitants in the center of the Earth, and what kind of individuals they were; for the idea shocked us, just the same as it does our readers. He studied us all for a moment or two and then said:

"Yes, I will tell you the facts now since the condition and demand to know the Truth are great within each one of you. You, as students on the Path who are really trying to understand Life everywhere in the Universe, must remember to keep the intellect often reminded there is no place in the Universe where Self-conscious individuals—and by that I mean individuals who know and are conscious of themselves as Creators with Free Will—may not go to explore and understand all Cosmic Activity. There is no place nor condition, I say, that they may not go, explore, and understand what is going on at that point—if they so desire.

"The idea that the center of the Earth is a mass of fire is entirely erroneous. Within the crust of the Earth for a certain depth there are conditions of the Fire Element acting; but within the center of the Earth itself there are Self-conscious individual Beings, who through many cycles of work and Self-effort have mastered the control of certain forces— with which they are still working—to accomplish the Fulfillment of the Divine Plan for that part of Earth. There are also Beings who are striving for that same Ideal, but working only within the conditions provided by Nature at the surface.

"You must understand and remember that the Ascended Masters are instructing and assisting in all grades of the outer experiences of Life in every condition found within and upon Earth as well as on the other planets of this System. Why should it not be a perfectly natural, normal condition that would permit some of Their number to be the Instructors of those who are working with forces at the center as well as at the circumference of the planets?

"This Revelation is not unnatural nor inconsistent with a Great, Infinite Divine Plan. The inconsistent, unnatural condition of humanity is the ignorance, the narrowness, the littleness, the darkness of a human concept that shuts the door upon the stupendous Marvels of this Glorious Universe and says, 'I don't believe it—that is impossible.'

"Only ignorance and darkness make mankind believe anything is impossible. The students of Light who know and really *accept* an All-powerful Source of Creation—and what reasoning mind can doubt It when one studies the marvels of the atom, as well as of the Cosmic Suns—know that the Wonders of Creation which face us everywhere on our planet are limitless, marvelous, and stupendous. These facts are True. There are many kinds of individuals expanding their Light on the planets of Our System, and just because one type has not yet had conscious knowledge of others is no proof they do not exist.

"Humanity must someday learn a little more of what abides in the Universe besides itself, and this Instruction contains part of that New Knowledge. It is True, every word of It, and no human ignorance or doubt can remove that Truth from Its manifestation in the Universe. Clouds may shut off the Sun's rays for a time, but they never will be able to put the Sun out of existence. So it is with human opinions and ignorance of the past and present. Someday the 'Light' must break through these clouds, and that day is here. It is NOW! Let the *Light of Truth* shine clearly through all preconceived human ideas and opinions. Facts will be revealed that compel all ignorance to disappear into the sea of forgetfulness and be replaced by the Great Light of the 'Mighty I AM Presence.'

"Now We shall continue with our other Work. The hour is at hand for the Ascension of this good brother," He said, referring to the white-haired elderly gentleman—whom we shall call David. "Because of previous attainment, he has so attuned his Life Stream that he may now enter a wider, or Cosmic Wave of Expression, and in this Great Activity he will express far more Transcendent

Phases of Individual Life than he can possibly do in this present existence. By previous growth and present Self-conscious effort in this Life, it is possible for the Assistance which We can render to be given him. Let us now go to the electrical laboratory."

As the door opened, we saw the room was flooded with Dazzling White Light. We stepped toward the Atomic Accelerator, and this time it was charged with the very Essence of Life. Permission has not been granted to give a detailed description of this Instrument at the present time, other than to say the Chair in which the one being raised sat, looked as if it were made of pure gold—but Saint Germain told us it was a combination of gold and several other substances as yet unknown to the outer world.

Saint Germain asked David to take his place in the Chair, and certain Currents of Light began to glow within the Chair itself. David sat with his body perfectly at ease, completely relaxed, with his arms resting comfortably on the arms of the Chair. There was no mechanism of any kind surrounding the Chair or within it, and it gave one a wonderful feeling of marvelous, regal comfort. It was positively a most ecstatic heavenly sensation one received about the whole arrangement.

When all were in readiness and we were very

silent, one of the Ascended Masters of Tremendous Glory and Power suddenly stepped directly out of the atmosphere. He placed those present in the proper position according to their radiation and asked that they join hands to make a complete circle around the Chair—the Mighty Master himself facing David. The persons on each side of the Master made Their connections with Him by placing Their hands against His back, just opposite the solar plexus, and Saint Germain stood opposite Him behind the Chair in which David sat. The Mighty Master then gave the necessary Direction.

"Let each one," He said, "close his eyes, focus the attention with all strength on the Almighty Power of the 'Mighty I AM Presence' within. Joyously give praise and thanks that David's body is now raised into its Divine Perfection, and that he now accepts and receives his Full God-given Freedom, Dominion and Mastery." He then spoke directly to me and asked that I observe the process closely.

I opened my eyes and at first could hardly see David's form as the Intensity of the "Light" increased. In a moment It became clearer, as I seemed to be in some degree lifted with It. Then I saw what almost made me start with surprise, for David's hair had returned to its original color (dark brown), the lines faded from his face, his flesh became the pink of perfect health, and his beard disappeared.

I could follow no longer, for the "Light" became so intense that I was conscious of nothing else. The most concentrated part was about his body, but It enveloped us all in the most Dazzling Radiance. The outline of his body completely disappeared, and involuntarily I closed my eyes. How long this lasted I never knew. Then our Beloved Saint Germain addressed us all, saying:

"David's body has been raised into its Electronic Perfection, and the Mighty Master, My Brother, has taken Him for the time being into that Realm of Light for which He has become fitted through the Perfection of His Eternal Light Body. Later He will return in that Ascended Form to minister to humanity under Divine Direction. Come, we shall now go to my quarters."

He led the way, and we entered the beautiful "Crystal Chamber," as I loved to call it, where we had eaten our wonderful precipitated dinner. Here we found the required number of chairs placed around the large golden table with the crystal top. This was really His audience hall, but at times He used it as a private dining room for special guests. He took the chair at the head of the table, asked Daniel Rayborn to take the opposite end, and then began one of His amazing Discourses.

"Tomorrow evening, you, My Brother," He said, speaking directly to Rayborn, "shall have a similar privilege as David had today. However, the Process in your case will not be completed; but it will start the raising of the atomic structure so when the time comes for what under other circumstances would be your passing through the change called death, you can have the necessary Assistance and raise your outer form into the Perfect Electronic Structure instead of casting it off.

"I promised," He went on, turning to Nada and Rex, "that there should be no sorrow at your father's passing. Now you can understand why. This is the way We take ourselves out of the hands of the reaper called death; and so We enter *consciously* into that Perfect Life which is the Divine Light and Eternal Inheritance of every one of God's children. Many have chosen to take a long time to come to this point, but all must make a beginning sometime, and all must do It eventually.

"This part of humanity's experience has received almost no acknowledgment. Neither has It been understood nor considered as possible of accomplishment until very recently; yet the Mighty Master Jesus gave the absolutely Perfect Example and Explanation of It two thousand years ago. He gave humanity the Proof wonderfully—conclusively, and said: 'The Works that I do shall ye do also, and

Greater Works than these shall ye do.'

"That Statement stands as an Everlasting Obligation upon humanity until all do it. Mankind has passed over this True Meaning and has taken the stand that It is not possible. While all do not need to accomplish It in exactly the same way as He did, yet every human being, sometime, somewhere, must raise the outer or atomic structure into the Imperishable, Electronic Body where no imperfection exists.

"A great many individuals now in physical embodiment are, or will be able to do this in the present Life—with a little necessary Assistance; and it is Our Great Privilege to give that. The Atomic Accelerator was perfected to help give this Assistance, and there is no invention or discovery that has or ever will bless mankind to so great a degree.

"The results you have witnessed in David's body are permanent, real and tangible. This amazing, real, physical machine is a mighty healing agent—as well as a means by which the body can be raised. It also quickly establishes perfect equilibrium in the brain structure, and through the balancing of the mental and emotional activities of a human being, dishonesty and crime of every kind can be prevented. It was used on Atlantis, although it was less perfect."

CHAPTER IV

Divine Romance

"NOW I am going to touch upon very important things which are sacredly personal," Saint Germain explained, speaking directly to Nada, Pearl, Rex, and Bob Singleton. "I do not wish you to feel that I intrude upon your sacred private affairs, or that I take of you because of the Power I possess and advantage use.

"However, there are certain things that I must make unmistakably plain to you. Rex and Pearl are 'Twin Rays' from the same Divine Flame. The Flame comes forth from the Heart of God, the Great Life Consciousness of the Universe, the Great Central Sun.

"When You, the 'Mighty I AM Presence,' will to come forth into an Individualized Focus of Conscious Dominion and use the Creative Word 'I AM,' Your first Individual Activity is the formation of a Flame. Then you, the *Individualized Focus* of the 'Mighty I AM Presence,' begin Your Dynamic Expression of Life.

"This Activity We term *Self-consciousness*— meaning the individual who is conscious of his

Source and Perfection of Life expressing through himself. Only the Self-conscious Individual has ALL the Attributes and Creative Power of the 'Mighty I AM Presence.' Only He can know who and what He is and express the Fullness of the Creative Power of God whenever He decrees, by the use of the Words 'I AM.'

"The outer human part of this activity is what we call the personality. It is but the vehicle through which Perfection should be expressed into the outer substance of the Universe.

"Within the Pure God Flame is a Breath that pulsates constantly. This 'Great Fire Breath' is a Rhythmic Outpouring of Divine Love, Its three Attributes being *Love, Wisdom, and Power in action.* These pour out constantly into the Infinite Sea of Pure Electronic Light. This Light is the Universal Substance or Spirit, out of which all forms are composed. It is intelligent—mark you—because It obeys law through the command of the individual who says or is conscious of 'I AM.' These two Words are the Acknowledgment and Release of the Power to create and bring forth into outer existence whatever quality follows that Acknowledgment. For Intelligence to act, there must be Intelligence to be acted upon; and the Universal Substance, being like a photographic film, takes the record of whatever quality the individual imposes upon It through his thought, feeling, and spoken word. The Words

'I AM,' whether thought, felt, or spoken, release the Power of Creation instantly. Make no mistake about this. Intelligence is Omnipresent, and It is within the Electronic Light.

"The first Fiat of Creation that went forth into Infinity was: 'Let there be Light!' and then Creation took place, for out of this Primal Light comes all manifested form.

"The 'Light' is the Central Point of Life or energy within every atom, composing the substance from which comes all physical manifestation. I speak of the atom because the lower rate of vibration composing the physical manifestation is the atomic structure which we have under consideration.

"When you consciously envelop or hold any person, place, condition or thing in the Dazzling White Light, you are penetrating, going through the atomic structure into the Electronic, wherein there is no imperfection. In this Use of the 'Light,' one penetrates the structure of imperfection, and that on which the attention is centered is then brought forth Perfect—not only as the Father sees It, but It is the Father's Perfection expressed.

"You, as the Son, are given choice, *commanded to choose and direct* where the energy—which is the Activity of the 'Light'—shall go. It is imperative to have your conscious thought, your firm attention on what is to be accomplished in order to give the needed direction to the Activity of this Mighty

Force which it is your right and privilege to use.

"When you use the Dazzling White Light, you are actually accepting the Electronic Structure which is then present in manifestation, for you are acting from the Plane of Action, or Perfect Manifestation. Your desire, when held steady, unwaveringly, becomes the Conscious Thought directing, for you cannot have a desire without Conscious Thought in the desire.

"Great strides have been made in the Higher Use of the Light at the Inner Levels in the past fifteen years. Your conscious great adherence to the Light shows you are ready for Its Highest Use. If in your use of the Light, you will know the Perfection of what you wish is already present in manifestation the *moment* you start the *dynamic action* of the Light, It will remove all uncertainty in your mind as to the positive assurance of the manifestation, or what you wish, taking form in your physical use.

"In clothing or visualizing any person, place, object or condition with the Illuminated Figure of Jesus Christ, or the Figure of any other Ascended Master, you are really unclothing, penetrating through the atomic garment—where you see, recognize, and accept the Perfection you now want present in form, for you have *swept aside* all imperfection in the action.

"The student should see and feel his body as if composed of Pure White Flame sending out long

Rays of Light. The Flame is your Real Self—'The Mighty I AM Presence,' the Full Christ Perfection. The Rays shooting forth are the Divine Mind, or 'Love in Action.' These Rays are what follow your Conscious Direction, carrying your thought and producing magical results when consciously directed, held firm by determined, unwavering, Conscious Attention. The 'Light' you thus visualize is the Electronic Substance the Hindus call 'Prana.'

"This Light is always directed by thought, but it is imperative that all learn to control and direct It consciously. This Conscious Control and Direction is how the Ascended Masters accomplish such Marvelous Results. Divine Love is a Presence, an Intelligence, a Principle, a Power, an Activity, a Light and a Substance. When we command Divine Love to go forth and do anything, we are setting into motion the Highest Form of Action—*the most Powerful Force.*

"This, however, does not require terrific effort; in fact, it requires just the opposite. It is a calm, steady, determined, conscious knowing. As this becomes a fixed consciousness, an *absolute certainty* in one's conscious awareness, he will find more and more instantaneous response to his demand and command. Never be afraid to demand and command anything that is a Universal Principle of Life.

"Make no mistake! The Light, the Universal Electronic Substance, is for your use—is at your command! Your 'Mighty I AM Presence' is a Self-Conscious Being of which your outer consciousness is but a fragmentary part. Therefore you can talk to your Mighty Master within as you would to a loving father who possessed limitless Light, Love, Riches, Power, Health, Happiness, or anything you could desire; for the more you consciously use this Mighty Presence of the 'I AM,' the quicker will It respond to you.

"Divine Love can control all manifestation! If in your use of Divine Love you are conscious that It has within Itself all Love, Wisdom and Power of this 'Mighty I AM Presence,' the fact is that you qualify this Principle which you command with whatever quality you are conscious of as being within It. You are given Dominion over everything in the air, in the earth, in the fire, and in the water—through the command of this 'Mighty Universal Principle' which is always at your Conscious Service and for your use.

"Love, Divine Mind, and Prana are One in the static or still state. Through the Conscious Action of the individual, Divine Love consciously directed, becomes Love, Wisdom and Power—in action. This is why Divine Love consciously directed to accomplish things produces such marvelous results. It becomes Instantaneous and All-Powerful as soon as the outer consciousness ceases to limit It.

"Now to return to the explanation of the Rays:

The Almighty God Flame, breathing within Itself, projects Two Rays into the Great Sea of Pure Electronic Light. This Intelligent Light Substance becomes the clothing, as it were, for these Rays of the 'Mighty I AM Presence.' Each Ray has all the Attributes of the Godhead within It, and no imperfection can ever enter into or register upon It. The Individualized Flame sends down into each Ray a Focal Point or Spark, forming a Heart Center upon which gathers the *Electronic Light Substance,* creating the Electronic Body. Around this It sends out Rays of lesser intensity that form an aura or force field. This force field is sometimes referred to as the Causal Body, and within It are deposited the results of all constructive effort during and between each embodiment. All Electronic Substance that has been used constructively by the personal self through physical experience is also deposited within It. Through It, the God Flame can send out into space a Greater Release of Its own Life Wave.

"The Causal Body, through the personality's journey in physical experience, becomes an Ever-expanding Sun and a Self-sustained Outpouring of Limitless Ideas, Love, Wisdom and Power, flowing out forever on Rays of Love to the rest of this Universe. This Sun is in reality a Reservoir of constructively used energy and substance, gathered through human experience and drawn upward, so

It becomes the Glory of the 'God Flame,' which mark you, never loses Its individual identity in the Universe. This is how the Beautiful, Joyous, Perfect, Limitless Activity of Life and Creation goes on— ever expanding Its Perfection.

"The Universal Substance and Energy which the personal self uses discordantly accumulates in the atmosphere around the physical body of both the personality and the Earth. Periodically it builds a vortex and can only be purified and returned to the Great Sea of Universal Light by the activity of the Fire Element.

"The purifying process of the Fire Element acting within the flesh of the human body to consume wrong qualities sometimes produces the sensation of pain if wrongly qualified by the personality; but if the Fire Element acts within the flesh of the human body to vivify and energize, It produces the sensation of Peace, Exhilaration and Ecstasy. If acting in the atmosphere of the Earth and within Nature to purify, It sometimes produces volcanic and cataclysmic conditions; when acting to vivify and energize in Nature, It produces marvelous growth and pure, rarefied air which vitalizes all.

"The personal self of every individual is endowed with the Power of Choice as to what it wishes to think, to feel, to create and experience. If one uses all the substance and energy of his Being constructively, then Peace, Expansion, Joy, Opulence, and

Glory are the return unto Life for the Outpouring of Its Gifts. If one chooses and creates otherwise, his misery and destruction return into himself and destroy his body.

"The personal self is a Custodian of Life, of Ideas, and of 'Light Substance,' Pure Electronic Substance. The very fact that one is in existence as a human being is an open acknowledgment to those who are able to read the Book of Life, that he has decreed to come into individual existence and accepted of his own choice the Responsibility of being a Creator. Everyone must carry the responsibility of his world. If he has created, because of the appetites of the physical body, things and conditions he does not enjoy, he has *all power* to purify and dissolve them by the *right use of the Fire Element—of which Divine Love is the Highest, Most Powerful, and Eternal Activity.*

"If he desires to set his personal self and world in order and therefore have Peace and create a world of Joy, Perfection and Glory, he must look to his Electronic Body for the Pattern of his Divine Perfection; for It cannot and never will be found anywhere else. There, and there only, can the personal self ever find security, rest, satisfaction, joy, and the Fulfillment of every constructive desire, for in the 'Fullness of the Presence' are the things that you desire.

"This Perfect, Eternal, Electronic Body abides

from twelve to fifty feet above the physical body of every individual, unless he be a very low or destructive type, when It withdraws still farther away.

"This is the Son and Sun of God, for the Electronic Body of every Individualized Flame of God is a Dazzling, Blazing Light of such intensity that the human eyes can only gaze upon It for the fraction of a second. *By adoration to the God Flame and purification of Its instrument—the personal self—the outer activity of the mind and physical body becomes raised in vibratory attunement to see the Electronic Body clearly within the Blazing Light of the force field around It.* The physical body or actual atomic structure of the flesh is the densest form and is the record of the outer activity of the mind.

"In certain phases of religious explanation concerning this Electronic Body, It has been referred to many times as the Guardian Angel. It is all of that and more when really understood and comprehended. To It, the personal self should look for the Supply of every good thing as a child looks to its mother. All that is within the God Flame flows into the Electronic Body, where the Tremendous Power and Intensity of the Light of the 'Mighty I AM Presence' is stepped down to a degree that can act in the vibratory octave of the physical world.

"From the Heart Center of the Electronic Body flows a Stream of Life Essence, or Liquid Light, which enters the physical body through the pineal gland and fills the nerve channels. This Liquid White Fire flows through the nerves as blood does through the veins. This beats the heart, moves the muscles of the body, and enables one to walk or raise the hand. It is also the Energizing Light within the brain cells.

"The Life Stream of the body has often been referred to as the 'Silver Cord.' So It is; for the Stream of Liquid White Light pulsates continually through the flesh body by way of the nervous system. At so-called death, the 'God Presence' withdraws the Stream of Liquid Light, and the flesh disintegrates. The reason the race continues to experience so-called death is because of the waste of this Electronic Light through emotional excesses, instead of retaining It within the physical brain and body to rebuild the cellular structure and supply the Motive Power for the entire body.

"Mankind does not like to hear this Truth, but the waste of the Life Energy through uncontrolled feeling is the cause of the disintegration of all physical bodies outside of violence. If one uses the Inner Sight to observe the Life Stream of a strong healthy child, he will see the nerves of the body full of this Dazzling Liquid White Light.

"Then if he observes the body of the same child when ill or fatigued, he will see the Light greatly diminished. In an old body, it is still more greatly dimmed, and if one wishes to observe the Soul passing out of the body at so-called death, he will see this Life Stream entirely withdrawn at the top of the head, until It becomes only a thin thread of Light which finally breaks. At that moment, the heart ceases to beat.

"Again, let us return to the explanation of the Rays: Nada and Bob Singleton are two other Rays of an Individualized God Flame. Whether you choose to accept this wonderful fact depends entirely upon yourselves. I do not even suggest—but knowing the secret feeling of your Hearts as I do, it is my privilege to disclose this much. It will explain some of the feeling which you have not understood.

"My sincere hope is that all four of you will be able to raise your bodies in this Life—with the outer attention consciously directed to that point. With the Assistance which We can give at the proper time, you will be able to accomplish the Final Attainment. I feel your gratitude, for which I thank you. In answer to your thought of why this Glorious Privilege is yours, I want you to know that it is because of previous growth. Your own Indwelling 'Mighty I AM Presence' commands It for your Safeguard and Illumination.

"I shall now give you the Explanation of the Law by which you are able to illuminate, raise the physical body, and express the Full Dominion, Victory, and Freedom of the Ascended Masters:

"The seed within man and woman is only

intended for the sacred office of creating a body by which another Soul may come into physical embodiment. At all other times, the Glorious Light within the body should be raised into the top of the head and allowed to flow up in adoration unto the 'Mighty I AM Presence.' Then by uplifted thoughts and feeling, one can do creative work at the mental level through glorious ideas, ideals of art, music, invention, discovery, research, and the creation of beauty and harmony of every description through a Service that blesses humanity, and therefore the individual who gives it.

"Instead of wasting the wonderful Liquid Light, the Marvelous God-given Essence of Life, in sex sensation and excesses, whereby the body becomes decrepit, flabby, crippled, face lined, eyes dull, the whole structure stooped and feeble, the brain inactive, sight and hearing impaired, and the memory not able to function—this Energy should be rightly used in wonderful, idealistic Creative Activity.

"In such constructive consciousness and accomplishment, the physical body would remain eternally youthful and beautiful, the brain and faculties keen, alert, and active; and the whole physical expression would become the Image and Likeness of the living God—truly the 'Temple of the Most High!'

"Your bodies are now calling for their accustomed rest. The chambers are in readiness. Sleep until you awaken. I commend you to the Embrace of your Glorious 'Mighty I AM Presence.' Rest in peace."

We returned to our beautiful sleeping chambers where all was in readiness. The most delightful fragrance of roses permeated everything, and we certainly never rested upon more comfortable couches, nor enjoyed such divine repose. Rex was very happy to find that Pearl was the "Twin Ray" of his own God Flame, and in speaking of her after he and I had gone to our room, said:

"Ever since we first met, I have felt a strange attraction to Pearl, and whenever in her presence, I am always conscious of a sense of quiet contentment. Our Blessed Saint Germain has certainly explained all most wonderfully, and I am deeply grateful."

"In giving this explanation to me some months ago," I replied, "He said to me: 'The Beautiful Love of one Ray for its Twin Ray is tremendously uplifting, exalting, wonderful, and infinitely more joyous than when the great Current of Liquid Fire, the Life Stream of the Universe, is turned downward and becomes passion.

"'This Mighty, Concentrated Electronic Force, or Life Essence, is a Liquid Light which flows wherever the attention directs It. The mind's attention is pulled this way and that by thought, feeling, sight, and hearing—in fact by the pull of all the physical senses. The True Understanding of what Mighty Power is at your command when you have full control over your attention cannot be overestimated. The Liquid Electronic Essence is this Mighty Energy, and It energizes whatever the attention rests upon.

" 'If one be doing intense mental work, the Liquid Light stays within the brain and flows forth through the center of the forehead between the eyes as a Ray of Light, and if the Inner Sight be opened, one can easily and always see It. If one be speaking, this Pure Mighty Energy flows forth through the Throat Center as sound. If one be pouring out Divine Love, this Liquid Light flows forth as a Radiance from the Heart Center.

" 'If one be sending out intense feeling, It flows forth from the solar plexus. Here It also performs the function of digesting the food. If one has the Inner Sight opened, he will see a Stream of Light pouring out from whatever center the energy is being used at the moment. This Pure Liquid Light becomes colored by whatever quality the personality imposes upon It through the thought, feeling, and spoken word. Here lies one's responsibility as a creator, and the means by which he can correct or purify whatever has been wrongly created.

" 'If this Life Essence is released at the generative center for sex pleasure instead of building a new physical embodiment for another Soul, the process of disintegration of the physical body is started, and the journey to self-generated dissolution of the body begins. It matters not what human opinion says to the contrary; this is the *inevitable, inexorable Law* of physical embodiment, and there is no person in the Universe who can change It.

" 'This is the *principal reason* for the condition that is called death within the race as a whole. Let anyone who disagrees with this Truth compare the brain and body of one who conserves this Liquid Light over a period of a few years with that of one who has wasted It over a similar period, and he will not need any other proof. The conservation of this Liquid Electronic Light and the conscious lifting of It by adoration to the "Mighty I AM Presence" and by the power of the mind through the control of the attention is the Way of Perfection, and is safe, sound, sensible and reasonable. It can have only harmonious, constructive results to the mind, the body and world of the individual.

" 'This is not a system of repression by the power of the human will. That is and will always be disastrous, for to dam up a highly-concentrated energy and then by thought, feeling and suggestion keep driving more of it to that point through thinking upon it in secret, must of necessity cause an explosion of some kind to take place. That method never was the original spiritual teaching of anyone who really knew and understood the Truth and the Law concerning it.

" 'Humanity has not except in a very small degree, understood this Truth, or thousands would have become Ascended Masters long before now. In order to rise out of the degradation, misery, poverty, and disaster in which the mass is now wallowing, the individual must come to a clear understanding of this Law in the outer activity of his mind. Through his conscious knowledge and control of the emotions, he shuts the door to the most dangerous and subtle suggestions from the psychic plane —which is the most unrecognized enemy and vicious activity of the sinister force in this world.

" 'The feeling nature of mankind is a reservoir of energy, and it is impossible for thoughts to become things until one propels them forth into the Sea of Electronic Substance—by feeling.' "

As we retired, the Glorious Illumination of our room faded out, and we were soon fast asleep. Such heavenly rest none of us had ever before experienced. We must have slept fully twelve hours when the most glorious tones of a bell sounded through the chamber, and the Dazzling Illumination gradually again filled the room.

When we had bathed and donned our Robes, we found a most delicious breakfast awaiting, served on an exquisite crystal-top table which neither of us had noticed as being there before. On it was food of which we had never heard, more delicate and

delicious than can ever be served by any culinary
artist of this world. The dishes looked as if they
were made of mother-of-pearl, with heavy gold
bands, and the rest of the service was made of
wonderful semi-transparent metal with pearl handles. We dined and were discussing the wonders
we had been experiencing, when the table with
its entire beautiful service disappeared before our
eyes.

Again the sound of the beautiful bell filled the
chamber. We went to the reception room and there
found Nada and Pearl awaiting us. They looked
radiantly beautiful. Youth always responds marvelously to the 'Mighty Magic Presence,' but in this
change a Transformation had taken place that was
more than usual with both of them revealing a
Radiance which had never been in either of them.
Both showed the awakening of a Great Love, and
while they had experienced the same wonderful rest
as we, yet they had undergone an even more wonderful change.

We had only been talking a few moments when
the great doors to the Crystal Chamber opened. We
entered and found twelve more Ascended Masters
present, making twenty-four with those whom we
had already contacted while in this Retreat. Saint
Germain presented us to Them, and I noticed
one Lady and one Gentleman around whom the
Light was dazzling, for Their Radiance shone

brighter than the others. They came directly over to Nada and Rex, and with Indescribable Grace, greeted them both.

"Beloved Brother and Sister," said the Lady, "We come directly from the Sphere in which your dearly beloved mother sojourns. It is not Her Home, but She is there for certain training. You did not know it at the time, but if you could have looked within the casket before your mother was supposedly placed in the sarcophagus, you would not have found her physical body. We were two of the twelve present who were with the Mighty Master Saint Germain when the Assistance was given that enabled her to be raised into her Eternal Electronic Body. She wishes you to know this—now that you have become aware of and have accepted the Great Ascended Masters' Way of Life.

"These, Our Blessed Ascended Brothers, have found that each of you can be given the necessary Assistance to raise your bodies as She has done when the humanly accustomed time of your earthly pilgrimage is finished. The third night here, She will come to you as We do now. Tonight, Nada and her father will have a very happy surprise."

Again the bell sounded, and our Beloved Saint Germain announced that all were to enter the electrical laboratory. Passing into that room we found the Marvelous Atomic Accelerator aglow with Great Currents of Light. He asked Daniel

Rayborn to take his place in the Chair. The two Radiant Masters stood at opposite points in the circle, one in front, the other behind Rayborn— Saint Germain standing within the circle of twenty-one. Again He asked me to watch the process closely.

In an instant, the Light within Rayborn's body began to increase, and his face revealed great joy. Within the Light around him were particles of substance, continually rising as the impurities in his physical body were thrown off and consumed. This lasted about ten minutes; then I saw his hair gradually return to its natural color, a dark brown, and his face become radiant and youthful. The Light within the Chair gradually disappeared, and the laboratory was again as usual.

Saint Germain extended His hand to Mr. Rayborn and he stepped down lightly, as if scarcely conscious of any weight. For more than an hour, the Radiance about his face and the Brilliant "Light" within his eyes was most remarkable.

"Words can never describe the Marvels I have experienced," he said, turning to us, "and for the first time in my Life, 'I AM' beginning to know the *real meaning* of Life. We do not dream in the unascended state what a small fraction of the Mighty Principle of Life we appropriate and use in our ordinary mundane experience."

"Each of you," said Saint Germain, "has been

tremendously uplifted through the Powerful Radiation of this Marvelous Atomic Accelerator."

We returned to the Crystal Chamber and noticed that chairs to seat twenty-four persons had been placed around the large crystal-top table. The two Radiant Masters took Their seats at the ends, our Beloved Master in the middle, and Nada opposite Him.

"Focus your attention upon Bob Singleton," He said, addressing Nada, "and request him to come to us." Almost instantly, a soft rose-colored Light enveloped all, accompanied by a most delicate fragrance of roses. In a few moments a beautiful blue formed around the rose-colored circle. This was followed by a radiance of gold around the blue. Then we heard a sound like the swish of wings, and Bob Singleton, in a tangible, visible body stood upon the table before us accompanied by the two Radiant Masters who before had been sitting at the ends of the table. I had not noticed that They had left until Their return with Bob.

As he stood there, I could see his form becoming more and more dense, until presently his body was as tangible as my own. Saint Germain arose and extended His hand to Bob as he stepped lightly from the table. We all rose to our feet, and Nada looked steadily at him an instant as the rest were about to offer their greetings. Bob put his arms around her and held her close to his Heart.

"My Precious Love," he said, "I have always seen you in my dreams. When you came to the mine, I knew you as my Angel Love, but you seemed so far beyond me, I did not even dare to hope. Now to hold you in my arms is the most divine thing I know. In the Glorious Freedom of this Inner Body I see the Light of Divine Love between your blessed brother and my dear sister. My gratitude is boundless."

Daniel Rayborn stepped forward with extended hands and gave his blessing to this Great and Divine Love; then turning to Pearl and Rex, gave them his blessing also, saying that in his highly attuned state, he realized all more clearly.

"Will I be able to remember this," said Bob, turning to Saint Germain, "when I return to my body?" and He replied:

"You shall do so if you wish. The Privilege granted you at this time is a very rare occurrence, for you are clothed in a temporary body. However, it is just as tangible as your own physical body and as the physical bodies of the others here."

Everyone came forward and congratulated the happy lovers, the Ascended Masters making a connecting link through which Assistance could be given at any time in the future in case of need. It was then we were told that the two Radiant Masters were also "Twin Rays." The Ascended Masters present knew Bob from contact with him in the

Higher Spheres, but he did not retain the memory of his acquaintance with Them. When Saint Germain stepped forward, Bob would have kneeled before Him.

"No, Bob," He said, raising His hand in protest, "your own 'Indwelling I AM Presence' is just as Great as the Ascended Masters who have found the way before you to complete Mastery and Freedom. To It belongs your First Love, Recognition, and Worship at all times—never forget that. 'I AM' your Elder Brother, that is all; and it is My Privilege to assist you to that same Freedom. It is at the Command of your own 'Mighty I AM Presence' that you are enabled to be here in this manner tonight. It is always a joy to be of any assistance that the Great Law of your Being permits.

"I wish you to come tomorrow night in this same manner, that you may meet your sweetheart's mother, for She will also be here at that time. Much is being done which you do not now understand, but your beautiful Love and Trust is opening wide the gates to Blessings of which you do not dream. However, the full understanding will come as you progress. Arrange your work at the mine so as to retire promptly at nine o'clock. Now you must return to your physical body." He then asked us all to form a circle about Bob.

In a few moments the Radiant Circle of Light in rose, blue, and gold again enveloped us. The two

Radiant Masters took Their places beside Bob, and in an instant, all three disappeared. The rest of us walked about in the Crystal Chamber, and in about twenty minutes the Radiant Ones reappeared in our midst.

Never in my whole existence have I ever experienced such wonderful joy and unspeakable Divine Love as radiated from everyone present. This finished our work until the following evening. The twelve Ascended Masters who had appeared last formed into a circle, and in a few moments, disappeared from view. The remaining six, after extending to us Their Blessing, vanished before our eyes.

We all gathered around our Beloved Saint Germain in boundless gratitude for the Marvels we had witnessed and the Limitless Blessing we had received.

"My Beloved Students," He explained, "do you not see how much easier, how much more joyous it is to rise above all human, earthly limitations and produce whatever you require direct from the Universal Substance—which is the Eternal, Omni-present Supply of everything you can ever desire? Each one of you who has been requested to come here can learn to do this much sooner than you dare to imagine in the outer activity of your mind. The time required to attain this Mastery is tremendously shortened when the individual comes to the understanding that his physical body is the Temple of the 'Mighty I AM Presence,' the GOD of the Universe; and the very Life Energy which moves his body across the floor is the Most High Living God! This is the Christ, the Only Begotten Son—*God in Action.* However, I find many who get tremendous results by thinking of It as the Ascended Master Within, or the 'Mighty I AM Presence' to whom they can talk. This 'Presence' is a Glorious Blazing Light. You can see Its Light within your outer mind and body—Its Visible, Tangible Presence resting a short distance above your physical body. You can speak to It and receive Its Definite Answers, Perfect Direction and Wondrous Revelation.

"You can thus always be God directed if you will only contact your 'Mighty I AM Presence' close enough and often enough. Its Mighty Wisdom, Intelligence and Liquid Light will flow ceaselessly into whatever you wish to accomplish if you will but hold your attention steadfast upon the 'Mighty Presence' *first* and whatever you wish to attain second. Then follow this up by determined, persistent insistence. Such Almighty Power and Intelligence is absolutely Invincible and can never fail.

"Human doubt and fear, which are subtle feelings, can keep you from accepting this 'Mighty I AM Presence' and Its Perfection if you let them, but the 'Presence' never did and never can fail. This is a simple formula for quick, certain attainment. You cannot possibly estimate what tremendous advancement is possible in a short time if you will— because you can—consciously, continually, and completely accept the Wonderful Love, Intelligence and Power of the 'Mighty I AM Presence' whose Energy is flowing and acting through your mind and body every moment of the twenty-four hours.

"There is one point that Real Students and those who wish attainment should know unmistakably, and that is concerning desire. No one can ever attain Mastery over human creation and gain the Ascension by an attitude of desirelessness, because without desire for attainment, attainment would not be possible. Remember forever that all Constructive Desire is *God in Action* in you; for if desire were not within the God Principle, manifestation would never have taken place. Until the Godhead desired manifestation, it could not come forth.

"The activity of desire is the forward-moving, or expanding motion of Life Itself, and can never be dispensed with. Life is Perpetual Motion, and the sustaining of that Activity is all Constructive Desire.

"However, be careful that you discriminate between desire and human appetite, for they are as far apart as Light and darkness. Appetite is but an accumulation of energy qualified by human feeling through the formation of habit in the sense organism only, and has nothing whatever to do with desire within God's Life; for all that abides within Life is Pure, Perfect, and Constructive. Constructive Desire is *eternally existent* within Life. It is impossible to progress or express Life without some form of desire.

"It is the student's duty to be alert and on guard, discriminating always as to his motive for doing anything. He needs to be severely honest with himself in his feeling and motive, for many times the outer activity of the mind tries to make one think he is doing a thing from the standpoint of reason, when all the time he is doing it to satisfy a feeling instead.

"As yet, the majority of the race are but creatures of feeling, for it controls them ninety percent more of the time than does the wisdom of the mind. That is why they are principally creatures of physical appetites instead of God-directed Masters of Circumstance and Dominion. Until the student takes his feeling body in hand and definitely controls it by the Love, Wisdom and Power of his 'Mighty I AM Presence,' he cannot and never will be dependable, nor can he make permanent progress to Freedom. The 'Mighty I AM Presence' stores Its Force in the emotional body, or feeling body, and depends on this Energy to accomplish the Fulfillment of the

Perfect Divine Plan of Life.

"Everyone knows the difference between a Constructive and destructive idea, and the difference between the feeling of Love, Peace, and Calm, and that of discord. So the simplest mind, even a child, innately knows the difference between the Divine Way of Life, a God Desire, and the human appetite for self-gratification. We are commanded to choose the Divine Way of Life, and if we do not compel the sense appetites to obey that Command, then we must suffer, experiencing chaos and destruction until we set our own world in order so it blends with the Great, Orderly, Harmonious Movement of the Whole. Purity, Order and Harmony are the *Law of Perfection* forever.

"When one wishes to give way to his own feeling of resistance rather than still that feeling and replace it by Peace, he destroys himself—mind, body and world—because the Law is that whatever discordant thought and feeling is sent forth by a human being, it must first vibrate through the brain and body of the sender before it can reach into the rest of the Universe. After swinging out, it begins the return journey to its creator. While coming back, it gathers more of its kind, and that becomes the accretion of which the individual's world is composed. This is *The Law,* and it is Immutable.

"When the Great Life Energy within the physical body is used constructively, the result is the greatest possible joy, happiness, and accomplishment—not only to ourselves, but to every person, place, condition and thing we control. Then the 'Mighty I AM Presence,' through the vehicle of the personal self, manifests Divine Love in action—and the firmer and more concentrated the attention, the more powerful the action and the more marvelous the results.

"Now all go to your well-deserved rest. The All-Powerful Illumination and Infinite Peace of the Most High God attend each, for I shall have much to say to you at the close of Our Work tomorrow night. Let everyone remain in his bath not less than fifteen minutes; it will be especially prepared. Then there will be food awaiting you. With My Peace, Strength, and Love I enfold you, and to your own 'Mighty I AM Presence' I commend you all. Good night."

We went to our respective chambers and found everything aglow with the vivifying Life of the "Mighty I AM Presence." The very atmosphere was charged with the Pure Electronic Light. Upon entering my bath, I was delighted by the very Living Presence within the water. It was like the magic caress of the Mother of all Life.

Every atom in my body was quickened into that

Radiant Peace that passeth all understanding. When we were ready for the meal, we stood before the mirror and scarcely knew ourselves—each looked and felt glowing and radiant. Our repast was heavenly, and after finishing it, we retired at once.

At five o'clock the following evening, we were awakened by the beautiful tone of the etheric bell sounding through our chambers, and we noticed the Radiance of the Light about us was much more dazzling than usual. It had been so quickened within our own bodies that Its Radiance emanated from our hands with great vividness.

The food provided was of the rarest quality and was like Concentrated Essence. There was a creamy, golden liquid that seemed almost like Liquid Light. As we partook of It, I said to Rex:

"You know, some unusually powerful experience must be about to take place, and we are given this Liquid so the body will not be burdened with unnecessary substance."

As we finished, a small crystal tumbler about the size of a wine glass appeared on the table before each, and with it came a slip of paper on which were the words, "Drink without fear." The substance in the glasses looked like Pure Electronic Energy. I picked up my glass and drained it without stopping. At first it seemed as though my being would never stop expanding, and then came a sense of being lifted to tremendous heights. I thought I was going to lose consciousness, but I did not. I soon became adjusted to It, and then I looked at Rex and saw him standing in a Flame of Blazing Light—his eyes were closed and his body swaying as though about to fall. I started towards him when the words flashed before me: "Have no fear!" Presently, he opened his eyes, and as he looked at me, two Rays of Light streamed through them. It was an amazing experience, and it was fortunate indeed that we did not fear.

In a moment, the bell sounded calling us to the Crystal Chamber. As we came to the large doors, they swung quietly open, and the most ravishing music greeted us. At the organ was seated the most Beautiful, Masterful Presence I have ever seen or imagined, and another, Its "Twin Ray," sat at the piano. No words can possibly do justice to those harmonies, for the music reached into the very depths of one's soul. We were not aware anyone else was in the room until the music ceased, and then we realized that ten of the Ascended Masters stood in our midst. Just beyond Them were Nada and Pearl, enveloped in a Brilliant Light that extended around them for about three feet. Another glorious flood of music followed, and suddenly in the midst of it, we all turned towards the door. Our Beloved Saint Germain and Daniel Rayborn entered with a beautiful Lady Master between them.

As They came in, the music ceased, and Nada and Rex exclaimed, "Mother!" The next instant both were clasped in Her arms. In a few moments Rex came to where I stood, and putting his arm around me drew me to his mother saying:

"This is our wonderful friend who came to us a few weeks ago. We could hardly love him more."

"My Dear Son," said his mother, "I have observed much that has taken place, and I am quite as grateful as you for such a true friend to my loved ones. I join the family in the great Love which they extend so sincerely. I see you reciprocate it radiantly. May God's choicest Blessings, Love, and Illumination enfold you always."

All came forward and extended greetings like one beautiful happy family. We suddenly felt an intense vibration, and looking up we saw the Master who had been playing the organ floating near the ceiling above us. It really seemed as if we were in the Etheric Realms instead of in the heart of a mountain on the Earth. Presently She stood on the floor beside us. We were presented to Her as Daphne, "The Child of Light." We met Arion, Her Companion at the piano, and Saint Germain remarked that They were from the Seventh Sphere, having long ago reached the Ascended State, completing their journey through human experience.

Daphne and Arion came directly up to Nada and Rex—a great Inner Attunement forming the bond between them. They asked if the children would sing to the accompaniment of the organ and piano. They replied in the affirmative, and Daphne asked Nada what they were going to sing.

" 'Love's Light Eternal,' " she said. "Rex and I wrote it." Daphne touched Nada's forehead a moment.

"I have it," She said, and stepping to the instrument, began. The children's voices were splendid before, but now there was a new power and beauty that was wonderful. Even the Ascended Masters expressed Their appreciation. Someone asked Nada's mother to sing and from the moment She began, a Thrill of Joy filled every Heart as She poured out Her Great Love to bless all through the song. It surely was the Glory of Heaven poured out upon Earth.

It was at this point that Saint Germain asked us to come into the electrical laboratory. When we had assembled around the Atomic Accelerator, He requested each one who had not raised his body to follow in turn and take his place in the Chair, beginning with Daniel Rayborn, Pearl, Rex, Nada and myself.

"The 'Mighty I AM Presence' within each will tell you when to leave the Chair," He instructed, "as no word should be spoken while the raising process is in operation."

Daphne took Her place facing the Chair, and Saint Germain directly opposite. Rayborn seated himself, and a dazzling blue-white Light blazed forth crystal clear. In perhaps ten minutes, his flesh looked perfectly transparent. Slowly a current of vivid blue moved up his spine and met the combined currents of the pineal gland, pituitary body, and the base of the brain, forming into a Dazzling Golden Light encircled by the most vivid blue I have ever seen. Then by the very Power of his own Light he arose and stepped forth from the Chair, and as he did so, he seemed to float rather than walk.

Pearl took her place in the Chair. In less than five minutes her form completely disappeared, so dazzling was the White Light. This lasted possibly ten minutes before she emerged from It. As she stepped down from the Chair, the Light followed, as if to caress her.

Next came Rex. At first there was a glow of soft rose Light, gradually changing into gold, blue, and then an intense white, with a glorious tint of blue still remaining. His form did not entirely disappear from view, but in about ten minutes he stepped down from the Chair, his eyes ablaze with the Light of the "Mighty I AM Presence."

Nada seated herself, and instantly the Light

became a dazzling sun, and her form completely disappeared within Its wondrous glow. Presently she seemed to float, so lightly did she step from the Chair, and Rays of intense Light continued to dart forth from the upper part of her body for some time.

Lastly, I took my place. I felt a million points of Light pierce my flesh as the greater force from within the electrons was released through the atomic structure. At first I wanted to jump right out of the body I was using and claim the Full Freedom of my "Mighty I AM Presence." Soon I became adjusted to It, and then a feeling of the most joyous exaltation filled my entire being—a sensation no words can describe.

I poured a Mighty Love to humanity and a prayer that all might be ready to receive this same Glorious Illumination—because no one can recede once he has entered into the Light in this manner. In this tremendously exalted state I consciously sent forth the Mighty Power of Divine Love to bless and illumine humanity more powerfully than I had ever conceived possible. If seventy-five percent of mankind could understand, be raised to this marvelous state and consciously send forth the Mighty Power of Divine Love for seven days, the Earth and all its inhabitants would be transformed. There would be no more selfishness—hence no more strife. Would to God that day were at hand now!

Our Beloved Master asked us to return to the Crystal Chamber. We did so and found the exact number of chairs for those present placed so they faced the eastern wall of that wondrous room. Saint Germain stepped to a cord hanging upon the wall and pulled it. The wall covering drew apart and disclosed a polished surface about twelve by twenty feet.

"This," He explained, "is a Cosmic Mirror in which any individual having reached a certain height of attainment may see his complete series of lives, the cause and effect of his conscious activity, and how the gradual process of Mastery is attained. Then, seeing the Divine Plan of his future, he will understand how to cooperate with the Great Cosmic Forward Impulse, and so, tremendously increase his power of service and usefullness by consciously expanding the Love, Light, Wisdom and Power of the 'Mighty I AM Presence' through himself."

Five of the chairs had been placed directly in front of the center of the Mirror. In these, Saint Germain seated Rayborn, Pearl, Rex, Nada, and myself, in the order mentioned.

"I ask you all to keep your eyes closed," He said, "except the one whom I shall indicate to do the observing, and at no time allow yourselves to speak.

I will speak the name of each one in turn as the preceding one finishes.

"I wish you," He said, indicating me, "to follow the observation throughout, because you are here to observe and understand all that transpires so this Knowledge may be given to the world. The others are here for their own individual growth." I am only permitted to chronicle fragments of the impersonal activities of what was revealed.

"As each one's name is pronounced," the Master instructed, "he is to throw his own Soul's Light into the Mirror, hold it there unwaveringly, and calmly observe the results, no matter what appears:

"Daniel Rayborn."

Immediately a spot of sapphire blue Light appeared upon the milky-white surface of the mirror and steadily expanded until it became crystal clear. Then Saint Germain explained:

"Life after Life appears, some in very great detail, others showing the terrific struggle of the outer self against the certain advance and expansion of the 'Great Inner Light.' This Light is expanding Perfection from the 'Presence.' This may be retarded, but never prevented from attaining Its Ultimate Eternal Victory and Dominion.

"In some cases, century after century and Life after Life pass with but very little progress because of the stubbornness of the outer self. When it becomes weary enough of the husks of existence, the unreality of things, and earnestly and gladly calls to the 'Mighty I AM Presence,' then all barriers disappear, and Its Great Inner Light is enabled to express more and more Perfection. Thus at last is Full Mastery attained." The screen revealed Rayborn's experiences, including even those of his present Life and our recent association.

"You see," He went on, "an Extension has been granted to this good Brother until he has finished certain outer work and the children are through school. These Extensions are only given where it is possible to raise the atomic structure of the physical body into the Electronic. When this takes place, he will be united with his beautiful Twin Ray, the mother of Rex and Nada. Then will They reveal Their True Service through the Mighty 'Magic Presence' of the 'I AM' as Their Radiance grows brighter and brighter. At an appointed time They will come forth with Their Ascended Master Authority and serve in Their Visible Tangible Ascended Bodies, holding positions as Great Teachers of the Light in high governmental offices, being Direct Messengers of the Most High Living God." The surface of the Mirror returned to white and Saint Germain said:

"Pearl."

A violet spot of Light appeared, expanded, and

covered the Mirror with a Wonderful Radiance. The entire action was very different. Out of the many lives shown, there were only three in which the outer self rebelled against the "Light." Both masculine and feminine embodiments were revealed. Many times, she was a very earnest teacher of the Truth to humanity. In one she was an eye witness to the crucifixion of Jesus. In another she watched the burning at the stake of Joan of Arc. Then came her meeting and union with Rex, the final Illumining and Raising of their bodies, and the ministry that was to follow. It even showed them always in touch with their parents as beloved friends —no longer in the parental relationship. Again the Light faded, the surface of the mirror became white, and Saint Germain said:

"Rex."

A disc of intense rose-colored Light quickly covered the Mirror, and a long series of lives followed. These gave also both masculine and feminine embodiments. In three of them he was a great teacher of the Truth of Life. Many times he was an officer of importance in large armies. In those, he was very active—especially during the time that the Greek civilization reached its apex. Another was shown in France and still another in England during the time of the American Revolution. Here the Master called our attention to an unusual condition.

"Rex's growth," He said, "has been so steady that he has had no very great struggle in any particular embodiment. This is a very rare thing when one considers the hundreds and sometimes thousands of embodiments that souls pass through in order to gain their Eternal Victory and Dominion. In three consecutive lives he was a renowned scientist and made many remarkable discoveries that blessed mankind.

"We now come to his present Life, which is just well started. Here is the close of his school days, his union with Pearl, and the call to go to the Masters in the Himalayas and the Far East. This will cover a period of at least two years. Notice the marvelous, vivid description of certain work that he will do in the future in which he will play a very prominent part in the government of America." Then with a flash, all vanished from the Mirror, and Saint Germain said:

"Nada."

Almost instantly a Light like a sun covered the Mirror, and as it cleared, Saint Germain continued:

"Here is a most remarkable revelation of hundreds of lives, the embodiments showing intense activity in which there seems always to have been a sincere dominant desire for the Light. In the particular Life now being revealed, it shows the meeting between Nada and Bob Singleton when they were together on Atlantis. At that time he was a nephew of one of the Great Master Rulers. In another, Nada was a priestess in Egypt. In the one now being shown, she was a daughter of an Arab sheik, and for many lives has been under My Care and Instruction.

"This is her present Life, showing our meeting, her contact with Bob, and the sudden end of her schoolwork. She will take up Definite Cosmic Work which Bob is not quite ready to do. Notice, as he awakens fully, the Great Light that blazes forth. Then they will become great teachers of Divine Wisdom. As you see, Bob will raise his body, as well as the others, with the Assistance of the Ascended Masters. Their Future Work from the Ascended State is beautiful indeed." Saint Germain next spoke my name.

Instantly I threw my Soul-Light upon the Mirror, and a revolving Light like a great diamond in the center quickly expanded to the outer rim. Far back in the past I saw my Real Self, the "Mighty Magic Presence" of the Great "I AM," utilizing one body after another through a long series of lives. Two of these were on Atlantis, one as an engineer of mining and aerial navigation. As the second came on the screen, He explained:

"In the last Atlantean embodiment, for the first time since going forth into incarnation, you came into contact with your Twin Ray. In Egypt, you were a secret teacher of the 'One God.' In Rome, you were a centurion during the Life and ministry of Jesus, closing that embodiment in what is now Great Britain—again in England, during the twelfth century—and the following Life was in a feminine body in France.

"Now comes your present Life, again in Perfect Union with your Twin Ray. This goes into the distant future, when in the Great Family of Ascended Masters you will still minister through Divine Love to those on Earth, assisting in their upward progress. The Blessing of Divine Service is a great privilege; but remember always, your First Service, the Greatest Service that can possibly exist is the Complete Acknowledgment and Acceptance of your 'Mighty I AM Presence'—the Mighty Light within and above you.

"I wish you all to remember especially what I am about to say on service, for it is one of the most misunderstood subjects. Many people consider various things as service which in reality are not service at all, but mere slavery to the human creation of themselves or others. The performance of *physical acts* for *gratifying* and *satisfying* of the *limitations* of the *human self* is *not* service, never was, and never will be. That is slavery to human creation and the treadmill of mankind's limitations. Please clear your minds once and for all time completely of that idea as a concept of service. I tell you frankly and truly, it is not. One of the Ascended Lady Masters has said:

" 'The First Service for any of mankind is praise and adoration of the God Self, the Great Master within each individual. In thus fixing the attention of the outer mind on the Only Giver of anything good we can ever receive, it raises the outer mind into the Full Acceptance of the Supreme Conquering Power anchored within the human form, which after all, is Divine.

" 'If, in man's service to man, he fails to hold his attention fixed on the "Supreme Source" of Love, Wisdom and Power, then he has failed in that service to a large degree.

" 'If, in the quest of things in the outer senses, he becomes so occupied that the conscious attention becomes fixed on the manifestation instead of the "Supreme Presence" that produces it, then again he has missed the mark.

" 'Again, if in man's great desire to serve, the overwhelming desire to serve his fellowman causes him to neglect to keep his attention fixed on the Supreme Producer, then that service too has failed to a large degree.

" 'The Only True Service is in holding the attention and acceptance so firmly fixed upon the "Great

Master Within"—the Only Producer—that the outer mind becomes so filled with the "Inner Presence," that naturally each activity of the day becomes, without considering it, the Perfect Divine Service of the moment. Then the "Great Master Within"—the "Mighty I AM Presence"—is always conducting the outer activity, until the entire action becomes Perfection expressed.

" 'The outer self, until fully awakened, has periods in which it unknowingly wants to strut its vanity and abilities over its fellowmen. This always invites a shock of some kind to shake up the outer self until it becomes aware of what it is doing. Then it wildly looks about for its Source of Power, which it has either forgotten or willfully pushed aside; for in our compulsory choice and the use of the Free Will, this "Great Master Within" will not intrude Itself unless welcomed and invited joyously to do so. I say "joyously," because the more joy we can put into the acceptance of the "Mighty Indwelling Power," the quicker manifestation follows.

" 'Our acceptance is a command which must be obeyed. It cannot be denied. The attention and acceptance must be *held long enough,* firmly enough, and steadily enough upon the "Mighty I AM Presence," until the shell of the outer self is completely shorn of the idea that it has any power of its own.

" 'The outer mind cannot argue against the fact

that all the energy it uses comes from the "Great Presence Within," no matter how that energy is applied. Never let any desire for service deprive you of the needed time—undivided—to fix your attention and acceptance on your "Great Master Within," knowing then that you will naturally give the right service and do the right thing. This is the Law of True Divine Service which says forever to the personal self: "Thou shalt have no other Gods before me." This is the whole of the Law applied.'*

"The personal self has absolutely nothing of its own, for it comes into embodiment without even clothes, and unless the physical body is illumined and raised, it passes through so-called death and leaves even the body behind. So the personal self really owns nothing. It cannot deny the fact that all it has is loaned to it by the Great Master Presence, no matter how much it misuses the marvelous gifts of Life.

"Keep your attention to the Heights, the 'Light,' and the struggle of the outer self will soon cease.

*This Instruction concerning service was originally given forth by one of the Lady Masters, also known as Nada, who raised Her Body 2,700 years ago and who does very Transcendent Work for the humanity of this Earth, as well as a Greater Work which She does in very much Higher Spheres. It was Saint Germain's Request that it be put into *The Magic Presence* at this point, for He gives it to all His Students and has placed it here that everyone who reads this Book may have the benefit of Her Radiation as well as His Own, and profit thereby.

You will find yourselves steadily rising into that glorified Ascended State where the Joy of Divine Service so far transcends earthly comprehension there are no words to describe It.

"This discloses the revelations of individual growth through hundreds of lives in earthly experience. It is a rare occurrence and privilege for any student to be shown this, and it is only permitted where the individual has reached a height of attainment and Inner Strength that will enable him to observe the experiences of the past without receiving suggestions or being in the least influenced by them, no matter how terrific they may have been."

Only a tiny fragment of all which passed upon that Mirror is recorded here; for the experiences of one individual alone through hundreds of embodiments would fill many volumes. Saint Germain then drew the covering over the Mirror, and taking His place in front of His guests, gave a most marvelous Discourse. Much of it was private Instruction and information for those present concerning their own work. I will give only a very small portion of it here.

"It is my wish," He said, addressing Pearl, Nada, and Rex, "that Pearl return with Nada to her school. "It is quite imperative at this time for her to take up certain studies which I will indicate for the year, until their graduation. At the end of that time I shall be very happy to have you accompany me to the Far East, where you are to remain for two years and make Certain Contacts which it is necessary for you to have.

"At that time, Bob will be ready to go with you. I will see that dependable men are brought to the mine and ranch. One year from today, July 28, 1931, we shall all meet again in the Cave of Symbols, and Daniel Rayborn will complete the raising into his Electronic Body and enter Perfect Freedom with his beloved Twin Ray, Nada, 'The Child of Song.'

"Each of you will receive Training and Instruction from time to time as you require it, and this will be your Path to Freedom. You all know there is but One Source to look to for anything, and that is your 'Mighty I AM Presence' within and around you to whom you can call—and you will never fail to get a response. From It, you may receive without limit Courage, Strength, Power, Protection, and Guidance which will take you through any ordeal you may ever encounter.

"I have not observed any weakness within you; otherwise you would not be here. Trials will arise from most unexpected places. You will, of course, remember that the sincere student is *never off guard*. The Inner Light will never fail unless you deliberately turn from It, a thing I trust none of you will ever do!

"Now will you join me around the Crystal Table? We still have another service to render our beloved brother Bob." When all were in their places, He asked Nada to call Bob with the "Inner Light." In about ten minutes he stood on the table before us. Rex extended his hand, and Bob stepped lightly down and clasped Nada in his arms. She led him forward and presented Bob to her mother, who had returned to the audience chamber with Daniel Rayborn.

She looked at him steadily for a moment, and with the sweetest smile held out Her arms and embraced him. As She did so the Light within Her blazed forth with such intensity that their bodies were hardly visible.

"My Beloved Son, in whom I am well pleased." She said, releasing him, "I congratulate you both on this discovery and the Love that enshrines your Divine Union. The Greatest Blessing My Power of the Ascended State can give enfolds you both forever. Always remember that Pure, Unselfish Love and Devotion form the Open Pathway to the Ascended State."

Nada asked Daphne and Arion to play again, and They assented. When They took Their places at the organ and piano, a Dazzling Light floated above Them near the ceiling. As They struck the first chords of a beautiful melody, a Glorious Tenor

Voice burst forth from within the Light. The control of the Voice was Perfect; its range seemed to be almost without limit.

Here we were listening to a Being we did not see, yet whose Voice was the most magnificent proof of the "Presence" and Its Great Gifts to mankind. When the first song was finished, the organ, piano, and Voice all modulated into "America." Instantly everyone arose, not only in tribute to America, but to the Great Master whose Wondrous Voice thrilled us all.

"America," said Saint Germain, "means so much more than most of Her inhabitants dare to dream; for She is the Heart Center of the Spiritual Progress on this planet. It is in America that the firm Foundation of the Cosmic Christ—the 'Mighty I AM Presence'—will find anchor in the Hearts of mankind. This Great, All-Powerful Light shall intensify and expand until not a vestige of selfishness or political intrigue will remain or be remembered. Many amazing things will take place in the coming years, until mankind will truly realize the time of miracles is not past, but is forever with us. We will then understand they are but the results of obedience to the Great Divine Plan of Life. We are just beginning to enter an age of so-called miracles which will reveal the glories 'The Magic Presence' holds waiting for Its Children.

"America is *the Grail—the Cup for this Earth—*that carries the Light of the Cosmic Christ which shall illumine the Earth and set it in Divine Order by the Power of the 'Mighty I AM Presence.'"

Bob was so happy, he asked if he might be permitted to meet our Beloved Master in the visible, tangible body before the school season opened, and Saint Germain replied: "It may be sooner than you expect, for your blessed friends will be at the mine shortly, and I will meet with you all at that time— let us say the tenth of August. Now, Bob, you must return to your physical body." Instantly the two Radiant Masters stood on each side of him. Bob said good-night to his sweetheart and those present, and they immediately disappeared. The rest of us gathered around Nada—the mother—who embraced each of Her loved ones. "It is time We must part," She said, "but on this occasion it is in joyous rapture instead of sorrow, as at our first parting."

"I wish you to return to your chambers," Saint Germain directed, "and rest until two o'clock to-morrow, and then return home. Proper food will be served when you are ready. It is My privilege to escort this Beloved Child of Song (indicating Rex and Nada's mother) to the Sphere where She is sojourning."

We watched Them closely and saw the two Forms

begin to fade from view, and in about three minutes They completely disappeared. Such is the Power of the Ascended Master to come and go in the Tangible Body and make It visible or invisible at will. In the intense interest of watching Nada's mother and our Beloved Master disappear, we did not notice that the other Ascended Masters had gone also, leaving only Daniel Rayborn, Pearl, Nada, Rex and myself. As we looked at each other, I do not think there was a dry eye in the whole group, for tears of the greatest gratitude and joy we had ever known filled our eyes and Hearts to overflowing.

We returned to our chambers and found the most appetizing dinner awaiting us. There was a delicious nut-loaf, an amber liquid, wonderfully refreshing, and a combination salad made of things we had never eaten before. As we lay down, the Brilliant Light in the room gently faded out until only a soft bluish-white Radiance like moonlight remained. Unless one has experienced something of this kind, it is not possible to describe the feeling of rest and quiet such Light conveys.

The next thing we knew we heard the etheric bell sound through our chambers, and when I looked at my watch I saw it was one o'clock. We put on our robes and sat down to the small crystal table in our room, laden with luscious fruits, among them peaches and strawberries such as I have never seen in the outer world. There was a substance like heavy whipped cream for the fruit, and every spoonful sent an electric charge through the body that gave one the Feeling of Strength, Courage, Power and Confidence which it is impossible to explain.

As we finished our repast, a slip of paper asking us to come to the Crystal Chamber at once floated down to the table. The great doors opened at our approach, and as we entered, Saint Germain and the others who had already arrived greeted us.

"Our work here is finished for the present," He said, as soon as we were seated, "for you have each leaped ahead in growth very rapidly because of previous attainment of which you are entirely unaware. Now you shall return to the ordinary routine and activity in the outer world, but you are no longer of it. Never again will the vibratory action of your minds and bodies be lowered to the point where they were before you entered the Cave of Symbols three days ago.

"Your friends will see and feel the Change, but will not know Its Cause. They will always be restrained from asking personal questions. You may now wear your clothes of the outer world, but always keep your Robes, as they are for your meditation and communion with the Ascended Masters.

"I have my own Way of keeping in constant touch with you. If you will come with me as soon as you are ready, I will take you to the opening of the Cave, as I must be in the Far East at five o'clock this afternoon. Henceforth, we are never separated."

We returned in our hiking clothes, and Saint Germain led us to the entrance. We tried to express our gratitude, but He raised His hand for silence and said:

"In the future let us refrain from attempting to express what is already known to the others. We, I trust, have gone beyond the need of human conventions. I know the Great Love and Gratitude in your Hearts. My own Love and Gratitude are just as great as yours—that you have found the Way into Eternal Light, Freedom, and Perfection. That I have been privileged to be of Assistance is my sufficient reward. All is at the Command of 'The Magic Presence' within you—the 'Mighty I AM Presence' of the Universe."

As He ceased speaking, His body grew less dense, became dim of outline, and finally disappeared completely before our very eyes. Our Love and Gratitude to Beloved Saint Germain is Boundless and Eternal; obedience to His Slightest Request is a Command to us and a Joy forever. He has helped mankind so continuously through the centuries that all in this world should give Him every possible cooperation.

CHAPTER V

The Great Command

A S we again looked upon the outer world, it was almost as if we had returned from another planet. We went down the trail to where the auto was waiting, with a joy singing in our Hearts that was unspeakable. We drove back and reached the Rayborn ranch at three-thirty that afternoon. I could not help but wonder several times while at the ranch how it was possible for Rayborn to be engaged in such a line of business and still be privileged to have the marvelous experiences we had witnessed while at the Cave of Symbols. In response to the question in my mind, Saint Germain had explained:

"While it is a very unusual thing to find one who is so nearly ready to be raised occupied in these lower activities of the outer world, yet it does happen occasionally—very rarely of course—that an individual who has had former growth does become entangled, so to speak, in some such outer effort, through business associations of the personality. In these unusual cases the Ascended Masters do give Assistance by instructing them in the use of the Consuming Flame, which enables the individual to consume a great deal of the human creation previously generated. This they must use of their own choice. In this way such an emergency can be taken care of and the plan of many lives fulfilled. We do not give sanction, however, to such avenues of work as the proper course for personal business activities. We do not want any misunderstanding about these conditions which the human side of mankind generates; for the raising of animals to kill for food is wrong from the beginning to end. But once in a while a soul of very great growth becomes enmeshed in some such activity through the suggestions and general conditions of the outer world. When this happens, the Great Divine Law, through the Wisdom of the Ascended Masters, provides a Way to help the individual who reaches forth for his Full Attainment and wants to be Free."

At seven o'clock on the morning of the ninth, we were to drive back to the mine. The day was unusually beautiful, and Nada's father suggested we go by a way of a high pass through the mountains where we could see one of the most beautiful views of the entire West. Far to the northwest stood the Grand Teton in the midst of a most rugged, beautiful scenic belt that is incomparable. To the south lay Pikes Peak, to the southeast Longs Peak and a host of others reaching skyward. I shall never forget it. Passing on down the mountain, we looked upon a perfect panorama of exquisite beauty. At seven o'clock we drove into the camp at the mine, but no one felt in the least tired.

We sounded the horn, and in a few moments Bob came running out to us at full speed. This time he seemed to have forgotten Pearl and rushed straight up to Nada. She stood very still as though not recognizing him at first. He stopped, turned deathly white; then Nada with her sweetest smile held her arms out to him, but it was some moments before he could speak.

"Darling," he said, "you gave me a terrible shock, and for a moment I felt my Experience in the Cave of Symbols was only a dream. Now I know it was not!"

"No, Love," said Nada, "it was very real—praise God—and I am deeply grateful. We shall both be grateful forever." Then as Bob looked up, he seemed to realize there were others present.

"My Dear, forgive me," he said, taking Pearl in his arms. "You know I would not neglect you."

"Beloved Brother," she replied, "I quite understand. It is all right." Bob gave each of us a bear hug, even to Daniel Rayborn.

"Bob," said Rayborn, "it does my Heart good to see you so natural and loving. Come to dinner with us tonight. From now on you are one of the family. Always dine with us instead of at the camp." That evening at dinner, Bob related his Experience at the Cave of Symbols, for he had retained every detail of it, and was perfectly fascinated by Nada's mother. It was very apparent that through it a Great Attunement had taken place. Then we discussed the work in the "Master Discovery."

"It is amazingly rich," he remarked. "We must have taken out over three hundred thousand dollars in value already."

We were about to leave the table when a piece of paper floated down in front of Daniel Rayborn. On it were the words: "May I have the privilege of dining with you tomorrow evening, and of supplying the food from the Universal Substance? I might suggest that you allow your housekeeper a vacation for the evening." It was signed, "Saint Germain." This idea was something quite new to Bob, and for a few moments he was very much perplexed. "Do you mean to tell me," he said, "that the Master will provide the dinner from the invisible?"

"Precisely that, Bob," replied Mr. Rayborn. "However, you will have ample opportunity to observe all that takes place, for a new world is opening to you." Then the table was cleared and we held a regular business conference.

"In all my life, Mr. Rayborn," Bob began, "I have never seen such marvelous harmony among mining men—or such Love and respect sent by everyone to the owner. I know it must be due to this Master.

"The new assistant, Dave Southerland, has arrived, and I would like to have you meet him in the morning. He was a classmate of mine at the School of Mines in Colorado and graduated a year after I did—with high honors."

"Better have him come now," Rayborn replied. Bob phoned, and in about half an hour there entered a fine looking young chap at least six feet two, well built, with a frank, open countenance that would win the Heart of anyone. He was a man of high honor and sterling ideals, and one felt he could be absolutely trusted at all times.

The next morning, Rex and I went with Bob to the office and found Dave already there. He seemed very grateful and appreciative for his opportunity to be with Bob and Rayborn.

"Gee, I never dreamed I would get so near Heaven," he said with frank enthusiasm. "Dave," Bob answered, "you don't know how near Heaven you really are!"

At a quarter to six we gathered in the living room and had been there for about a quarter of an hour when someone tapped very gently on the door. When Rex opened it, Saint Germain stood before him in a beautiful white flannel suit, a perfectly groomed gentleman of the modern world.

"I thought I would give you a little surprise," He said, greeting us all with His loving, gracious smile.

"Well, Bob," He said, looking at him quizzically, "why don't you do it?" Bob seemed confused for a moment, and coming up, threw his arms around the

Master and gave Him a big hug.

"My Beloved Brother," He went on, "the first step to Perfection is to be natural, for all things are right when the motive is Divine." Bob saw at once that Saint Germain knew his inmost thoughts.

"Now if we may all take our place at your table, we shall dine. The linen and entire service required tonight will be permanent and will be presented to Pearl and Rex as a gift from One who loves them very much."

Daniel Rayborn seated our Beloved Saint Germain at the head of the table, Nada at His right and then Bob; Pearl, Rex and myself at His left, he taking the other end of the table. All bowed their heads in silence as the Master gave praise and thanks for an abundance of everything they required.

As we raised our heads, the most exquisite white cloth covered the table, with napkins for each. In the center was a beautifully carved jade vase filled with roses, some of them buds just opening, and their wonderful fragrance filling the entire room. A crystal goblet containing a Golden Liquid appeared at each place. Saint Germain raised His glass and gave a toast in which we all joined:

"To the Full Illumination, Glory, and Perfection of each one of you and of all mankind!" Bob drained his glass rapidly, and as the Essence rushed through his body like lightning, the expression on his face revealed his surprise.

Next came the plates, cups, saucers, and other dishes of the most exquisite china we had ever seen. It was like the substance of pearls, with embossed golden leaves of wonderful design. The knives, forks and spoons were made of a rare white metal with carved crystal handles. On the place of each appeared what looked like an individual meat loaf, but when we tasted it, there was no meat in it.

"This loaf," Saint Germain explained, "contains a combination of substance not yet known upon Earth. You see, there is a definite reason why We never eat meat, and why human beings should not eat it either. This is because the atoms of which it is composed are the condensation into the substance of this world of mankind's own vicious thoughts and feelings of the past.

"Animals were not in existence upon this planet during the first two Golden Ages. They only began to appear after humanity had generated the discord that followed those first two periods. The First Creation, described in Genesis, referred to these two Golden Ages, and they were described as 'very good.' Then the mist arose, and the so-called fall of man came about by the attention of the intellect becoming focused upon the appetites of the body, through the feeling.

"Thus the outer mind became more and more enmeshed in the world of things, and hence forgot the Source and Powerhouse of its Being, which is the 'Mighty I AM Presence.' The Plan of Completeness, or Divine Way of Life, was lost sight of, and more and more discord has continued to creep into the feeling of humanity ever since.

"As long as human beings insist on killing animals, they will never be able to break the vicious habits within their own feeling by which they have bound themselves; for they are constantly destroying their own bodies and shutting out the finer mental impulses. The Love of mankind for domestic animals is raising and purifying some of that past creation and releasing that stream of Life into a more harmonious phase of existence. As humanity becomes more harmonious and pure, all animals will disappear from the Earth. Even the weeds and blight upon plant life will be removed, and the Earth once again return to her Pristine Purity described as the Garden of Eden—meaning obedience to the Divine Wisdom.

"The great harm of meat-eating is that the flesh of the animal records the feeling of fear it experiences when killed. The animal has an emotional body, and the vibration of fear recorded previous to and at the moment of death qualifies the flesh—and that quality is absorbed by the emotional body of the human being who eats it. It also causes a certain substance to condense into the brain which dulls the intellect and prevents the finer impulses from flowing into it from the 'Mighty I AM Presence'.

"This substance even an Ascended Master will not interfere with because the individual does these things of his own free will. Fear, in its many subtle phases, is the predominant feeling within mankind today, and it is the wide-open door through which the sinister force holds its control in the personality and does its destructive work. The teaching that it is necessary to eat meat in order to obtain strength is vicious and entirely untrue; for the elephant, one of the strongest creatures on our Earth, is a non-meat-eating animal.

"The idea that serums made from animals can produce health and perfection or protection against disease in a clean child's body or that of an adult is another consciously directed activity of the sinister force in this world. It breaks down the health and resistance in the race, that the destructive feeling may hold sway and destroy the ideals of mankind. The medical profession has been unknowingly made a cat's-paw for this destruction, under the guise of science. It is only because of the persistent stubbornness in the sense appetites, which are feeling in the human body, that the race keeps using its marvelous mental capacity and the wonderful Pure Energy from the 'Mighty I AM Presence' to create more and more destruction.

"When human beings will spend the same

amount of time and energy studying Perfection and
the wonderful Miracles of Creation that face us
everywhere as they now do in gratifying the physical
appetites and whims of the personal self, they too
will produce the same Miracles the Ascended Masters are able to do. However, before fifty years are
past, mankind will look back upon the meat-eating
habit of today as we now look upon cannibalism.

"There are several things that leave a substance in
the brain which must be cleared away if the Full
Perfection from the 'Mighty I AM Presence' is to be
released through the personal consciousness. These
are, in the order of their importance: narcotics,
alcohol, meat, tobacco, excess sugar, salt, and strong
coffee.

"Now we come to the remedy for these things, for
I will never point your attention to any consideration of imperfection without showing you the Way
to transcend it and replace it by Perfection brought
about harmoniously. I want you to realize always
that whatever needs to be changed in the physical
experience—if you will call your 'Mighty I AM
Presence' into action through your mind and body,
the result will always be produced without suffering
or discord of any kind.

"The Way of Perfection, which is the Activity of
the 'I AM Presence,' never demands of the personal
self anything but the letting go of its chains, its

discords, its limitations and its sufferings; and this change is always brought about harmoniously and through Divine Love.

"The way to purify the brain and body structure, if the personality has been putting these substances into the physical body in the past, is to call to your 'Mighty I AM Presence' to pour through your mind and body Its Violet Consuming Flame, using the following Affirmation:

'Mighty I AM Presence'! Blaze through me Thy Consuming Flame of Divine Love. Take this desire out of me; annihilate its cause and effect, past, present and future, and replace it by the Fullness of Yourself, Your Perfect Satisfaction, and hold Your Full Dominion here forever!

"This same Affirmation can be used for another with the same miraculous and permanent accomplishment. Then spend a few moments at least three times a day visualizing yourself standing within a pillar of Violet Flame—rushing from the feet to some distance above the head and extending for at least three feet on each side around the body. Hold this picture as long as you can comfortably do so, and feel the Flame, which is the Purifying Power of Divine Love, penetrating every cell of your body. This dissolves all impure and unnecessary substances in the cells of the body, thus clearing and illumining the consciousness. This is part of the Knowledge of the Sacred Fire which has only been taught in the Retreats of the Great White Brotherhood throughout the centuries. It is the way the Ascended Masters purify, heal, and harmonize mankind and the very Earth itself. It is the Power by which so-called miracles are performed. It can never have any other effect in either the brain, body or affairs but great ease, comfort, peace, and eternal good.

"In my reference to the animal creation of this world, I wish you to understand that the birds were originally created by the Ascended Masters as messengers for the use of humanity. What destructive qualities they sometimes express are due to the radiation of discord from human beings. As the New Age comes in, these qualities will disappear. Nature, and by that I mean the plant and mineral life of this Earth, is created and brought forth by the Great Cosmic Masters who design and direct the Creation of a planet at Cosmic Levels.

"Nature within herself is forever pure, and if humanity did not impose its own discord and impurity upon the very atmosphere in which plant life grows, there could not be poisonous weeds or plants in existence. There was a time upon this Earth when everything in Nature affected the minds and bodies of human beings harmoniously.

"Within Nature is a Self-purifying, Self-protecting Immortal Activity which tolerates only for a time man's vicious genius for destruction. Cataclysmic disaster is Her method of Self-defense, in returning to man that which he has imposed upon Her in the centuries past. Thus, through Life after Life, man continually meets his own creation turned upon himself, until he builds his Universe according to the Pattern of Divine Perfection which is the True Expression of his own Divinity.

"Age after age Nature is continually throwing back upon man, through cataclysmic action, his own iniquity; and She is stronger than any opponent because She is the Direct Creation and Outpouring of the Ascended Masters. In this way, man's own discord destroys and buries himself, and Nature in Her Pristine Purity goes on serenely expressing Her Immortality. Notice the many civilizations that have been built upon this Earth, and the fact that Nature has so completely obliterated all traces of man's work in them—until only in tradition and myth is there the faintest record of some of these activities.

"Man, if he has attained Wisdom, which is the constructive use of all knowledge, may have the perfect cooperation of Nature's gigantic forces, and through them make his accomplishments Immortal also. He must stop the stupendous slaughter of animals for food and the business of raising them to kill."

A few moments after we began our dinner, a tiny loaf of bread appeared in front of each one—Nada's and Bob's coming together, and Pearl's and Rex's also. This was followed by a delicious vegetable salad, entirely different from anything we had ever tasted. For dessert, there was a most wonderful fruit-whip made of a combination of peaches, plums, and other fruits unknown to us. Blended into this was something resembling whipped cream, but sparkling like frost, just deliciously cool—another unfamiliar delicacy.

"Now," said Saint Germain, "you shall have something which I feel sure you will prefer even to coffee." As He spoke, an exquisite container appeared before Him, filled with an amber liquid, steaming hot. Cup after cup arose from the table, passing to Him, being filled, and then returned as if held by invisible hands. "This," He said, "does not require cream, and please do not be alarmed by the sensation of the first taste. It is not intoxicating but is one of the most nourishing of beverages." We sipped it very slowly and felt a thrill as of an Electric Current rush through our bodies like Living Light. It was most delicious.

The service for each course disappeared as soon as we were finished and before the succeeding one arrived. At the close of the dinner, Bob could not restrain himself any longer and burst forth: "I have never been so amazed and happy in all my Life. To think that we are living in the very midst of these Marvels all the time; and yet to be so unaware of it is almost unbelievable. The possibility that one may attain this Understanding and have such limitless use of God's Energy and Substance to produce everything we require—as has been done here tonight—thrills me through and through. I want to understand the use of this Great Law more than anything in the world! I am willing to try to do whatever is necessary to attain it. Will you, Beloved Master," he exclaimed, turning to Saint Germain, "help me?"

"My Beloved Brother," He replied, "you have just spoken from the Great Inner Self. It is the 'I AM' within you, and Its Great Wisdom and Power you shall learn to use when you do accept this 'Magic Presence' in Its Fullness. Then you will do these same things as easily as you have seen me do them here tonight.

"Remember in regard to this, that the Ascended Masters never use darkened rooms in which to produce that which They create direct from the Universal Substance. Whatever cannot stand the Light is not of the Christ and should be instantly dismissed! Let no one who serves the Light ever sit in darkened rooms trying to produce phenomena. That which is of the Light always works in the Light; and whatever cannot stand It certainly does not serve the Constructive Path or the Way of Perfection. All that requires darkened places to produce its phenomena is of the psychic plane, and will sooner or later ensnare those who try it in the net of misery and destruction which exists there. If you will follow the Instruction that will be given from time to time, you will have reason to rejoice throughout eternity.

"I shall now keep my promise to you," He continued, turning to Rex and Pearl; and in just a moment, all the service that had been used during the dinner reappeared upon the table as if placed there by invisible hands. "We do all our cleansing," He replied, "by the use of currents of energy, a means that many will also use in the New Age we have entered. This delicate-looking china and crystal service which I present to you is unbreakable." With this remark, a glass and plate fell to the floor without being damaged in the least.

"The table cloth and napkins will never soil nor wear out," He went on, "but never allow anyone to care for them but yourselves. Now I wish to have your attention further. Only because this is a double union of two sets of God's Twin Rays may I produce for your instruction that which will follow." Holding out His hands, in just a moment, a disk of gold about the size of a twenty dollar gold piece appeared in each one.

"Gold will always respond," He remarked, "to your call—if you understand the Great Law governing its production. I wish you to examine this carefully," He commented, as He passed the pieces around the table for each of us to look at closely. We handed them back, and He went on, "Look again!" Immediately, a perfect blue-white diamond formed in each palm, which He offered for our examination; and then taking a piece of gold and a diamond in each hand, He closed His fingers—waited a few moments. When He opened them, a beautiful diamond ring lay in each hand. He handed one to Bob and the other to Rex, saying:

"My Love to you. Wear them always. Please observe again." Here, He held out His hands, and in a few moments there appeared, as though suspended in the air, a pearl necklace above His left hand and a diamond one above the right. Gently, they settled down into His palms, and He continued:

"These are of equal value, and in the commercial world would bring a fortune. I present them to My Beloved Students Pearl and Nada with a *far greater purpose* than that of any monetary value." He handed the pearl necklace to Pearl and the diamond one to Nada, with His Blessing: "My Love to you. Wear them always.

"Now your consciousness is anchored so I can give you the 'Great Command.' With It you can command the body to manifest Perfection, having dominion and use of certain elements, Currents of Electronic Force, and Rays of Light. Thus you can govern your Life and affairs in Perfect Divine Order. This is strictly Private Instruction to you while here in this Retreat, and is never to be given to anyone—except by Me."

He proceeded to explain the tremendous use of the "Great Command," for Its Simplicity is so wonderful and Its Power so stupendous. He then took each one separately and asked us to give the "Command," and to realize fully how impossible it was for anything to result from It but the greatest possible Harmony and Blessing to everyone.

Each of us had instantaneous results, and we were almost speechless before the enormity of Its Power. We took a vow before the Mighty God Self in each that we would never use It except in the Service of Divine Love.

"You have all heard the phrase often, 'With God all things are possible.' I tell you that you can so perfect yourselves, so raise your consciousness into the Pure Essence of God that all things with YOU are possible—as soon as you learn to direct this gigantic Power by the Love and Wisdom of your own 'Mighty I AM Presence.' The 'Mighty I AM Presence' within you is Supreme and Victorious over everything in Heaven and on Earth. Place It *first* always, and contemplate this Mighty Truth whenever you have a quiet moment."

It was now nine o'clock, and it had grown very dark out of doors; yet no one was aware that the Light within had steadily increased as the Light outside grew less. No one thought of turning on the lights, as Saint Germain had illumined the room by His Control of the electronic force.

"I want each of you," He continued, "to so train yourself that you are never surprised at My Appearance. I may come at any time—anywhere—when it is necessary to give Assistance." Here, He looked directly at Bob.

"No, Bob," He said, "a student is never given anything by Us that he is not ready to receive. An Ascended Master makes no mistakes, of that I can assure you! In regard to those who are sometimes called Masters, I wish to give an explanation that is of very grave importance to the Students of Light and Truth.

"In the first place, there are those called Masters, some of whom have attained a very high degree of wisdom and maintained Life in the physical body for nearly two centuries, yet have not raised the body—as Beloved Jesus did. There are also many who call themselves masters who have not the faintest concept of what a Real Master is.

"Of one thing you can be absolutely and eternally certain: that no one who is a Real Master will ever say so, and that an Ascended Master never accepts payment of any kind for the Help He gives—because the First Qualification of True Mastership is to do all as His Glad Free Gift of His Service of Love to the world.

"The Ascended Master is absolutely Infallible at all times because He has passed out of the octave of vibratory action in which mistakes can occur, for He has become wholly Divine. By the raising of His Body, all atomic structure has been changed into the Electronic. He sees with Limitless Vision and knows all because He uses—only—the All-Knowing Mind of God.

"Those Masters who have attained even a very great degree of wisdom but have not yet raised the atomic body, can and sometimes do color what they give out by their own personal concept; for no one becomes infallible until he functions in his Electronic Body, or the Body of Pure Light, where no contamination or personal concept can exist.

"Bob, you are quite worthy of all you have been privileged to experience. Ever strive to make yourself more worthy of the 'Mighty I AM Presence' that beats your Heart and gives you the use of every good thing.

"I wish to suggest that Nada, Pearl, and Rex return to school, and this good brother," indicating me, "remain at the ranch with their father until their graduation and his Ascension. After that the five of you may always consider the Diamond K Ranch your home. Your activity after three more years will be such that the world will be your home, for you will be required to serve wherever your assistance is needed. One year from the tenth of the coming September, I wish Nada, Pearl, Rex, and Bob to accompany me to the Far East, India, and Arabia, and to remain there for two years.

"Bob, it will be well to prepare Dave Southerland in the meantime to take full charge of the mine during your absence. As to our plans, please be absolutely silent. I will meet with you all once more at the ranch just before the young folks leave for the University, and I wish you, Bob, to make arrangements to be there also. I will let you know the exact date later.

"Your Great Love and natural sincerity has opened wide the Door of Illumination. Be ever faithful to the Great Light Within, the 'Glorious I AM Presence.' Always ask, and then listen for your Inner Guidance. It will and must come clearly, definitely, and correctly. I rejoice to have been the guest of such noble, faithful friends. My Love and Blessings shall always be with you. Good night."

As He spoke these Words, the Dazzling Illumination of the bungalow faded out. Rex stepped across the room and turned on the lights. Saint Germain had gone. We returned to the dining room, and before us upon the table stood all the marvelous crystal, china, linen and silver. These people—who are still my beloved friends—have these beautiful Gifts in their possession today.

"Oh, the Glory of this night! It shall stay with me forever!" exclaimed Bob in his natural enthusiasm. "It transcends anything of which I have ever heard or dreamed, and it is real, true, and attainable for each of us! I am so grateful these two great streams of happiness should come to me at once—Nada, and this Great Revelation of Perfection and Power. To have the Gift of the Highest Love possible and the Glory of my Twin Ray in one who has this marvelous True Understanding is a miracle to me—and a thing I have been craving all my Life!

"The happiness of having found the 'Mighty I AM Presence' within myself is beyond words; and when I think of the Assistance from our Beloved Saint Germain and my financial freedom through you, my Blessed Friends, my gratitude is endless. My cup of happiness is surely full to overflowing! I feel as though I could flood the world with that

'Mighty Inner Love,' which I see so clearly is the Great Solvent for all things."

The first thing we heard next morning was Bob saying, "Oh joy! I still have it!"

I asked, "What?"

"My ring!" he answered, and that started the day joyously for us all.

Rex packed the wonderful Gifts of Saint Germain and placed them in the car when we were ready to return to the ranch on the morning of the fifteenth. Great tears filled Bob's eyes as he held each of us to his Heart in wonderful gratitude for all his happiness. When he came to Nada, his strength almost failed; but as he looked up, he saw the face of our Beloved Master, and instantly he was sustained. With a wonderful smile, he assisted each of us into the car and waved good-by.

We reached the ranch the following day. When Rayborn awakened Saturday morning, he found a Message from Saint Germain asking all of us to meet Him in the Tower Room at eight o'clock that evening—and informing us that He had invited Bob to come also.

At twenty minutes to eight we went to the Tower Room, and as we approached it, the door suddenly opened. There stood our Beloved Master in His Seamless White Robe, every line of His Being expressing the Majesty and Dominion of Love. The rest of us wore the Robes we had been given in the Cave of Symbols, except Bob, who had not yet received his. Saint Germain's Radiance enfolded each one as He greeted us. "I see you are prompt and faithful in all things," He said, handing Bob his Robe as He stepped toward him, and then continued, "Accept this with My Blessing." Bob returned in a moment looking like a Being from another world, he radiated such grace and power, and we took our accustomed places.

"Let each one focus his consciousness upon the Light within the Heart from the 'Mighty I AM Presence." In a few moments, we opened our eyes and could both see and hear within the World of the Ascended Master—through the raising of our consciousness during the meditation.

Each one could clearly see his own "Mighty I AM Presence" smiling down upon him serenely. This made us realize deeply what we could become as we hold steadfastly to the acknowledgment and acceptance of the "Magic Presence" and the use of Its Limitless Wisdom and Power. This is the *Only Presence* in the Universe which can raise the human side of us and draw us into Itself. Thus, by Its Love, Light, and Power do we become wholly Perfect. Surely there can be no greater incentive to mankind than to reach with all its strength, determination and devotion to this "Mighty I AM Presence," that we may be raised above limitation of every kind. Then shall we be enabled to live as was originally intended and render Service that is truly Divine.

The opportunity to see, even for a few moments, our own Electronic Body, is a Blessing and Privilege that cannot be overestimated; for it gives us strength and encouragement, drawing us like a magnet— until at last we enter the Holy of Holies and become One with the Source from which we sprang.

After a few moments of contemplating that "Mighty I AM Presence," Saint Germain lowered the vibratory action until most of that Higher Consciousness faded from our sight.

"Do you not see, My Dear Ones," He explained, "how easy it is to consciously lift your consciousness until it expands and encompasses everything you can possibly desire to know?

"This is the method I wish you to use, and by so doing raise your awareness to where you do actually comprehend the Great Law and attain Its complete use and operation. Do you not see how you can utilize and direct this Mighty Energy without limit? You will soon be doing it quite easily yourselves. I have shown you the Individualized 'I AM Presence' of each one, that you may understand what a small fragment of your own God-given Dominion you are using in your physical experience. This Glorious Presence is ever urging you to arise, receive your

Crown of Glory, and wield your scepter of Complete Dominion over Its Vast Domains and be Free *forever* from every limitation. This Transcendent 'I AM Presence' which you have just seen is your own Real Master, the Pure Christ Self. It is all Majesty and Mastery in Full Eternal Dominion over all worlds, over all created things.

"I have a few Directions to give before I leave you tonight. It is my wish that Nada, Pearl, Bob, and Rex meet the rest of us in Washington, D.C. for the holidays between Christmas and New Year. Your father and this good brother," indicating me, "will be there a few weeks ahead of you for work We have to do.

"Alexander Gaylord, your father's friend, will visit you here tomorrow. Remember as you return into the association of the outer world, the *Only True Service* is to understand and use in Perfect Divine Order the Mighty Energy of God within and about you. To consciously direct this perfectly is the only important activity of your lives. All else is secondary. Again I enfold you in the Eternal Light of Love, Peace, and Complete Illumination with My Sincere Blessings." With these parting Words, the body of our Beloved Saint Germain steadily entered into that Higher Vibratory Octave and disappeared.

CHAPTER VI

The Messenger of the Great White Brotherhood

THE prospect of seeing our old friend Gaylord delighted us, for his friendship with both was one of long standing, and it formed a sort of Inner tie. Rayborn and I felt his visit was to be of great importance. Mr. Gaylord arrived at eleven o'clock the following morning, greeted us cordially, and as I was about to thank him for having brought me in touch with the Rayborns, he looked into my eyes steadily and remarked,

"You have our Beloved Master to thank."

"You know Saint Germain then?" I asked.

"Yes," he answered, "I have known Him and been under His Direction in specific matters for some ten years. He is drawing certain of His students together for important work that is to begin this year. This concerns a very serious crisis affecting the entire world, and especially North America. Yet it is possible that certain things can be averted, and if they are, the world at large will never know the vicious danger that threatens and the

169

overwhelming disaster that it will have escaped.

"There is a certain sinister force at work within the atmosphere of Earth that is trying to destroy the beautiful Christ Light which is growing like a flower in the Hearts of more than sixty percent of humanity. The greater portion is in America, but there are many in all nationalities."

We went into the house where Gaylord greeted Rex and Nada as if they were his own children, and was then presented to Pearl.

"May I be excused," he asked immediately. "I have matters of a private nature to discuss with your father, and will you," indicating me, "remain within call?"

In about an hour I joined them, and it was then I realized how important his visit really was. When we were seated, Mr. Gaylord revealed some of his activity as a Secret Messenger of the Great White Brotherhood and presented his credentials. His work in this capacity had extended over a period of seven years. He had his own avenues of personal contact with some of the higher official and diplomatic circles in Washington, as well as many other places of importance. It was because of his personal influence in these channels that he was able to be of such great assistance to the Brotherhood when need arose.

"Saint Germain," Mr. Gaylord began, "is concerned with certain activities in Washington at the

present time. It is His Request that we three reach
there the second of October, and He will meet us on
our arrival. He says it is possible to use you,"
glancing in my direction, "in certain ways which He
cannot do with His other students—a slight example
of which you both experienced when the attempt
was made on Mr. Rayborn's life.

"Remember always," he went on, directing
his conversation entirely to me, "that our Eternal
Motto and rule of conduct is: 'To know, to dare, to do,
and to be silent.' Your trust in your own 'Mighty
I AM Presence' may be severely tried within the next
few months; but you must realize the Messengers of
the Great Ascended Masters may only make Themselves known at the right time—which moment
those in charge of the activity decree."

With a few more personal directions to me, the
meeting was over. After dinner Rayborn and
Gaylord went to the Tower Room. We met again at
breakfast the next morning and I learned they had
both been present at an important Council of the
Ascended Masters in Arabia. Rayborn, with Mr.
Gaylord's assistance, was enabled to go forth in his
Finer Body while their physical bodies remained
undisturbed and protected in the Sacred Chamber.
As Mr. Gaylord was leaving, he remarked:

"I am glad you have all entered the Pathway of
Light, for there alone will you find Permanent
Happiness. Henceforth we shall meet often at the

most unexpected times and places, and from now on distance will be no barrier for any of us." He said good-by, entered his car, and waving his hand, was gone. "How long have you been aware that Mr. Gaylord knew and was under the direction of Beloved Saint Germain?" I asked Rayborn.

"About four years," he replied. While I had known Gaylord a long time, it was only now that I was beginning to see the real magnificence and Inner Character of the man. In referring to this later with Saint Germain, He said:

"Little do people realize how often they are in close contact with greatly illumined souls who are many times Messengers of the Ascended Masters— but are totally unaware of it until some unusual event opens the door and causes them to reveal the Great Inner Light. One might live for months or years under the same roof with a Messenger, and not know him until some crisis arose that caused him to reveal his power."

The young people left for school the next day, and Bob returned to the ranch with us to receive directions from Mr. Rayborn about the work at the mine, and orders to be ready to return early the following morning. That evening we three had a quiet, confidential talk that revealed still more of the nobleness of Bob's character. Arrangements were made for him to come to Washington, D.C., at Christmastime for the meeting with Saint Germain.

Rayborn and I had many enjoyable evenings discussing the Instructions Saint Germain had given us. One evening about a week after Bob had left, we were deep in the study of re-embodiment when Rayborn read to me some of the material on this subject which Beloved Saint Germain had given him. I quote it exactly:

"If human beings only understood that human embodiment upon this Earth is an opportunity given the personal self—by the Great Law of Balance—to correct the mistakes made in previous lives, they would use every experience and extract the lesson from it instead of rebelling against circumstance and being used by it.

"This constant return to physical embodiment, or garments of flesh, would be an endless circle of cause and effect if it were not that man has the 'Presence of God' within him.

"This part of you which says 'I AM' is the Life, the Intelligence, and the Power that moves through your physical body. When the discordant habits of the atomic consciousness of your physical body build to such a momentum the Light of the 'Mighty I AM Presence' is no longer allowed to expand, and through that, maintain the Fulfillment of a Constructive Plan of Life, the Master Self begins to decrease Its supply of energy, and eventually withdraws.

"There is only one thing that ever causes what

the world calls death, and that is the lack of enough Liquid Light within the nerve channels. It radiates the Cohesive Power which holds the atoms together that make up the flesh body. This Liquid Light is owned by and comes only from the 'Mighty I AM Presence' of the Universe. The outer garment is the receptacle into which this 'Presence' pours Its Light for a constructive purpose and use only. When that purpose is continually interfered with, the Light is withdrawn; and the flesh body, which should be the Temple of the Most High Living God, disintegrates.

"The experience called death is a constant re-proof to mankind and a reminder to the personal self of its disobedience to the original God Plan, the Divine Way of Life.

"If the student really wants to know the Truth about re-embodiment and Life, he must go to the Source of Life—the 'Mighty I AM Presence'—and study there; for only as he receives Wisdom from his All-knowing Mind will he ever BE Its Light.

"We may have mental concepts and ideas by the thousands, but unless we have become One with a thing through feeling it, we never really know. To gather facts from the world of sense and form, or the outer activity of the mind, is but accretion. Eternal Truth, Law and Intelligence come only from the 'Mighty I AM Presence,' the 'Light of the Universe.'

"If one desires to prove to himself the Truth of re-embodiment, that proof can only come from his own actual experiences—revealed to him by his own God Self. No amount of argument or phenomena will ever be proof to anyone. To the one who wishes to have this proof, I give the following, and it is infallible; for the Ascended Masters have attained Their Perfection of the Ascended State by its use, and others may do likewise if they so choose.

"If the student, with unyielding determination, will acknowledge and accept his 'Mighty I AM Presence'—call to It constantly, and sincerely reach up to It, love It, and be grateful for Its wondrous Life which he is using every moment, waking and sleeping—he will cause his outer consciousness to be so raised that he will know, see, and experience first hand the answer to every question and every problem confronting him.

"The greatest and most important Activity of Life is Love, Devotion, and Gratitude to Life for all Life gives us. As our outer consciousness becomes lifted by being held in constant adoration upon the 'Mighty I AM Presence' and continual acknowledgment given only to the Perfection of Life, all human habits and miscreations disappear, and we express only Light. This is the Ascended Master Consciousness.

"The outer activity of the mind and physical body becomes the visible, tangible form of whatever we think and feel. Man becomes that upon which his attention rests. If he meditates upon the 'Mighty I AM Presence,' he will become the Full Outpouring of that Perfection. If he spends his time and energy, through his attention, upon the appetites of the physical body, trying to satisfy their insatiable demands, he destroys his temple. No man may say him nay, no matter what his choice. The responsibility of his choice is unescapable, for it is inherent within Free Will.

"The Paramount Command of the Eternal is: 'Be ye Perfect, even as your Father in Heaven is Perfect,' for Life will return you, the individual consciousness, again, again, and again into human embodiment—until you fulfill the Supreme Edict of Life. When that Decree is obeyed, we shall find the Manifestations of the Constructive Way of Life have become Immortal.

"The Cosmic Activity and Light from our Earth is being expanded at this time. Many feel this greatly increased energy, and unless it is used in a constructive way, the individual qualifies it with his own feelings of irritation and resentment against persons, places and conditions. This but creates greater turmoil in his own mind and body, which constantly disturbs himself and others.

"During the present Expansion of the Light throughout the Earth, it is absolutely imperative for the individual to keep an iron control over his own thought, feeling and spoken word—compelling them to be constructive, and giving recognition to nothing else—if he is to avoid continual distress and countless loss to himself and his world. At no time in the history of the planet has this been so important as it is at the present moment.

"The Earth is passing through the throes of a tremendous new birth, and in the few years just ahead will be in a transition period. It is changing now in a Cosmic Way—from the attitude of war into that of Peace, from hatred to Love, from selfishness to unselfishness—and into the full recognition that in the future the people must exert strength enough to live according to the Law of Love.

"The hour strikes in the evolution of every planet and its humanity when they must express the Full Peace, Harmony, Perfection, and the Divine Plan of the System to which they belong. When that hour strikes, humanity either moves forward and fulfills God's Plan, or whatever portion will not come into alignment with the new activity removes itself to another schoolroom of the Universe—until those personalities learn obedience to Life.

"The Law of Life is Heaven, Peace, Harmony and Love to every created thing. Even the ethers of infinite space express this Harmony everywhere. Human beings are the only creators of 'hell.' They can accept and obey the Law of Life, and enjoy every good thing of the 'Kingdom,' or they can disobey that Law and be broken as a reed before the storm by their own self-generated discord. Each individual carries his own heaven or hell with him every moment; for these are but the results of mental and emotional states which the individual has created because of his own attitude. There is no other cause for them.

"Over the humanly generated chaos of the past there are being poured out by the Ascended Masters and Great Cosmic Messengers, Great Streams of Love and Harmony upon which Peace depends. Mankind, having so long pulled against the Great Cosmic Current of Love which ever seeks to bless, is now being compelled to turn around and seek the Light in order to survive in the midst of its own destructive emanations of the past. The constant Command of the Ascended Masters is: 'Let the Great Light of the "Mighty I AM Presence" enfold the humanity of Earth—quickly—that its sufferings may cease.' Misery, darkness and ignorance exist only because of lack of Love."

Mr. Rayborn and I were the only two left at the ranch for the next few weeks. We received splendid letters from Nada and Rex, and occasionally one from Pearl. They were deeply grateful to Beloved Saint Germain for the beautiful apartment which He, in His Love, had provided for them; and among its many blessings were two of His other students who acted in the capacity of chef and maid. They had come from Arabia, and while in their activity as servants, were the very essence of loving help.

When the twenty-fourth of September arrived, Rayborn and I made a visit to the mine for the last time before leaving for Washington. The trip was beautiful, and we felt tangibly the overshadowing Power of the "Magic Presence" which filled us with unspeakable joy and happiness. We found Bob expecting us, as Saint Germain had left him a message saying we were to arrive that evening.

Mr. Rayborn's purpose in coming at this time was to contact the men more closely and give a Radiation that would bless all. He spoke to the three shifts as they came off duty, telling them of the new superintendent, Dave Southerland. They deeply appreciated Rayborn's kindness and generosity to them, and as he thanked and encouraged them in their work, he seemed more like a brother than an employer. I never ceased to marvel at the Power of Love to bless men and their business—when they really accept and live It. Rayborn was a living proof of its efficiency and wisdom in the practical daily experience of the business world.

That evening Rayborn spent much time telling Bob many things Saint Germain had revealed to him during their hours of Instruction. Bob was as happy as a schoolboy, deeply grateful for all he received. The next morning we three said good-by with Hearts full of Love. Rayborn and I reached the ranch after an uneventful trip and retired early.

The following morning he suggested we take the beautiful Arabian horse out for exercise, that I might see the part of the ranch that lay among the foothills. He asked me to ride Pegasus; and as the groom led the horse out, he broke away and came to me at full speed, rubbing his nose against me as though to express his joy at not being forgotten. Rayborn mounted the black horse belonging to Rex, and we cantered off. We were returning along the foothills when suddenly Pegasus planted his feet and would not move.

"Let him have his own way," explained Rayborn. "He knows a rattlesnake is near. Give him the reins and then watch." He moved a short distance forward very slowly and then stopped. We distinctly heard the rattle, and looking a short distance away, saw a huge rattlesnake.

"Don't touch the reins," warned Rayborn. "You will see a very unusual thing." Raising his right foot, Pegasus began to strike at the snake slowly, at the same time watching it closely. Suddenly the snake struck, and quick as a flash down came Pegasus' foot on its head, severing it from the body completely. I hugged him—I couldn't help it; but he was quite calm. I dismounted to get the rattles and found there were twelve. "You had better give me those rattles," said Rayborn, "Pegasus will never let you carry them on him; he has a violent antipathy to them."

The next morning we left for Denver. We went directly to the Brown Palace Hotel where Gaylord had left word for us to come immediately to his suite of rooms. We obeyed directions and were greeted graciously by our host. He called a porter to check our trunks, and when the man returned, he knew before he accepted the checks that one was missing.

"My good man, you have not checked one of the trunks," he explained. The porter saw his mistake and returned later with the missing check. We boarded the train at nine o'clock and found that he had engaged three adjoining drawing rooms. Gaylord excused himself almost immediately. "I wish to retire at once," he explained, "and leave my body, as I must go to Arabia for further directions; but I will be with you at breakfast."

The next morning at the first call, Gaylord, Rayborn and I went through to the dining car. While we sat at breakfast, a dark, handsome, wiry sort of man passed our table, accompanied by a beautiful woman of striking appearance.

Involuntarily, we all noticed them. We finished our breakfast, and Gaylord asked us to come at once to his drawing room. "That man and woman," he explained, as soon as we were seated, "are two of the communist representatives with whom we have to deal. We are perfectly safe because they do not know how to protect themselves or their secrets by the Power of the Inner Light. They do not serve the 'Light,' and are therefore unable to use It as we do, and so release Its Power. However, we must be on our guard from the start so that at no point will they be able to sense anything of our activities. The man's companion is one of the cleverest, most dangerous and notorious persons known in Europe.

"Put on your Armor," he said, speaking to me, "for in handling this woman, when the time comes, you will need to use all your powers of diplomacy. You have a part to fulfill—more important than you dream; but I know your courage, poise, and the assurance from the 'Mighty I AM Presence' within. That will take you through victoriously.

"Through my visit to the Far East last night, it is very evident that we are getting into action here none too soon. Those who are the claws of the sinister force are already polluting and corrupting wherever possible by their deceit and treachery. Now you can realize how great was Beloved Saint Germain's Wisdom in His three days' Preparation and Attunement of you while in the Cave of Symbols. I know of the place; I have been there many times."

"Will you," I asked, "tell us whatever of your experiences you are permitted to reveal?"

"I will be glad," he replied graciously, "to relate whatever I am permitted to reveal for your instruction and enlightenment, but not just for entertainment. We change trains at Chicago, and after leaving there, which will be about nine o'clock tonight, I shall be glad to visit you again. When we reach Chicago, have all the bags taken to your compartment and wait for me, as I expect to have important communications for both of you." When the train pulled into the station, Mr. Gaylord stepped off the car and disappeared immediately in the crowd.

"He must have drawn the Cloak of Invisibility about him," I said to Rayborn; "he has gone so quickly." We changed trains and went immediately to our compartment. As the train pulled out of the station, we heard Gaylord enter his compartment. In about ten minutes, he tapped on our door and asked us to join him.

"It was just as I thought," he explained. "Our adversary has a powerful tool in this city, one of the high political officials who is receiving large sums of money for the assistance he is giving to their destructive activities. However, he is under surveillance and will be taken into custody in the morning. No one will dare to announce it publicly because of others with whom he is connected—and whose prominence makes it too dangerous for them to allow his name to be revealed. It is the same old story: when the battle grows too fierce in the camp of the unvirtuous, it is each man for himself, and each man's deeds trap him in his own net.

"The man and his companion whom we saw at breakfast the other morning have taken the compartment next to you," he continued, indicating me. "However, you will know exactly the right thing to do at the right moment, and I know you will do it. Now I will explain, for your instruction, one of my experiences that began in India, reached its height in Arabia, and finished in America:

"Some years ago, when the aftermath of the war was spending its fury, I was selected by the Council of the Great White Brotherhood in India to act in the capacity of Messenger. This work necessitated taking my physical body with me, for at that time I was not able to levitate and transport it through the atmosphere as the Ascended Masters do. However, now I can leave my body consciously at any time, as you are both fully aware and this good brother," indicating Rayborn, "has physically observed.

"Obeying the Call from the Council of India, I sailed for France, the first part of my journey. At that time I was not so clearly sensitive to the Finer Vibratory Action as I am now and had to be led more or less intuitively. Little did I dream in those days that I was obeying—as definitely as I am now. The first morning at sea, I found a most distinguished looking gentleman seated at my table as I came down to breakfast. He arose as I approached and introduced himself. 'I take the liberty of introducing myself,' he said. 'I trust I am not intruding!' I liked him very much the moment I shook hands with him; and we chatted on generalities for a few moments when he remarked:

" 'I presume you are traveling for pleasure, possibly on a mission?' and as he pronounced the word 'mission,' he looked at me very sharply. Instantly I felt something tighten within and I was on guard at once.

" 'I enjoy water travel very much,' I replied, 'especially in the month of May.' A slight smile passed over his face and an amused look came into his eyes. Still, the feeling that I liked him grew stronger, and somehow I could not help it, nor explain the cause. Suddenly he shifted the conversation, began speaking of a certain young prince, and asked if I had met him.

" 'Only as a small child,' I replied, 'but I have always felt he was a great soul.'

" 'Just what do you mean by that?' he asked.

" 'I mean he is one who has lived many lives and attained certain Inner Knowledge through much experience,' I replied.

" 'Then you believe in re-embodiment?' he questioned again.

" 'I not only believe it, but I know it to be True,

and a certain phase of one activity of the Great Cosmic Law,' I answered.

" 'You speak with great assurance,' he continued.

" 'In this respect, I speak from actual knowledge,' I retorted.

" 'Oh, you do? Now for instance, do you think you and I have ever met before?' he went on, and there was a sort of quizzical, half-teasing note in his voice—yet a loving kindness in its quality that denied any real opposition to my thought.

" 'Yes,' I continued, 'we knew each other before the last cataclysm on Atlantis, and also in Egypt. Now we have met again and shall work together many times for our mutual good.' I spoke with an Inner Impelling Power and a Feeling of Authority that amazed me. I was surprised at my own words.

"He extended his hand, looked at me with a smile that would have melted anyone, and gave me a sign which I knew came only from one of very high authority in the Great White Brotherhood. I was deeply grateful and very happy.

" 'You passed the test splendidly, My Brother,' He explained, 'and it is well you are on guard so naturally. This makes it possible for the Inner Presence to act at all times. Remember, the "Mighty I AM Presence" is the Only Power which can guard you in the outer activity, for it cannot be done by the personal will.

" 'Never fail to maintain this Continual Guard,

for it is imperative in the work you are to do. The Great Life Stream and plan of our work has brought us together for the next few months. Your "I AM Presence" spoke the Truth about our having been together in former lives. I rejoice, as I see you do also, that our outer activity unites us again at the present time. Let us go to my cabin, and I will give you some idea of our work. You will receive further instruction in detail from the Council in India.'

"As we entered His cabin I felt a sense of exquisite beauty about everything around Him. I did not know then, as I have learned since, that it was not so much the furnishings as the wondrous Radiance He shed over them. His Blazing Aura penetrated, charged, and illumined everything in the room.

" 'The first important thing I have to tell you,' He explained, 'is that I am detailed, with your assistance, to prevent the assassination of the young prince we mentioned some time ago—whom we both love because of his Inner Light. The second duty is to prevent a great indignity to Arabia by certain European powers. The third thing is the activity of the sinister force with which we are dealing now. We shall stop two days in Paris as we pass through France and there shall make important contacts to help us accomplish our work.'

"The days passed all too rapidly while I was in association with this Remarkable Man, and the only promise He exacted from me at any time was when He introduced himself—by requesting that I never reveal His Name to anyone. I have never done so to this day and never shall, except with His Permission.

"I thought at the time when I saw Him perform what the world calls miracles that He was the most wonderful person in the world; but He revealed only a fragmentary part of His Knowledge and Power at that time. When I mentioned these things to Him, He replied: 'This sort of activity is the least important Work the Members of the Great White Brotherhood are able to do; in fact, there is nothing They cannot do when necessity and the Divine Law permit.'

"The boat arrived at Cherbourg, and as we disembarked I saw a man who looked like an Arab give my Friend the Sign of the White Brotherhood, which He answered. The Arab led us to a magnificent auto that we entered at once, he taking the wheel.

"Inside the car sat a closely veiled woman to whom I was presented, not by name, but as the 'Brother from the Far West of America,' and She merely as 'Sister of the White Brotherhood.' As nearly as I could see and sense, She seemed very young, not more than seventeen years of age. We were hardly seated when She said:

"'We can reach Paris much more quickly this

way,' indicating a road into which we turned immediately.

" 'We are being followed,' She warned a moment later; and looking around, we saw another car following at full speed. At once there arose from the ground a Wall of Vapor between the two cars.

" 'They will not pass that barrier until we are well out of their reach,' She assured us.

"We arrived in Paris a few hours later and stopped at an old castle-like residence from which we could see dimly the Eiffel Tower. It was situated high up, and from its many windows one had almost a complete bird's-eye view of the city. It seemed as if it had been built for that purpose in the first place.

"The Veiled Lady led the way through the entrance and up a grand staircase. We entered what looked like an audience chamber, and passing through a side door, came into a large library.

"A tall, handsome man, turning from one of the bookcases, came forward and greeted us with a courtly grace that is not the custom of our time. Later I realized why. He was one of the Great Ascended Masters who had made His Ascension more than five hundred years ago. His eyes sparkled with Kindness and a Wisdom that seemed as old as eternity.

"The Veiled Lady who had accompanied us, He

explained, was His daughter in a former life and a pupil of His in this one. She had been in the Ascended State more than three hundred years, yet She looked not over seventeen. I can never tell you the effect those experiences had on me. Every new Revelation stirred a feeling within that I never knew existed.

" 'My Beloved Friends,' our Host said, as soon as we had been presented and greetings had been exchanged, 'please be seated. Luncheon will be served immediately, and afterwards I will convey the Instruction which I am to give you.'

"A few moments later two youths in cream-colored robes appeared and served our meal. It was very delicious and was the same kind of precipitated food that we have all been privileged to eat at Saint Germain's Retreat in the Cave of Symbols.

" 'Tonight,' said our Host, 'you are to be my guests, together with eight of the Brothers who will be here to meet our American Brother. They know him, but as yet he has not recalled the memory of Them.'

"Promptly at eight o'clock our Host led the way to the top floor, and we entered a circular room where everything was decorated in soft milk-white color. In the center stood a white onyx table, and around it had been placed twelve chairs. We stood for a moment, one at each corner of the table, with heads bowed; and when we looked up, the eight

Brothers were there in living, tangible Bodies. I was presented to each in turn, and then the group sat down.

"They all knew my Friend of steamship acquaintance very well. Many problems of national and international importance were brought up for solution, and in every case, a real remedy worthy of Their time and attention was found to meet the requirements.

"It was during this time I learned that our Host was Chief of the Council of France, although He was not a Frenchman. Each Brother was given specific direction which it became His duty to carry out. As the Council adjourned, everyone said good-by with the Blessing: 'We enfold you in the Potent Power of the "Magic I AM Presence" to whom all Brothers of the Great White Brotherhood look and receive without limit.' We bowed our heads, and the Brothers disappeared as silently as They had come. We bade our Host good-night, and were shown to our rooms.

"We had breakfast early the next morning and were ready to leave by nine o'clock, the Veiled Lady accompanying us as before. We arrived at the docks in Marseilles just in time to ask God's Blessings upon our fair Sister and take our leave.

"We boarded the steamer and I asked my friend why I felt such an attraction to the Veiled Lady and what was the meaning of it, for She seemed always before my vision and about me ever since we had entered the automobile in Paris."

" 'Have patience,' He answered. 'You will soon know.'

"Our cabins adjoined, and we settled down to enjoy our trip on the Mediterranean to the full. We were bound for Bombay by way of the Suez Canal and the Red Sea, with visits to Alexandria and Cairo. It was a trip one could not forget in a thousand years. Not a single thing occurred to mar its beauty and our joy, and being extremely fond of water travel, I reveled in my newly-found happiness.

"As our boat came alongside the pier at Bombay, I was intensely interested, for this was my first trip to that part of the world. Since those years, the Orient has become quite familiar.

"I had expected that we would make the last portion of our journey by train, but to my surprise, we had scarcely left the gangplank when a hand-some young Hindu dressed in white approached. He gave us the Sign we knew so well and led us to a large, beautiful auto. He opened the door in quiet dignity and waited for us to enter. To my astonish-ment, within the car sat another veiled lady—who looked very like the one we had left in France. To my intellect that seemed impossible, so I put it out of my mind. I was presented to her in a similar manner as to the other lady. It was not long until our fair companion answered my thought with the question:

" 'Why, My Good Brother, should we think anything impossible where the Understanding of the individual is complete?'

" 'My Good Sister,' I replied, 'you are so like a lovely lady we met in Paris that I can hardly believe you are not the same person. Yet we left Her there, so She could not be here.'

" 'You think not?' She questioned again, and my Friend suggested:

" 'We had better watch the beautiful scenery, for we may not pass this way again.' The view was powerful and majestic, and a very delightful source of inspiration and enjoyment. It was ten o'clock in the morning when we left Bombay. We drove until six in the evening and by that time had reached a quiet little city. We drove to a large native residence. The man in white driving the auto waited for us to alight and then drove away immediately.

"Again our veiled sister led the way to the dwelling. A stately, white-haired English lady with a youthful face and figure opened the door.

" 'Welcome, my Good Sister and Brothers,' she said, greeting us cordially. 'I was anticipating your arrival. Your rooms are ready, and the attendant will show you to them if you care to refresh yourselves after so long a drive. Dinner will be served in twenty minutes.' Presently, the soft tones of a bell announced the meal, and we proceeded to the dining room. Imagine my feelings as we met at dinner when I found that the Veiled Sister who had driven with us from Bombay was the same Lady we had met in Paris! As soon as I saw who She was, I greeted her with:

"'My Beloved!' I had no intention of saying any such thing and felt greatly chagrined and confused. I apologized profusely and tried to restrain an almost irresistible impulse to talk. She did not seem to mind the familiarity in the least, but replied, 'I deeply appreciate your sincere greeting.' I managed to collect my thoughts enough to ask,

"'Will you please tell me how you were able to reach India before us?'

"'I have a means of transportation,' She explained, 'with which you are not familiar. However, you will be taught to travel as I do. We are able to transport Our Bodies to any distance We desire without using any physical conveyance.'

"The next morning we were on our way at daybreak. The day was very warm outside, but within the auto it was comfortably cool and delightful; deliciously cool drinks were always provided for us. We had been driving in the mountains for some time and were climbing steadily when we entered a deep gorge, the walls rising at least two thousand feet on each side. It looked as if a giant fissure had been cut through the mountains for nearly a mile.

"We drove through this crevasse and came out into a basin about four miles in circumference, surrounded by towering peaks. Never before or since have I ever seen a more beautiful spot on Earth. It was a Perfect Paradise.

"On the west side of this basin, facing east, stood a magnificent palace of white marble, unlike any building I have ever seen in the outer world. Saint Germain had not said so, but I have always thought it was a Precipitated Substance. A large golden dome covered the central portion of the roof, and there were four smaller domes, one on each corner. When the morning sun flashed upon these domes, the whole scene became an indescribable blaze of glory, a daily, silent symbol and acknowledgment by Nature of the 'Great Light' and Wisdom that poured out constantly upon the Earth from this Temple of Beauty.

"We drove to the eastern entrance of this magnificent palace and two youths in snow-white garments came out to greet us. They were the picture of perfect health, youth, and beauty. Their hair was especially attractive, one being a soft wavy brown, and the other a most wonderful gold. The latter welcomed us:

"'Beloved Sister and Brothers, you are expected and most welcome. Will you please follow me?' We entered and were greeted again by one of the Ascended Masters who is greatly beloved in the outer world, and who has worked ceaselessly for many centuries to bring enlightenment to the race of mankind. He has a very kindly face, a smile that would melt a heart of stone and makes one feel at once that He wields a Power that solves all things.

"Other attendants came forward in graceful, rhythmic motion and led the way to our rooms. The interior design and furnishing of this palace were exquisitely beautiful. Since my first visit to that wonderful spot, it has been my duty as well as my pleasure to contact many important places throughout the world because of the work of the Great White Brotherhood with which I have been associated; but even the most elaborate have never approached the Exquisite Perfection of this White Marble Palace of the Ascended Masters.

"The whole interior of this wonderful building was made of an imperishable material, milk-white in color, with here and there touches of a very delicate gold, violet, green, and an intense electric blue. This produced the most artistic effect imaginable. Everything remained immaculately clean because within and around the building all was so powerfully charged with Electronic Force and the vibratory rate was so high, the Power of the 'Light' repelled everything imperfect, and kept all in a self-sustained state of Beauty and Perfection.

" 'Dinner will be served in your rooms,' explained the youth with the golden hair, 'and you are requested to wear the silken Robes and Sandals that will be provided.'

"When the dinner arrived, it consisted of several kinds of fresh fruit, among them berries served with a substance like whipped cream, similar to that which we have eaten at the Cave of Symbols, and a delicious drink of golden liquid a little less heavy than honey.

"As soon as we had finished our repast, we were summoned to the Council Chamber under the central dome. On entering, the great table in the middle of the room caught the eye at once—because of its massive size. It was made entirely of jade, heavily veined in gold, exquisitely beautiful in even the smallest detail, and around it had been placed sixty chairs made of solid gold, and upholstered in a fabric of soft violet color that looked like silk velvet.

"We stood a moment admiring the Beauty and Perfection of it all, and as we looked around saw Beloved Saint Germain. The entire Council entered in little groups of three to twelve. When all but one had arrived and taken Their places around the table, our Beloved Master spoke.

"'Let us bow our heads in silent praise and gratitude to the 'Mighty I AM Presence' which is lifting the Hearts and illumining the minds of mankind.' As we raised our heads, a Most Marvelous Being stood in the place that had been left vacant at the head of the table. He was One of the Great Ascended Masters to whom it is impossible to do full justice—because the Great Majesty and Authority to which He has attained surpass all human powers of description. His Robes looked like a glittering mass of jewels, but as I became more accustomed to the Brilliancy of His Light, I saw that what looked like jewels at first were points of Dazzling Radiance emanating from His Body and Robes. The Love He poured forth was so All-encompassing that It seemed to flood the Universe, so far-reaching was Its Scope.

"'Beloved Sisters and Brothers of the Great White Brotherhood, I greet you,' He said, giving the Sign of the Order that acknowledges only the Omniscience of the 'Mighty I AM Presence,' the Omnipresence of the Undying Flame of Life, and the Omnipotence of the Shadowless Light.

"'My Brother from America, I bid you welcome. Please accept My Love and Gratitude for the service you have performed. I shall speak with you at length at the close of the meeting.'

"This Mighty Brother of Light proceeded to give Definite Instruction concerning the most important activities of the Earth, principally the Inner and outer changes that needed to be brought about for humanity's advancement. Many of the Councils from all over the world were represented by those present. The Chief of each Council received orders direct from the Presiding Master and gave His Directions to the ones under Him. When the outline of Their activities was finished, He asked each one to turn his chair about and face the west.

"In the atmosphere before us began to pass living pictures of the problems the Great White Brotherhood held under consideration, or were working on at the time. They showed the individual Brothers who were concerned with them and would continue to work on special assignments, giving the principal details and means of solution. The work of protecting the young prince previously referred to, and the Brothers who were concerned with it, was one of the many scenes that passed before our vision. The method for readjusting conditions pertaining to Arabia was also shown and excited my admiration greatly.

"When the greater problem of dealing with the sinister force which is trying to keep humanity from recognizing and manifesting the Perfection and Blessing of the 'Mighty I AM Presence' was revealed, it was the most astonishing thing anyone can imagine. It really showed the Unlimited Force of the Cosmic Christ Light dealing with darkness, and no words can portray the Majesty, Power, and Victory of the 'Presence of the Infinite I AM.'

"At the present I may give no further details, but the Glory and Supremacy in action of the 'Mighty Presence of the Infinite I AM' transcends all imagination, just as Light transcends darkness. The pictures came to an end, and the Presiding Master— He of the Dazzling Radiance—turned to the Sister from France and myself:

" 'Come, My Beloved Children,' He said. We stepped forward, and He extended both hands, His left one to Her, and His right to me.

" 'My Brother from America,' He went on, 'I bless you exceedingly. You have not yet realized the Eternal Perfection that is now yours in the outer activity. Our Beloved Sister is your Twin Ray. This is one of the Greatest of God's Mysteries and explains the mutual attraction between you since your first meeting in Paris. If the humanity of Earth could have the God Understanding of this part of the Divine Plan, it would do more to purify the chaos of the outer world than any other thing We know.

" 'The time is nearing when the Truth concerning the Twin Rays must be thoroughly understood and Its Mighty Wisdom and Power utilized. No Individualization of God does Creative Work at Cosmic Levels in the Fullness of the "Mighty I AM Presence" until that one's Twin Ray has made the Ascension. Earthly choice has nothing whatsoever to do with it. Each Ray must, by Conscious Understanding and the use of the "Great Command," purify, perfect and illumine all the human creation

by which it has surrounded itself. It then becomes
the Ascended Master who forever has Conscious
Dominion over the Earth and all that is therein.

"'When both Rays have made the Ascension,
They are of the same state of Purity, Freedom and
Perfect Dominion. The Two are then able to work
at Cosmic Levels. There, They can project great
Cosmic Rays of Love, Light and Wisdom, focusing
them with such Power, They create and control
Cosmic Activities and reveal the Great Glory of the
"Mighty I AM Presence."

"'Our Beloved Sister has seen and known of this
for some time, patiently awaiting this divine moment. After the raising of your body, your Work
together will be very transcendent.' He raised His
hands above us in Blessing, and His voice, beautiful
as a bell, with a tone of Eternal Authority uttered
the Supreme Decree of Love Everlasting upon our
union:

"'By the Command of the "Mighty I AM Presence," I join these Twin Rays of the Eternal Flame
of Life in Supreme Love, Light, and Perfection.'

"As the Master said these Words, a Dazzling Shaft
of Light enveloped us; and in this, the Mighty Flame
of our Twin Rays set Its Eternal Seal upon our
Cosmic Pathway of Life. In that moment we were
fully conscious of ourselves as only that 'Magic
Presence of the I AM.'

"This closed the Council meeting, and in the hour that followed, we met the members of that Retreat and received Their congratulations. They assured us our Unlimited Cosmic Service would now begin. The next day the Master who was our host explained some of Their Work and revealed the Perfection that had been maintained there for centuries. In explaining the origin of Their Work, He said:

" 'This Council of the Great White Brotherhood was created centuries ago by the Great Brothers of Light, that a Powerful Focus of Their Help and Illumination to humanity might be brought about and perpetuated for a definite period of time. The wonderful semi-tropical climate you find here will last as long as We desire to retain this place as a Retreat.'

"That evening we were shown the perfected instrument for television in operation. I could not help remarking what glories and marvels humanity could and would experience, if it would only reach up consciously and sincerely to the 'Inner Light,' and the individuals open their Hearts and feelings to the 'Mighty Magic Presence of the I AM.'

"Early the following morning we returned to Bombay, whence we were to sail for Arabia. The trip to the coast was delightful, the atmosphere in the car always remaining cool and comfortable no matter how warm it became outside. I knew this was due entirely to the deep understanding of my Beloved and my Friend. We went back to Bombay by an entirely different route from the one by which we had come. The following morning we sailed on a small boat for Egypt, stopping at the port we wished to reach on the west coast of Arabia. When it reached the Red Sea, as we began to sail north on its placid waters, my Friend suddenly became charged by the Electronic Force so powerfully that we all noticed it.

" 'For some reason,' He said, 'I have contacted the period in which Moses led the Children of Israel through this sea; for the living pictures are all appearing before Me here in the Etheric Records. What a time of wonders that was in the midst of such a very great distress. Moses truly made a most wonderful contact with the Ascended Masters who were assisting and who wielded Tremendous Power through him to accomplish that undertaking.

" 'I see for the first time the Great Ascended Master to whom Moses knowingly addressed his petition at that time for help. The Majesty and Power of that Mighty Being can scarcely be comprehended by the human mind, so marvelously does it transcend the ordinary experience of humanity.

" 'How little the modern world knows, realizes, or credits those marvels actually performed by such wonderful Servants of God for the enlightenment and uplift of mankind. These stupendous so-called miracles are, after all, only the Activity of a Law that humanity has not yet tried to study or understand.

" 'When one speaks in terms of Universal Truth, there is no such thing in Infinite Creation as a "miracle," for what the world calls miracles are only the operation of Divine Law, which, because of Its very nature of Perfection, sets aside all humanly established laws of limitation. It is to bring the Full Understanding of the operation of 'Divine Law' into the minds of the children of Earth that the Ascended Masters have labored in the past—and for which they still do labor unceasingly with the inhabitants of this planet.

" 'Today, all unknown to the outer world, there are still more wonderful things being done than in those days of long ago. So far as this vast, deeper Knowledge and Power are concerned, the majority of mankind are but babes. However, the hour is rapidly approaching when humanity must awaken to the All-Encompassing Inner Presence of God acting through the individual.'

"At last the boat stopped at our seaport on the coast of the Province of Hejaz, a sort of peninsula jutting out into the northeast edge of the Red Sea. We landed at this quaint place and again were given the secret sign by a tall, slender Arab in spotless white garments who stood beside a large powerful auto, opening the door for us to enter.

"Without a word, we were driven away at unusual speed over a hard, sandy highway. There were lovely refreshments already provided within the car. Late in the afternoon we entered a small mountain village and drove up to a low, snow-white house. Our silent Arab guide opened the door and motioned us to enter. He knocked upon an inner door that was opened immediately by a white-haired elderly gentleman with brown skin and very kindly eyes.

" 'Sister and Brothers,' was his greeting, 'you are expected. Refresh yourselves, and food will be served as soon as you are ready. After nightfall a Brother will call and take you to your destination. I trust the Brotherhood will not fail in Their Assistance to our country.'

"I was about to speak when my Beloved grasped my arm firmly. I understood Her signal and kept silent.

" 'The Light of God never fails,' my Friend answered our host in a voice that made the very air tremble, so great was the Power and Truth with which His spoken Word was charged, and so definitely did He utter that Almighty Decree. The effect was like magic. The old man fell on his knees and bowed his head to the ground before my Friend. At nine o'clock a handsome young man wearing the native white Arab dress over which was thrown a long Indigo Cloak, appeared at the door.

" 'Friends of the West,' He said. 'Come, the way is open.'

"We followed immediately without a word. We walked a short distance and found camels waiting. We mounted silently and set off at great speed toward a high mountain. Later I learned that these were the famous racing camels; and the one on which my Beloved was mounted was snow-white. We sped along in silence for nearly two hours, and then came to a hut made of heavy stone and set close against the mountain. As we dismounted, a man appeared from out of the darkness to care for the camels. Our Guide entered the hut and motioned us to follow.

"We reached the opposite side of the room and He raised His hands and placed them against the wall. They at once became a Blazing Light, so great was the Power He directed. They were as dazzling as an electric light bulb, only much whiter. He pressed a certain section of the wall and it turned on a pivot, disclosing an opening into a tunnel of intense White Light.

"We stepped into this, and the opening closed behind us. We followed him for several hundred feet and came to a metal door. Our Guide placed His hand upon a certain symbol on it, and the door, weighing many tons, fully eight inches thick, opened slowly, and we entered a long narrow room whose walls, ceiling, and floor were all made of untarnishable steel.

"In a few moments a door opened in one wall, where an instant before none could be seen; and a man entered, motioning us to follow him. With our Guide still leading the way, we went some distance and at last came to another solid wall. It opened at our approach and admitted us into a marvelous chamber, fully a hundred feet long and about forty feet wide, furnished in a most extraordinary manner, but artistic, exquisite, and beautiful as a dream.

"In the center of the floor was a great circle enclosing a marvelous zodiac, and around this had been placed large soft cushions for twenty-eight persons. Our Guide stepped to a room at one side of the great chamber, asking us to follow. Within was a sparkling bath, beside which lay Robes and Sandals provided for our use. 'When you are ready, send me your thought,' said our Guide, and left us. We finished our preparation and sent the mental message as requested, and immediately an attendant appeared with delicious refreshments. We finished our meal and then re-entered the great

Council Hall, where twenty-four of the Sisters and Brothers had already assembled. Our Guide presented us to the Members, and all took their places around the circle.

"To my amazement I discovered that the Brother who had acted as our Guide was none other than the Chief of the Council of Arabia, a Great Ascended Master of whom I had heard many times. He arose, gave the Invocation, and addressed the Assembly:

" 'Because of unusual agitation,' He explained, 'in the political circles of Arabia at the present moment, great secrecy has been imperative in bringing outside members into these Councils. That is why there has been a constant watchfulness on our part while our visiting members have been en route.'

"Matters of grave importance were presented for discussion, especially the one nearest to the Hearts of these people. The Chief directed their attention to my Friend.

" 'This Brother,' He said, 'holds a solution to the problem concerning our beloved land of Arabia'; and He asked Him to present it.

"My Friend outlined His plan briefly, and when He had finished, everyone in the room except our Chief was surprised at its daring and ingenuity. The Chief smiled reassuringly and continued:

" 'The plan is feasible, remarkable as it is. It shall be carried out quickly and successfully. The entire Great White Brotherhood of the Earth will watch over the meeting that is about to take place; and you can rest assured, this plan will be set into operation at once.

" 'The Sister and Brothers who have come under special guard are to rest here tonight and tomorrow. On the third day I will go with them to the British Consulate where our negotiations will take place.' A wave of joy swept over the whole meeting as this outline of Their Work was finished. Other matters concerning their various activities were disposed of, and the meeting came to an end—the members disappearing one by one. The Chief then arose and came to where we sat.

" 'Beloved Sister and Brothers,' He said, 'I did not reveal myself to you at first for reasons that you will soon learn. I welcome you with Great Joy to this Retreat of the Great White Brotherhood. All is at your service. Brother from the West, retire to your quarters and sleep until you are called.'

"I awakened twelve hours later at the signal, feeling like a new person, so charged was I with new Life and Light.

" 'I think you will be interested in this Retreat,' our Host said—'to learn something of Its history and the part It plays as a Center of Power on this

Earth. It is one of the oldest Foci of Spiritual Power on this planet. You have only seen a fragment of it so far. A year from now, a Great Council of the White Brotherhood is to be held here. At that time each member will be shown through this vast unknown citadel.' He spent a long time showing us Their tremendous accumulation of Records which They have preserved for the enlightenment of humanity. It was truly a privilege to be shown these Treasures hour after hour.

" 'You will leave here at two o'clock,' He explained. 'Go now and put on your garments of the outer world, for by then it will be time to proceed to where the camels are waiting at our entrance.' We obeyed, and when we returned, found the Chief dressed in a beautiful blue flannel suit, wearing a long Indigo Cloak over it. Except for the marvelous texture of His skin and the brilliant, piercing, loving Light in His eyes, one might easily have thought Him to be a man who belonged to the outer world of business.

" 'Why may I not look like yourselves?' He remarked, as He saw my thought. 'I am an individual like yourselves, only of greater Experience and Wisdom which I have applied longer. That is all. Wisdom is of no benefit to anyone unless it is used, and through that use, the individual manifests Perfection, so he can live above every limitation.'

Our Beloved Ascended Master Jesus

Our Beloved Ascended Master Saint Germain

"By this time we reached the gate where the camels were waiting. When all were mounted, we sped through the night—with the wonderful white camel always leading the way. We made even greater speed than before because we arrived at the hut, the starting place of this particular part of our journey, at three-thirty. The auto was waiting, and just as we entered, the driver said something to the Master that I did not hear.

" 'Have no fear!' the Chief replied, 'We shall draw the Cloak of Invisibility about ourselves and the car, and pass them unnoticed. Let us proceed.

" 'Spies,' He explained to us, 'have been stationed along this road to seize the car and prevent anyone from discovering us afterwards. The *right use* of knowledge, which is True Wisdom, always sets us Free, as you will soon observe.'

"It was not long until we approached the spot where the spies had been placed, and in an instant a dense white vapor arose all around us like a fog, enveloping the machine completely. A peculiar whirring like the sound of an airplane was heard overhead, and while the guards were looking up to find the source of it, we shot by silently like an arrow.

"It was a marvelous experience for me, because while we could see them through the Cloak of Invisibility from within, those on the outside could not and did not see us.

" 'How is it,' I asked, 'that they did not seem to hear us?'

" 'Sound,' He explained, 'does not penetrate the Cloak of Invisibility; otherwise it would be of no use to us. The *Tales of the Arabian Nights,* My Brother, are only too true, for when really understood, they are Revelations of Divine Law instead of the silly, literal interpretation the outer world in its smug ignorance has chosen to place upon them. They are not folklore for children, but Inner Intimation of accomplishments that are perfectly possible when the student is sincere, worthy, and humble enough to be trusted with the Power and Truth they reveal. The great monster—doubt— and his nefarious associates: ignorance, pride, ridicule, skepticism, fear, and many other useless barnacles, have so fastened themselves upon the mentality and feeling of humanity, they have become like fungi hanging from a tree and rotting its trunk.

" 'If it were not for these vampires, mankind would see and know, within the very Light which animates the physical body exists an Intelligence and Power that can and will carry out perfectly whatever the mind directs—when Harmony is maintained and all direction is constructive.

" 'Love, Wisdom and Power are the primal

attributes which Life uses to build a Permanent Creation, and when mankind ceases its self-created discord, all Life around it and in Nature will express Permanent Perfection.'

"We drove along the seacoast on a splendid highway, and at last entered the city that was our destination. We registered at the best hotel, and early the next morning called at the British Consulate. My Friend said He had been sent as a Representative of the Arabian Government to present a certain solution for the impending crisis, which He trusted would satisfy all concerned, and prevent a very great injustice and indignity to Arabia.

"The British consul asked for His credentials, and instead of presenting them Himself, the Chief of the Arabian Council stepped forward and presented them in His stead. An appointment was made to meet with the British Representatives at eleven o'clock, and we returned promptly at that hour. After the conference had progressed with its usual method of suavely yet persistently shelving everything which did not give them the best of the arrangement, my Friend, at the opportune moment, arose and presented the proposal of the Arabian Government.

"He was calm, masterful and kindly, yet everyone realized unmistakably that He was somehow in command of the situation, and all the dignity and power of the conference had centered itself around Him. His opponents were not just altogether comfortable: He was too keen and honest for their usual method of diplomatic fencing; but somehow they could not present their ideas in a very favorable light in the face of His frank scrutiny and open kindness.

"They played for time by various kinds of strategy, when suddenly I was conscious of the entire conference being held within a Great Circle of Blazing Light—so bright it seemed to me everyone must see It. Then I realized what a Gigantic Focus of Power the Great White Brotherhood had directed into that room.

"Less than an hour later, my Friend's solution was accepted, the documents drawn up and signed by both parties, and the meeting adjourned in Peace and happiness. The news flashed quickly throughout Arabia, and there was great rejoicing. As we returned to the hotel, my Beloved came forward to greet us:

" 'Noble Brother, I congratulate you,' She said, 'on your dignity and splendid accomplishment.' The next day, the Chief of the Council of Arabia bade my Beloved and me good-by, and we boarded the steamer returning to France. That evening we sailed on the Mediterranean under a full moon. To me it was the most peaceful night I ever experienced.

"We landed at Marseilles, left immediately by train for Paris, and spent the night with the wonderful Master who was the Chief of the Council of the Great White Brotherhood in France. The following morning He drove with us to Cherbourg. Here we said good-by to my Beloved, whom I was not to see until years later. When we next met, it was never to part again. We boarded a liner for New York, and that voyage stands out as one of the most remarkable of my entire Life, for my Wonderful Friend taught me the most marvelous Use of the Ancient Wisdom. He instructed me, and the results I had from the use of the Great Command were simply amazing.

"We arrived in New York and hurried at once to Washington, where my Friend presented the results of the Arabian matter to the President and his cabinet. The news had already preceded His arrival. That ended my first personal contact and observation of the stupendous and marvelous Activity of the Great White Brotherhood."

As Gaylord finished relating his experiences, we saw daylight just breaking on the eastern horizon.

"Let us go to your drawing room," he said, referring to me, "for one of the Ascended Masters has much to do in the work we are to accomplish next. The lady and gentleman—who are but pawns of the sinister force—have in their possession certain documents and records which they have stolen. These papers contain information we need which they intend to use against innocent people for blackmail purposes. We must have that information in order to protect others whom they seek to injure and to bring into their clutches through the power of fear." We then returned to my compartment. I wondered what Mr. Gaylord intended to do next. We waited a few moments, and soon heard the man and woman go into the dining car.

"Now watch carefully," said Gaylord, "and do not move or speak while I am operating."

We sat down, and he focused his attention upon the door that led into their compartment. In a moment he directed a Ray of "Electronic Light" upon it. He steadily increased the Power, and we were enabled to look within the room. A traveling bag lay upon one of the seats. Gaylord held the Force steadily until he saw what it contained. The expression on his face indicated he had found the information for which he was searching, and in an instant, he released the Power and said:

"In three days they will be ready for the proper authorities to welcome them to a long rest from any further activity of that kind. With those papers in their possession it makes their escape impossible.

In this case, the newspapers will not be able to break through the Wall of Secrecy and Invisibility of the Ascended Masters—who control all human law by the One Eternal Law of Divine Justice."

Saint Germain had indicated the hotel in Washington where we were to stay, and when we arrived, He welcomed us in person. His appearance was changed so that He did not attract undue attention.

"My Beloved Brother," He said, as He went up to Gaylord, "I do sincerely congratulate you and give praise and thanks for your splendid success— because you have broken the backbone of a very destructive activity, at least so far as that group is concerned." Turning to Rayborn and me, He greeted us in that Loving, Gracious Manner that is such a distinguishing characteristic of all Ascended Masters, and particularly of Beloved Saint Germain.

"May I have the privilege of providing your breakfast?" He said. "I trust it will be quite satisfying and delicious. Will you come to my rooms?" After breakfast He suggested that we retire and get our much needed rest—yet while in His Marvelous Presence we were never conscious of needing rest.

The third day after our arrival, Rayborn, Gaylord, and I, accompanied by Saint Germain and certain members of the Secret Service, went to the rendezvous of an important group of those who were willing channels for the sinister force. There were present the seven principal leaders in America. We reached the place and stood for a moment outside their rooms. We could hear an excited discussion going on in undertones as we approached the door. Suddenly it burst open and we walked in upon them, Saint Germain charging the atmosphere with an Electric Force that held them immovable. Their drawn guns dropped to the floor where they stood, and their arms hung motionless by their sides.

Saint Germain raised His right hand, made the Sign of Cosmic Protection and Power, and in a Voice that penetrated every atom, even of the building itself, uttered the Eternal Fiat of Truth before which all destructive forces bow and are forever silenced:

"Tell those who have been associated with you and all who come after you that 'THE LIGHT OF GOD NEVER FAILS!' "

As His voice carried that Decree into their consciousness, they turned ashen with fear from their own creation and their bodies shook like leaves in the wind. The members of the Secret Service stepped forward and took them into custody—where they shall remain until they serve THE LIGHT.

CHAPTER VII

The Mysterious Message

"I WILL be with you two weeks longer," said Saint Germain as soon as we had returned to our hotel. "With your permission I will devote a part of each day to individual Instruction, which I can see with the Inner Unlimited Sight you are going to need.

"Our interference with the plans of the sinister force and the imprisonment of their tools that took place in Washington recently has drawn the attention of certain forces to you—especially to Gaylord and this Brother," indicating me. "You both have certain faculties developed in former lives which can be used in many remarkable ways. It is because of this the sinister force will try to strike at you.

"However, you will be protected in every way and kept perfectly safe so long as you keep poised and free from anger, hate or fear. This is why I wish to give you certain definite Training along the line of Self-Protection.

"The most important and imperative thing for you to remember always is to fully accept and realize the 'Mighty I AM Presence' is *'The Magic Presence,'* and that It is focused in, through, and around

219

you at all times. You have seen your Glorious God Self of Dazzling Light—the very Life of your own Being—while you were at the ranch, so there is no excuse for not accepting It completely.

"The outer activity of your mind is the bucking bronco. This you must bring under subjection and make it perfectly obedient to the 'Mighty I AM Presence' in every way. For those who have not been privileged to see the God Self, there might be some excuse, although It is speaking constantly through the Heart to every human being that ever was born into this world; but after an individual has once seen his 'Perfect Self,' the Blazing God Light, there is no reason for ignoring that 'Presence' afterwards.

"When Its Form and Light have once been recorded in the outer activity of the mind through the sight, the individual can at any instant recall that Picture consciously and at will, and again release that Power into all earthly problems.

"The sincere student can draw the Full Power of the 'Mighty I AM Presence' into any condition, and so charge all things with Perfection. Thus he can live once again in the Father's House—in the Glorious Freedom that was originally designed for him. This is the *only* predestination there is.

"Having once seen your 'Mighty I AM Presence,' your own vision is one of the most powerful faculties you have for bringing invisible activity into visible, physical form. The architects of your business world are doing this constantly. They receive an idea, which is an invisible activity; they then draw a picture of it. It is but a very short time until the substance is drawn together and the invisible idea has become a visible, tangible building.

"The individual's ability to use this Law is absolutely unlimited; but it is only when the student consciously sets to work to control his faculty of sight so that he closes it to the picturing of negative conditions, that he begins to have Freedom and puts his world in order.

"The average person's thoughts and feeling are nothing but a mass of chaotic pictures and negative suggestions which he has accepted from the world about him, and keeps repeating and feeding them by his own energy through his attention. Order is Heaven's First Law—Harmony and Peace, the Cohesive Power of the Universe. These come from One Source *only*, and that is the 'Mighty I AM Presence' of the Universe, your God Self.

"Limitless Substance and Invincible Power are forever about you. You must understand how to raise or lower the atomic vibratory action by the Power of the 'I AM' to produce whatsoever you can possibly desire. There is no one to say what shall come into your experience and world but yourself.

"The Limitless Omnipresent Substance is always about you waiting to be acted upon. You, the individual, are the channel through which the 'Mighty I AM Presence' wishes to expand Its Perfection. It pours out ceaselessly the Limitless Light, or Energy of Life; but you are the governor of its use, the director of its destination and of the result it is to bring forth to you.

"It can and will produce anything you wish instantly if you will but keep your personality harmonized so thoughts, feelings, and words of discord do not interrupt Its ever-flowing Perfection. Life is Perfection, and It contains all Perfect Manifestation within Itself. The only duty of the personality is to be a 'Cup' that carries and reveals the Perfection of Life. Until one obtains obedience from the outer senses and maintains a feeling of peace within himself, he pollutes the Purity and Perfection of the Life that is flowing through.

"It is your duty to know the Wisdom of the 'Mighty I AM Presence' always directs your use of Its Power and Life. It alone knows what is Perfect for you—except an Ascended Master. He, being ONE with the All-knowing Mind of God, is ONE with your 'I AM Presence,' no matter whether It acts through you or through Him. Thus only your own 'I AM Presence' or an Ascended Master knows what is right for you at all times. Only these two Sources, which are really one, can see down your entire Life Stream and know all the forces that play upon your problems, and the cause of your experiences, past, present and future.

"The lack of discrimination in distinguishing the True from the false is the thing which makes mankind fail everywhere in the outer world. *The one who determines to attain Perfection must train the outer activity of his mind to listen to no voice but that of his 'Mighty I AM Presence.' He must accept only Its Wisdom and obey only Its Direction. He must hear the Light—see the Light—feel the Light—and BE the Light of the 'Infinite I AM Presence.'*

"While there is a different Individualization or Flame of God governing each human body, yet these Individualizations are, have, and use the One Universal Mind, Substance, Wisdom and Power. This is how there is but One Mind, One God, One Substance and One Power ever waiting to be consciously acted upon and directed by the 'Mighty I AM Presence' through the conscious mind or outer activity of the individual.

"If the feeling and thought of the personality is kept harmonious, then the 'Mighty I AM Presence' expands Its Perfection through the outer activity of the individual. If they be discordant, the personality becomes like a steam engine without a governor and destroys itself. The latter is the condition the larger part of humanity is expressing today. Everyone is constantly using this wonderful, limitless Energy

—the Greatest Force in the Universe.

"The responsibility for its use rests entirely upon the individual, for he is a Creator. If this tremendous Energy be used with the Conscious Understanding of the Love, Wisdom and Power of the 'Mighty I AM Presence,' the individual can only express Freedom, Perfection and Mastery.

"We all know there are thousands who desire this Instruction—that is true; but no individual in Heaven or on Earth can fail to attain It if the desire for the 'Light' be earnest enough, determined enough, and strong enough to hold the attention of the intellect upon that Light. This must be the Paramount Idea of Life upon which to focus all one's energy. To the one who has this great determination, undreamed-of ways will open to bring about the fulfillment of that desire.

"If human beings seek the Light with one eye and the pleasure of the senses with the other, they will not receive much Light. The Great Ascended Masters have become Perfect and All-Powerful by dwelling or thinking upon Perfection and obeying the One Law of Life—Love. They are That upon which They have meditated. Today mankind is *that* upon which it has meditated, or focused its attention in the past. Human beings would not live to be over twelve years of age if it were not for the continual Help of these Great Luminous Beings of

Transcendent Attainment and Love. They give the same wonderful care to the inhabitants of Earth that loving, unselfish parents give to their children, and help all individuals who have a sincere desire to live constructively. To such persons an opportunity is always open so they may attune to and contact the 'Mighty I AM Presence' within themselves, anchor to Perfection, and thus come into the Ascended State also, if they be determined enough.

"The Ascended Masters always work in perfect cooperation with the Cosmic Law of Love. Students often ask, 'Why, if these Masters are All-wise and All-powerful, do They not correct the discord upon Earth and make humanity's suffering cease?' They do help the individual who wishes to serve the Light to harmonize his thought and feeling, and bring the body into obedience to the 'Mighty I AM Presence.' They protect him thousands of times from destructive currents of force and activities of which he has no knowledge; but They cannot and do not fulfill his Plan of Life for him.

"Each individual knows a thing only when he attains the consciousness of it by the expenditure of his own energy, for then he feels it. An Ascended Master never, never intrudes upon the Eternal, Sacred Prerogative of the individual's Free Will. Whenever a destructive force of any kind gathers a certain momentum or accumulates pressure, whether it be done by an individual, a group of individuals, a nation, or in Nature, the Great Cosmic Law allows it to spend its force in order to annihilate the focus, balance the pressure, and release the misqualified energy back into the Universal Reservoir. There it becomes purified by the Great Flame of Life and can be used again.

"The personality, if it be obedient, can, by the Conscious Command of the 'I AM Presence,' release the Consuming Flame of Divine Love and willingly purify its own miscreation. Thus the individual avoids the necessity for compulsory balancing and purification by the Action of Cosmic Law.

"The willingness to right a wrong, correct a mistake, balance and purify any miscreation, will always open the way for an Ascended Master to give Assistance and bring permanent attainment. This willingness can come in a group, a nation, or an entire humanity just as well as it can in the individual; for the Infinite only acts and controls the Universe through Its own Individualization—through the Being who says 'I AM.' Creation could never have taken place if the Infinite had not acknowledged Its own Being through the 'Individual I AM.'

"When the individual determines to express the Perfection of Life, he must be loyal enough to his own 'I AM Presence' to stand back of his own Decree in the face of all outer experience. He can then give the 'Great Command,' and Life yields to him the fullness of every good thing—so long as the 'Mighty I AM Presence' is acknowledged as the Owner and Doer of all that is good.

"If one refuses to accept his 'I AM Presence,' he refuses all Good and the Source that gives it. As Life is the Great God Flame from which all proceeds, he—by this attitude of thought and feeling—refuses Life. Hence disintegration is the self-chosen experience which the individual permits the outer activity of his consciousness to impose upon his own Stream of Life.

"If thoughts and feeling of anger, hate, selfishness, criticism, condemnation and doubt of the 'I AM Presence' are permitted to remain in the consciousness of any human being, the Door to Perfection closes, and his existence becomes but a process of sleeping and eating until the energy drawn by the outer consciousness spends itself, and the body is left to dissolution.

"Then the individual makes another effort to express the Fullness of Perfection through another body, and continues this effort for aeons, if necessary, until that Perfection is fully expressed. It is to avoid such continual re-embodiment into limitation, that it is so imperative for the individual to have Conscious Understanding of the Purpose of Life, because the Knowledge of how to release Love,

Wisdom, and Power enables him to fulfill that Purpose perfectly.

"I can assist you to attain this, because by the use of the Consuming Flame of Divine Love for the purifying and blessing of humanity, you can always free yourself.

"I am delighted with Bob's progress. It is a long time since I have contacted anyone with such determination and whose desire for attainment is so intense. His advancement is truly wonderful.

"I have tickets to the opera of *Parsifal* tonight," He continued, changing the subject abruptly. "Will you be My Guests?" That evening in His wonderful Presence, *Parsifal* became something far more than an opera. It was the struggle of the individual through human embodiment. The Instruction He poured out to us as the drama of the soul and the Victory of the "I AM Presence" unfolded Itself in music and allegory was one of the most marvelous experiences I have ever had. As the performance began He said:

"Observe what can be done for those who are sincere and loyal to the highest ideals through their art." The two who played the part of Parsifal and Kundry were the fortunate ones chosen for this remarkable Blessing. They had been singing a short time when Saint Germain turned on a Great Stream of Spiritual Power, and instantly one could detect the change in their voices. They became more remarkable in quality; the timbre increased so powerfully, the singers themselves were visibly delighted and amazed. One could feel the Charge of Electronic Light penetrate everything. The audience felt the change too, thrilled with delight and enthusiasm, and called them back again and again in its appreciation.

"What will be the result," I asked at the first opportunity, "when they find their voices are not the same the next time they wish to sing?" "This added Power and Perfection will be permanent," He replied. "Former growth permits it to be done for them at the present time. If they had not made previous effort, it would not have been permissible to use them in order to give you this Instruction. The beloved sister and brother will think that Divine Providence has come to their assistance, which is literally true; only in this case, I happen to be the Director of Providence."

As scene after scene was presented that night, Saint Germain showed us the true meaning of what was being portrayed in a manner we can never forget. By the time it came to a close I was raised to a tremendous spiritual height, and the exaltation was so great that it lasted for hours. We returned to our hotel filled with unspeakable joy and gratitude.

The following two weeks passed rapidly while our

Instruction continued. Then one morning our Beloved Master announced that He was leaving us for a time, and that He had retained His suite of rooms for the use of Nada, Pearl, Rex, and Bob over the holidays. Bidding us a loving good-by, He disappeared.

Next morning, Gaylord came to me with a letter which he had found on the table in his room requesting that he come to a certain address in New York at once. He seemed concerned about it, and yet he sensed an uncertainty, something that was not altogether as it should be.

"I don't understand how the letter got on my table without going through the mail," he explained. "I have inquired, and no one seems to know who placed it there." As he continued to ponder over it, there increased within me a sense of uneasiness. I said so frankly, but his only remark was, "I must go and find out what it means, and shall leave by the next train." I wanted to accompany him, but he explained it was not necessary, so I determined to follow my own Inner Direction. As soon as he had gone, Rayborn and I discussed it, and I decided to follow him.

"I am leaving at once by airplane," I said. "He will be in great danger I feel certain, and why he has not sensed it himself, I do not know. At any rate, I shall watch events and may call you by telephone." Fortunately I had noticed the address in Gaylord's letter and hastened at once to the flying field where a plane left immediately, reaching New York long before he arrived. I went to the address, looked the place over thoroughly, but saw no sign of anything unusual. At last I saw Gaylord get out of a taxi and enter the building. The place was a high-class apartment hotel, and as he inquired for the number, I heard the man at the desk say: "They are on the tenth floor."

I followed and kept well out of sight. The door to the apartment opened, and a beautiful woman admitted him. I waited a long time, but he did not come out. At last I was about to go to the door, when it opened and two tall, fine looking men and the beautiful woman with Gaylord came out. They went down to the lobby, passed quickly through, and entered a waiting auto. I saw Gaylord was very pale, but poised and calm.

They drove rapidly away. I jumped into a taxi and followed, giving the driver orders to keep them in sight. Their car arrived at a pier from which a transatlantic liner was sailing. They went aboard at once. I made inquiries and found that the boat was to leave at ten o'clock for Cherbourg.

I was positive by this time that Gaylord was being forced to accompany them, so I went direct to the transportation office, and after considerable argument and tipping, finally secured passage. I wired Rayborn of my sailing and sent a letter explaining. I provided myself with a grip and clothing, boarding the steamer at nine-thirty.

I asked the "Magic I AM Presence" to see that my stateroom was near Gaylord's. Not knowing the name under which these people traveled, I secured a passenger list and asked the "I AM Presence" to show me which staterooms they were in. My attention became focused upon four names, and the Inner Light corroborated my feeling. I looked up the location and discovered that one of them adjoined mine.

I made it my business to watch and listen, and was rewarded the second morning about four o'clock by hearing voices, and among them at intervals, Gaylord's—in an undertone just barely audible. I put my ear close to the wall and used all the Power of the "I AM" so that I might miss nothing and be able to give him assistance if necessary.

There was evidently some argument, and very determined pressure was being brought to bear upon him in several ways, for at last I heard his voice raised to a pitch that indicated he was giving an ultimatum that did not work to their advantage. At last he spoke so anyone passing outside could hear him.

"No," he was saying, "I will not intercede for

your accomplices, even if you kill me."

"We shall see," replied a man's deep voice, "when we get you in the hands of our assistants in Paris."

In those few words enough was revealed to show they were trying to force the release of the others who had just been seized in Washington. I sent a wireless to Rayborn to be silent and wait, for I had learned the necessary details.

Then in the quiet of my room, I sent a message to Saint Germain and the Brotherhood that some of Them might meet me when we landed at Cherbourg. I was not conscious of any answer, but I felt at ease and peace after the effort, and rested in that feeling of accomplishment. It was then five o'clock in the morning, and I lay down to get a few hours' rest, for I knew I would need all the alertness and strength possible.

While sleeping I dreamed, or I thought so at the time, that I met the Master of whom Gaylord had told me many wonderful things—He who had been sent by the Brotherhood to take him on his first trip to the Himalayas. He said to me distinctly:

"Be at peace, My Brother. I will meet you when the boat lands at Cherbourg. All is ready, and the control of this situation is in the hands of Those who never fail." I saw Him so clearly in the experience that I felt sure I would know Him anywhere. The whole experience was too real and tangible to be a dream, and I knew that I must have gone to Him in my Higher Mental Body while the other body slept. I awakened later, wonderfully refreshed.

All that day I kept close watch of their staterooms but learned nothing. I got up at four the next morning, and at five was rewarded by seeing the two men come out. I saw them very plainly, so I was certain I would recognize them again anywhere. They walked the deck for awhile and returned. The woman left the stateroom and took her turn at exercising in the fresh air.

I had hoped they would all go out at one time, but they were too shrewd and kept Gaylord very closely guarded. The fourth day was very stormy, and I saw no one. That night I spent listening intensely every moment, hoping for some kind of revelation. Finally at midnight they argued with Gaylord again, but he was adamant. They told him where they would take him, and I noted the address carefully. It was strange that they did not seem to suspect that someone might follow them, except that they kept strictly to themselves during the entire trip.

The fifth morning the woman came out to walk on deck a short time, and during that interval, I heard the men discussing her. She was evidently an American, and socially prominent in Paris. As near as I could judge from their conversation, she was under their influence, and through her they were avoiding any suspicion being directed to themselves. I realized there was no opportunity of reaching Gaylord without endangering the whole matter, so I trusted to my Inner Feeling and relied upon the Brotherhood and Saint Germain to guide me further.

I thought the masked ball during our last night on board might draw them into association with the rest of the passengers, but nothing induced them to come out of their seclusion. The last night was a brilliant social affair.

The next morning I was up at four o'clock, but nobody left the stateroom until we came alongside the pier. As our steamer docked, they all came out together. I did not dare to let Gaylord see me lest we betray ourselves, but I felt help was near at hand and followed them as closely as I could. They hurried away from the pier and my heart began to sink—when a hand touched my shoulder. As I looked up, the Master of my dream stood before me.

"Come quickly," He said. "I will explain as we go." We followed the others rapidly and kept them in sight until they entered an auto. At that moment, a car drew alongside of us, and the Master motioned me to enter. We drove along rapidly, keeping the other car clearly in sight.

"I am Gaylord's Friend of whom he told you," He continued, while we sped along. "I received your message, and also one from him shortly after." He introduced himself and requested that I never reveal His Name.

"My Son, you are a True Brother of the Great White Brotherhood, and out of this experience will come good of which you do not now dream." There were not many other cars on the road, so it was an easy matter to keep them in sight without attracting attention. They drove at a normal speed, and we soon reached the outskirts of Paris.

A few moments later, a large car came alongside of us. The Master opened our door as the two cars stopped, and a man stepped from that machine into ours, while His car turned at the next corner and disappeared. As He sat down, the Master explained:

"This is another 'Brother of the Light' who will stay on guard when Gaylord reaches his destination."

At last their car came to a large villa with beautiful grounds surrounding it, but the building was falling into ruins. As we saw them pull up in front of this place, we stopped in a secluded spot. They went into the building, and their machine drove rapidly away. The "Brother of Light" got out of our car to observe.

"Watch every move," the Master said to Him. "You know where and how to reach Me. I will take this Brother where he can have peace and rest. He needs it very much. I give you My Blessing. May the 'Magic Presence' seal you in Its Ray." Then speaking to our driver in a language I did not understand, we drove away at a speed that I did not believe was ever allowed in any city.

"These two men who have Gaylord in charge," the Master explained further, "are to wait there for five of their accomplices, two of whom are on their way from Russia. This group cabled from New York that they would arrive today, and those from Russia will be here the day after tomorrow."

Our car soon came to a beautiful villa, and as we stepped out, the most delightful fragrance of roses filled the air. We entered the house and were greeted by a beautiful young lady, the Sister of the Master who had brought me. As I thought how very young She looked, He smiled.

"My Sister is much older than she looks," He volunteered. "My Good Brother, my Sister and I have both lived far beyond the allotted three score and ten years. Our Understanding has enabled us to utilize certain Laws, direct and maintain certain currents of energy in the body, erase all signs of age, and remain eternally youthful and beautiful. I have retained this body for three hundred ten years and my Sister for three hundred. You see, from the human standpoint, we should have passed through the change called death long ago, but that reaper has no terrors for us. It can never touch us now.

"We have had the benefit of the Atomic Accelerator in the Cave of Symbols in your Beloved America. You are surprised that we have been there? Why? We saw you and your friends in that marvelous Retreat quite recently. The joy and marvelous Love your Hearts sent forth was one of the most beautiful and encouraging experiences we have had in many years. In the near future we shall be there again to complete the raising of these bodies into that Eternally Perfect State of the Ascended Masters. Then we can come and go freely as They do, and work above all limitation.

"Of course you understand that after having been given the benefit of the wonderful Accelerator, it is imperative that the student maintain always a constant state of *Conscious Harmony,* no matter what the condition may be within or about him. Once this Assistance has been given to the outer self, it must keep that Power flowing through the body from the 'Mighty I AM Presence.' To some students this is quite a struggle, but it will be short if one has real determination to hold to the Great Light. Come! we are forgetting the joy of hospitality. I will show you to your room, and as soon as you have refreshed yourself, we shall dine."

He showed me to an exquisite room and bath, and I could not help but notice how these Great Ones who are the Carriers of the Light always are surrounded by Beauty, Harmony, and Perfection in every part of Their special activity. I remarked about this once to Saint Germain, and He replied:

"When Life is lived as it was intended, all is Peace, Harmony, Beauty, Opulence, and Happiness. To conquer the desire to feel or express inharmony shuts the door to inharmony. Therefore it cannot act within the personal self nor its environment. It is a joy to know that humanity has the strength to do this, and thus receive the untold Blessings of Life."

We had dinner, and the Master urged me to go to my room to sleep until called. I obeyed, and was awakened at seven o'clock the next morning by sweet chimes sounding through my room. They thrilled my body as if a charge of Electronic Energy had come through the sound. I dressed quickly and joined the Master and His Sister in the drawing room. I felt so wonderful it seemed as if there were no such thing as being weary. Much had taken place during my rest. Word had been received that the tools of the sinister force were arriving to join their accomplices the following day.

"All must be in readiness to act quickly," the Master explained. "The Brothers of Light who are members of the French Secret Service have been instructed to be thoroughly prepared, and there must be no publicity about the seizure of this group."

You can imagine my joy, when two days later as I entered the drawing room, Saint Germain greeted me serenely and as graciously as usual. A moment later, as the Master and His Sister entered, a Dazzling Light flashed through the room.

"Come," said Saint Germain, "all is ready. Let us go." As we approached the rendezvous, there was not a movement or sound. Saint Germain went up to the door, extended His hand—the lock clicked, and the door opened noiselessly. He led the way as though familiar with every detail. He approached massive double doors and again extended His hand. They fairly flew open, so great was the force He had focused. Before us stood the seven tools, Gaylord, and the woman.

As we entered, the seven drew weapons, and for a fraction of a second the battle was one of mental forces. Suddenly a Circle of Blue Flame surrounded them; their hands dropped to their sides, and the Brothers of the Secret Service entered. In less than another minute the tools were in handcuffs, within closed autos, and on their way to a certain place of restraint where no other prisoners can ever contact them. Gaylord was surprised and overjoyed at the speed and quiet with which his release and their capture had come about. They had tried to force him to use certain legal authority that was his to have their co-workers in America released.

"Beloved Brothers," he said, "I can never thank you enough for saving this body for further service. They were deeply in earnest, I can assure you, and would have destroyed me when I refused to help them. However, in their unguarded conversation I learned much that will be of value to us in the future." He embraced each of us with great tenderness, Love, and gratitude. "The woman was guarded by us," Saint Germain explained. "It is not necessary to punish this child; she has been but an innocent victim of their villainous treachery.

"My Dear Sister," He said, "we do not wish to harm you. You have been but the plaything of this sinister force. You shall have complete Release and Freedom forever from its influence and control."

Instantly a Blue Spiral Flame encircled her from head to foot. Her body swayed as if she would have fallen to the floor, and yet could not because she was held in the Embrace of Its Marvelous Power. She stood thus fully ten minutes, and then the Flame slowly faded out. Her body trembled violently a moment, and her eyes opened with a pleading, appealing expression.

"Oh, where am I?" she asked.

"You are with friends," Saint Germain replied, as He took her hand in His.

"You are forever released from a condition far worse than death. Come, and we shall take you home."

"No! no!" she replied frantically, "I can never go home again after all I have done and all that has happened. I cannot—I cannot!"

"Yes, you can," Saint Germain answered with a Conviction and Power of the Truth that changed all resistance into instant obedience. "You will find everything changed, for your good husband understands and will welcome you home. Your daughter, an invalid who has suffered so much, shall also be restored, and your home will be a happy, wonderful place once again."

We went out, entered the car of Gaylord's Friend, and drove to a beautiful residence in the best residential section of Paris. We entered and were received by a tall slender man whom I knew instantly to be an American. He had been handsome in earlier years, but now his face showed deep lines of care and sorrow. With tears streaming down his face, he held out his arms to his wife. She rushed into them, sobbing as though her heart would break. Saint Germain waited a moment, and when she became calm, presented us to him.

"Beloved Friends," He said, "let us go to your lovely daughter, for we have further Work to do." We entered a lovely room where a girl once beautiful lay upon the bed so drawn and deformed that she hardly seemed human.

Saint Germain stepped to the bedside, took her left hand in His, and placed the thumb of His right hand on her forehead between the eyes. He stood in this position for about five minutes while the rest of us looked on expectantly. Suddenly the girl gave the most unearthly scream; her whole body straightened out on the bed and she lay as still as if in death.

"Have no fear," He said. "She will be conscious in a few moments. Then I will give her strength to stand and walk." Presently she opened her eyes with the sweetest smile of Love and Gratitude—and the Light of her "I AM Presence" streamed out in Blessing to Saint Germain. He extended His hand, assisting her to rise and stand on her feet while she received the loving embrace of her father and mother. Saint Germain picked the child up and carried her to a soft couch in the drawing room. He gave directions for her care and said He would be with them the following day.

We returned to the home of our wonderful Friend and a full explanation was given to Gaylord of all that had happened since he had left Washington. His gratitude was very great, and he discussed his own feeling and reaction during the trip on the boat.

"The only feeling I had during the entire experience," he explained, "was to trust wholly in my 'Mighty I AM Presence' and the Great White Brotherhood."

"My Beloved Students and Brothers," said Saint Germain, "do you not see how unfailingly the Great Law of God acts? In this case, the sinister force tried to compel a Member of the Great White Brotherhood to serve it—and therefore darkness. You see, our Good Brother became the decoy, and his 'Light' the channel by which seven more of their destructive talons were cut off from any further activity; and a very great joy and happiness was restored to a wonderful, blessed family.

"I have news that will surprise you still further. The man to whom his lovely wife and daughter were this day restored is Arthur Livingston, the uncle of our beloved Brother Bob Singleton. This man is the most highly inspired mining engineer I know. I mean by that, he is well directed by the 'Mighty I AM Presence' in his mining work.

"I wish all three of them to return to America with you, for you will find they will become very earnest fellow students. Tomorrow I will arrange a return passage for you, but during the next week you are to remain in Paris until your boat sails."

During that time, we were the guests of Gaylord's wonderful Friend and His Sister. The next day we accompanied Saint Germain to the Livingstons. When we entered, the Transformation was greater than the human mind believes possible.

Mr. Livingston looked ten years younger; the daughter was radiantly beautiful and happy, gaining strength and the normal use of her body with amazing ease and rapidity. The mother's wonderful Love was now fully reawakened, and her devotion to her family was very great. She wanted so much to make amends for all the suffering that had come to them through her.

"This suffering," she said to us, "that so nearly wrecked everything for myself and my family, was the result of my desire for social supremacy wherever we have lived. As I look upon the whole experience now, I can see that my desire for social influence was an intense craving that completely absorbed all my time and attention. It very nearly did irreparable damage to us all. I promise you I shall never forget this lesson. I shall try to make amends for it all by greater devotion to my family and Eternal Service to the Light."

"I wish the three of you," said Saint Germain addressing the Livingstons, "to sail with these friends to America—where I desire you to make your permanent home. It will help you to forget the experiences that have caused so much suffering here." Their joy was unspeakable, and their gratitude to Him is everlasting.

A week later when we said good-by to Saint Germain, Gaylord's Friend and His Sister, we could not find words to express what was in our Hearts, for Love is the only thing that expresses the gratitude one feels under such circumstances.

We went aboard the steamer at four o'clock and enjoyed every moment while crossing the Atlantic. Gaylord asked me several times to relate with full details all the experiences we had passed through, and after each story, his only comment was:

"How marvelous! How wonderful!"

On our arrival in New York, Rayborn met us at the pier, and I never saw a happier man. When he was introduced to Arthur Livingston as Bob's uncle, he was delighted indeed. We went directly to Washington, D.C., where the Livingstons were to establish their new home.

Thus does the Great White Brotherhood ever continue to bless humanity in this marvelous, silent manner, and through Its Unconquerable Power and Intelligence, forever fulfill the Law of the Eternal: "The Light of God never fails."

CHAPTER VIII

The Conquering Power

OUR return with the Livingstons to Washington, D.C., was followed by many weeks of pleasant study while receiving the Great Wisdom of our Beloved Saint Germain. We were very busy during this time, and days sped by on wings, for during our contemplation of the "Light" and the Ascended Masters, we transcended all sense of time. After all, only as human events call our attention to it are we ever aware of time. We had arrived in Washington on the second of October, and the Christmas season was now approaching.

"For some reason," Rayborn said to me one morning, "Saint Germain wants the children to come here earlier than was originally planned. Let us wire them to be here by the twenty-first of December. He said arrangements had been made to have them excused a few days earlier. He did not say why He wanted them, so I did not presume to inquire."

We sent the wire, and late in the afternoon of the twenty-first they all arrived. Bob's train came in half an hour ahead of the others. We all went to the hotel where Nada and Pearl were given the suite of rooms Saint Germain had engaged. During the evening, with a twinkle in His eyes, Saint Germain asked the four of them to sing a certain group of songs.

"I sent for those songs and have been practicing them for three weeks!" Bob announced.

"So have we!" chorused the other three. "Why should we all have chosen the same songs?"

"That is very good," said Saint Germain, smiling knowingly; and then He revealed His surprise.

"We have been planning to attend a concert on Christmas Eve," He began. "Two of the soloists will be indisposed. I know the man in charge of the entertainment, and at the opportune moment, I shall offer to supply the artists to take their places." Bob looked at Him in positive fright.

"I have never appeared in public in my life," he said. "I should be scared to death!"

"Bob, do you not have confidence in me?" said Saint Germain as He stepped up to Bob and put His hands on his shoulders.

"Of course, I have all the confidence in the world," he answered, as his eyes filled with tears.

"Then leave it to me," Saint Germain replied. "All fear will be gone when you awaken in the morning. Be at peace."

The next morning at ten o'clock, a telephone call came from His friend in charge of the concert, who was in great distress because two of his soloists had been taken ill and would not be able to appear.

"Be at peace. I think I can help you out," Saint Germain replied. "I can send you a quartet, two of whom are splendid soloists." The manager knew that He understood what was needed but did not know He was an Ascended Master. However, he accepted the proffered assistance without question. He made the announcement that a quartet would appear in place of the soloists.

Christmas Eve came, and the great auditorium was packed to capacity. As the curtain rose there were exclamations of appreciation here and there in the audience as a gorgeous fairyland scene was revealed before them. Saint Germain kept in touch with the manager at intervals, and all felt a curious state of expectancy, feeling that something unusual was about to take place. The feeling grew stronger as time passed. The other artists sang, and then came a sort of hush. A second curtain lifted, revealing a marvelous setting of Bethlehem in the background with a Brilliant Star shedding its wonderful Radiation over the entire scene. Just at this point an airplane in the shape of a great white bird floated down and landed midstage. Out stepped the quartet in beautiful Arabic costumes.

They first sang "Holy Night," and the audience compelled them to repeat it. Then Nada sang a solo, "Light of Life, We Look to Thee." The enthusiasm of the audience continued to increase as they showered applause upon her. The quartet sang the next number, "Master Jesus, We Follow Thee." The fourth number was Rex's solo, "In the Light I Rest Secure." Handkerchiefs were waved, and some rose in the audience calling for him to repeat it. The quartet sang again, and then the manager stepped to the front of the stage and announced his surprise for the closing number.

"Allow me to present our Guest Artist of the evening," he said, "singing 'I Come on the Wings of Light.' Prima Donna Nada."

We all gasped with surprise as the mother of Nada and Rex entered, wearing a gown glittering with jewels. Her own beauty far transcended that of the gown She wore. The applause and greeting from the audience was tremendous. She raised Her hand for silence; the audience responded instantly, and She began.

She sang with tremendous Power and Glory as Her Radiation was released to flood out over the audience and the city of Washington in Blessing. From there it has spread like a Mantle of Peace and comfort over America and the Earth. At the close of Her song, the audience was gripped in silence a few seconds, and then burst forth showering their deep appreciation and joy in loving gratitude upon Her. They called for Her again and again. After She had sung it for the third time, She raised Her hand for silence and spoke to them.

"Your joy and gratitude is so sweet, so sincere, that I shall sing for you something I love which expresses My Feeling for you. It is called, 'I Love You.'" In this, Her Voice took on a Beauty and Power that acted like magic. She sang as only an Ascended Master can sing, and it was no wonder the audience in its enthusiasm and appreciation tried to call Her back again and again.

However, at a signal from Saint Germain, the final curtain was lowered. We rushed to the wings and such a greeting and reunion followed that no words can describe. Rayborn was almost overcome by his joy.

"Come quickly," said Saint Germain, as He threw a Velvet Indigo Cloak about Nada's mother; and we stepped into the auto, driving away rapidly. It was not a moment too soon, for the audience was rushing to the stage entrance. We arrived at the hotel and went directly to the master suite. In a few moments reporters besieged the place, wanting to know who the singer was. Saint Germain stepped to the door and greeted them.

"Prima Donna Nada," he said, "is the wife of a western mining man, Daniel Rayborn, and the two soloists of the quartet are Her son and daughter. That is all," and He dismissed them.

"After such loyal, splendid service from each of you," He explained, closing the door behind Him, "I thought you were all entitled to this happy surprise." He congratulated the quartet, and smiling quizzically at Bob, remarked, "You see, your trust did not go unrewarded."

"You know," replied Bob, "I never thought of stage fright."

We all gathered around the Mother of Nada and Rex and asked Her to tell us something of Her Work and where She had been.

"I will tell you briefly what I can, for I must leave you at two o'clock; but I will come tomorrow night for a visit from eight to twelve.

"The Sphere in which I dwell might be called a Stratum, for there are several Strata which enfold the Earth, holding it in their Embrace. The place where I am receiving certain training is just as real and tangible as your physical Earth—but I serve in the Strata below the one in which I am studying.

"When I thought I was passing through the change called death, I lost all feeling of Life for a few moments, and then awakened to find myself surrounded by twelve Ascended Masters, whose Light was almost blinding in Its Dazzling Radiance. Among Them was our Beloved Saint Germain— who had instructed me for several years previously.

"As soon as I became clearly conscious of the Ascended Masters, I was shown how I could be assisted and how I could assist myself in raising the atomic structure of my physical body—then and there—into the Pure Electronic Body, the

Seamless Garment which remains forever Pure and Perfect.

"As the process of Raising gradually took place, I became more and more aware of Blazing Light filling my entire body, and I felt the most marvelous Radiant Energy surge in and through me sweeping away every vestige of resistance and imperfection, and quickening my consciousness.

"I became more and more aware of my 'Mighty I AM Presence,' until finally It stood before me—Visible, Tangible and very Real. Steadily and powerfully, I felt my physical body drawn into and enveloped by my Glorious God Self, and when I stepped out of the cemetery, I could scarcely realize how Transcendent I had become. The old human, limited activities of my consciousness were raised into that alert sense of Freedom and unlimited use of Wisdom and Power. I was shown very clearly, now I was aware of this Greater Activity, that I must put It to use. Then came a still fuller sense of the Freedom, Beauty, Joy, and Service that I must render to those who still remain unascended.

"My first desire was that I might know more of these Ascended Masters who had so lovingly ministered to me. Instantly, one after another stood before me, and without a word being spoken, conveyed Their Names and Thoughts to me. With this marvelous 'Thought Language' there came certain attendant pictures in color and the true interpretation of them.

"This *Communion by Thought* was just as clear as human beings now use by the spoken word—in fact much clearer, for there can be no mistake when thought contacts thought. Misunderstandings come about through the use of words—for after all, they are but receptacles to convey thought and feeling. When thoughts and feelings are not limited by words, many imperfections and much resistance disappear entirely.

"At one time during a former Golden Age, mankind still had the Full Use of this Inner Communion by thought; but as the personalities looked away from the Light, the substance of their bodies became denser—until it reached the condition of the physical atom of which the human body is composed today.

"This substance vibrates at too slow a rate for thought to pass through; hence words or sounds which could register in this lower rate had to be used as a means of communication. Even today the individual could again draw forth this same Perfect Way of Communication by releasing a Ray of Golden White Light from within his own 'Magic I AM Presence' by conscious command—visualizing It passing through the brain structure from the Electronic Body. This Wave of Greater Light would increase the vibratory rate of the atoms of the physical body to the point where thought would register and be comprehended without the spoken word.

"Thought waves are always being catapulted, as it were, upon the flesh of the body, both from within the individual's own consciousness and from the thoughts of others; but how many people comprehend that fact enough to read the thought whose impact is felt? Mental telepathy is a slight part of this activity, but how many people can interpret the thoughts received and know from whence they come?

"It was weeks before I ceased to marvel at this wonderful threefold means of Inner Communication through the sight, the thought and the feeling. The Glorious Freedom of the Ascended Master is so marvelous that We long for every human being to understand and enjoy that same Great Happiness. This is the Final Crowning Glory of all human activity, the Ideal and Reward for which all human experience is sought and endured. If mankind could but understand and look toward this True Ideal of Life, the self-created chains and limitations that have bound the race for hundreds of thousands of years would drop away in less than a century.

"It is the Determination of the Ascended Masters that 'The Light,' which is the Ancient Wisdom, shall flood the Earth and its inhabitants *now*—and whatever cannot stand the Radiance of that Light must disappear as mist before the morning Sun.

The Law of Life of the whole Universe is the 'Law of Light'; and before Its Blazing Glory and Invincible Power, all discord and chaos are consumed.

"My first Experiences that seemed to Me so marvelous proved to be but fragmentary compared with what has been revealed since My Ascension into this far greater and more wonderful Activity of Life.

"Please keep this fact clearly in mind: that in the Ascended State, each Revelation of more expanded Activity always contains the attendant Wisdom and Power for its right use. This is a never-ending Joy and Wonder to the Sons and Daughters of The Light.

"After I had become somewhat adjusted to the new condition, Saint Germain took me to the Place for which I was best fitted—where I assimilated the new experiences for a short time. After this I was given the benefit of Illustrated Instruction. Then I began to enter into my Real Activity, my True Service.

"One of the ever-increasing Joys of the Ascended State is, that as We study any particular condition, it is always accompanied by illustrations of the exact Activity We are to use, and there can never be any mistake, for the end is seen in the beginning. However, this remarkable means of Illustrated Instruction does not occur below a certain state of consciousness—which can only be known as it is attained. IT IS A DEFINITE POSITIVE FEELING AND KNOWING.

"You beloved ones do not realize how fortunate you are in having the Blessing of the wonderful Atomic Accelerator—one marvelous result of the Love and Work of our Blessed Saint Germain. Great has been His Love, His Service, and the Gift of Himself to humanity.

"The beauty and rapid progress of each of you is due to your sincere and intense gratitude. It is the certain pathway to great heights of attainment and the easiest method by which to achieve every good thing. Gratitude to Life for all Life pours out to you is the wide-open Door to every Blessing in the Universe.

"It is because humanity has forgotten to be grateful to Life for all the Blessings upon this Earth that it has shut the door to Peace and become bound by the chains of its own selfishness. The mass of mankind seeks the possession and holding of things, which is an inversion of the Law of Life. Life forever says to the individual, 'Expand, and ever let Me pour Greater and Greater Perfection through you forever!'

"The Law of Life is to GIVE, for only by giving of one's Self can one expand. To give the intense Love of your own 'Mighty I AM Presence' unto all mankind, to all Life, is the Mightiest Activity we can use to draw the human into the Divine. In this Divine Love

is contained every good thing.

"There have been thousands of platitudes written about Divine Love, but only when the individual knows Divine Love as something more than an abstract principle does he realize that he can generate It at will and direct It consciously to accomplish whatever he decrees. The Ascended Master knows Divine Love as a 'Presence,' an Intelligence, a Principle, a Light, a Power, an Activity, and a Substance. Therein lies the Secret to Their Supreme Authority and Power, for there is nothing to obstruct the approach of Divine Love anywhere in the Universe. When the student understands how to draw forth the Flame of Divine Love from within his own 'Mighty I AM Presence' at his own Decree, he knows it is but a very short time until his constant use of It raises him into the Ascension. Only enough Love can accomplish that for anyone, but It must be first projected forth before It can release the Blessings within Its Heart unto the sender.

"Divine Love, being the Eternal, is the Unquenchable, Invincible, Unconquerable 'Presence of the I AM,' and therefore Master of all, now and forever!

"All the joys and pleasures of the outer world are as but dust compared to the limitless, ever-increasing Wonders of Creation in Cosmic Space which the Ascended Master may observe and enjoy consciously and at will. One of the tremendous Blessings of the Ascended State is the entire absence of any criticism or condemnation of human frailties or mistakes. If the student of Light will train himself to forget everything that is useless or that is in any way undesirable, he will not only make rapid progress, but it is imperative if he is to free himself from human limitation. For the student to drag after him unpleasant memories is but one of the many ways by which he creates over and over again the same experiences of misery from which he is really seeking to be Free.

"The Light does not receive inharmony into Itself. As the student enters the Light, he becomes all Light, hence all Perfection. *To have inharmony drop away from the body or affairs, the personality must let go of all thought, feeling, and words about imperfection.* An Activity that will always bring *complete Freedom* is for the student to pour out *Unconditional and Eternal Forgiveness* to everybody and everything. This does what nothing else can do to free everyone, as well as the person who sends it out. Forgiveness fills all with Light's Perfection.

"When Forgiveness is sincere, the individual will find his world reordered as if by magic and filled with every good thing; but remember that unless a discord is forgotten, it is not forgiven, because you cannot loose it or release yourself from it until it is out of your consciousness. So long as you remember an injustice or a disturbed feeling, you have not forgiven either the person or the condition.

"When the forgiveness is complete, the feeling nature or emotional body is serene, kind, happy, comfortable, and like a Mountain of Light. It is so powerful that one abides within it as impregnable as in a fortress. Even though he stand amidst the wreck of worlds, yet will he remain untouched by anything but Perfection in the Light.

"Remember, what your consciousness is held firmly upon, you bring into existence in yourself. It is impossible for your Life to contain anything that is not your present or past accumulation of consciousness. Whatever you are conscious of in thought and feeling stamps itself upon the Universal substance in and around you and brings forth after its kind—always. This is a Mighty Cosmic Law from which there is no variation or escape.

"Truly, it is the very greatest joy to be with those you love, so tonight My Joy is great indeed. The time is near at hand when you will understand that all human relationship is but a creation of the physical world. In the Ascended State, all are truly Brothers and Sisters, Sons and Daughters of the Most High Living God. In that phase of Life, the True Meaning of Friendship is understood and lived, and when rightly understood, it is the most beautiful relationship in the Universe.

"Now I must leave you until tomorrow night at

eight, for I have work to do. Hold yourselves steady within the Mighty Glow of the Cosmic Light, the 'Mighty I AM Presence' of the Universe, that your pathway may be illumined by Its Wondrous Radiance." As She spoke the last few Words, Her Body gradually grew dim until it completely disappeared.

"Beloved Students," said Saint Germain, smiling lovingly, "tonight I have shown you the higher ideal of entertainment. It is not only very enjoyable, but tremendously uplifting because of the 'Magic Presence' whose Limitless Power it releases. You see, when the proper channel is opened, there is no limit to the Blessings an audience may receive wherever the condition is made possible.

"You have realized that with sufficient understanding it is possible to cause your body to respond instantly to the higher and unlimited use of the 'I AM Presence' within you. Your body is the instrument upon and through which you can let the 'Mighty I AM Presence' play Its Great Song of Life—knowing no limitation nor defeat in anything. Or you can let the thoughts and feelings of limitation and discord sent out by other personalities play upon it and reap accordingly. Your body is your radio; your thought, feeling and spoken word are the ways by which you can tune into or out of any condition or activity you do or do not want. The only real difference is that your body is capable of being tuned to a very much greater height, inconceivably greater than any radio now in existence.

"You are the director of your own radio through your consciousness. You have the programs of the Universe from which to choose. Your world today reveals what you have chosen in the past. If you do not like that program, choose a new and better one from your 'I AM Presence.' "

Our Gratitude and Love were greater than ever for Saint Germain, and we realized as never before that in the Presence and Wisdom of the Ascended Masters, there truly is Heaven on Earth. We bade each other good-night and went to our rooms. We breakfasted the next morning at eleven and spent the afternoon showing Nada, Pearl, Rex, and Bob many places of interest in Washington. In the Raised Consciousness we were in during this time, the appreciation and intensity of our enjoyment were keener than usual, and it seemed we saw beauty everywhere.

We returned to the hotel at four o'clock, as Beloved Saint Germain had invited us to dine with Him later in the suite of rooms occupied by Nada and Pearl, saying the time had arrived for the Instruction of the Livingstons to begin. At six o'clock we were ready, the Livingstons had come, and all were awaiting Saint Germain's arrival when a most delicate bell sounded through the rooms.

"Saint Germain is approaching," said Pearl immediately.

"Who is He?" asked Zara Livingston.

"The Wonderful Man who healed you," Pearl replied, "and saved your mother from such a terrible fate. If my feeling is correct, you will soon see Manifestations of His Transcendent Wisdom and Power besides what you have already experienced." At this moment He was announced in the same way as any other guest arriving at the hotel. He greeted us all graciously and then explained:

"It is my wish that these good friends, the Livingstons, become accustomed to the Higher Use of the Law of Light. We shall now begin by realizing first that everywhere about us is a Universal Substance which We call 'Cosmic Light,' and which the Bible refers to as Spirit. This is the One Pure, Primal Essence out of which comes all Creation. It is the Pure Life Substance of the First Cause—God. This is Infinite, and we may draw upon It at any time for anything we can ever require. This Pure Electronic Light is the Great Limitless Storehouse of the Universe. In It is all Perfection, and out of It comes all that is.

"Now if you will gather about the table, we shall dine—so you may see, feel, taste and know this Wondrous Omnipresent Substance so often talked about, but so little understood."

Saint Germain went to the head of the table, seating Zara, Bob, Nada, and myself on His left, Mrs. Livingston, Arthur, Pearl and Rex on His right, and asked us to bow our heads in silence before the "Mighty Presence of God in Action."

Each felt the powerful Current of Divine Energy —"Liquid Light"—surge through his mind and body and fill him with a feeling of Infinite Love and Peace. As we raised our heads, a beautiful snow-white, rose-patterned cloth covered the table, made of a fabric none of us had ever seen. It most nearly resembled silk with frost upon it, both in quality and appearance.

Arthur Livingston turned white with surprise, as the moment before he had seen only the polished top of a walnut table. Now this exquisitely beautiful cloth covered it with napkins to match at each place. There followed the rapid appearance of an entire service for the meal. The dishes were milk-white and made of substance that was like satin in appearance, but very hard and unbreakable. Upon each individual piece were strange mystic designs embossed in gold. None of us understood them, but they were extremely beautiful. The knives, forks and spoons were made of a metal that looked like frosted silver, with wonderfully carved jade handles. Goblets of jade with beautifully carved stems appeared at the right hand of each guest, filled with a sparkling crystalline Liquid that was the very

Essence of Life—"Condensed Light."

"Do not be alarmed," Saint Germain said, "when you drink this Liquid. It quickens the vibratory action of your atomic structure tremendously, and if you should feel faint, it will only last a few moments." Then raising His own goblet, He proposed a toast.

"To the Peace and Illumination of all present, and to all mankind!"

We raised our glasses and drained them. It was with difficulty that we refrained from a gasp of astonishment at the effect of this Liquid as the Electronic Essence charged through our bodies. We felt as if we were being raised from our chairs.

A seven course dinner followed, the empty dishes of each course disappearing as soon as it was finished. The food was most delicious and extremely vitalizing to the body. Our dessert was similar to what we had for dinner at the Cave of Symbols.

"You see," said Saint Germain, as we finished the meal, "it is not difficult to produce what you desire direct from the Pure Universal Substance *so long as no element of selfishness enters in.* We have dined here tonight on delicious food. It has all come from a supply that is ever at hand. Yet it is but a fragment of what can be produced."

He extended His hand and a disc of gold formed in it which He passed around for all to examine. He held out His other hand and a beautiful blue-white diamond formed within it, a truly Perfect Jewel, so dazzling was its refractive power. He held them both in His closed right hand a few moments, and when He opened it, a beautiful necklace lay within, exquisite in design, with the gorgeous stone as a pendant. He handed it to Zara and said:

"Will you accept This as your Talisman of Light? The stone is not an ordinary one. It is really 'Condensed Light'; hence, it is a Real Talisman of 'The Light.' It will bless you greatly. Now let us go further. The service which has been used tonight, the Ascended Host present to Nada and Bob."

As He spoke these words, the service began to reappear on the table until all was complete. Suddenly a goblet fell to the floor, and when it was replaced was found to be uninjured in any way.

"This service," He went on to explain, "is unbreakable, as you see. Care for it yourselves always, and may it ever bring you great happiness.

"Now, about this good brother," He continued, indicating Mr. Livingston. "He is a very efficient mining engineer. In about six months he will be needed in Bob's place at the mine. May I suggest that We take the matter up tomorrow and make the necessary arrangements in detail. It will do his loved ones a world of good to spend two years in the West.

"I suggest they go out to the ranch about the

middle of April. Zara will find her Twin Ray awaiting her there. When she sees him, she will recognize him instantly. The drawing together of these sets of Twin Rays is one of the most remarkable things it has ever been my privilege to accomplish.

"My Dear Livingston, as you take up the study of these Mighty Laws, you will understand everything clearly. What today seems strange and perhaps unreal will become more real than anything else in your Life because there is no doubt within you. That condition makes it possible to give you definite Instruction, with your permission."

"Great Master," said Zara, "I cannot begin to express my gratitude to You for my Healing and for the opportunity to have this Instruction. The wonderful manifestation You have shown us tonight has awakened a dim memory within me, as though I had somewhere, sometime known about these Laws."

"My Dear Child," He replied, "you have known a great deal about them, and the complete memory of what you have known shall return to you." Then suddenly we became aware of other persons in the room, and a soft, sweet laugh reached our ears. The mother of Nada and Rex stepped in from the adjoining room in marvelously beautiful Garments —Her very Presence radiating Peace and Blessings to all. She held out Her hand to Rayborn. He bowed low and kissed it.

She greeted all graciously, and the Livingstons were presented, their admiration being frank and sincere. Saint Germain explained Her Ascension to them in detail, the training She had been receiving since Her Ascension, and the Service She was constantly giving to humanity. It was the most divinely happy Christmas night I had ever experienced, for it was filled with marvelous Radiance and deep Instruction.

At twelve o'clock, the Mother Nada bade us good-by until we should all meet again in the Cave of Symbols in July. She and Saint Germain had Work to do together, and as They disappeared, His last Words were a request to Livingston that he meet with us at two o'clock the next day.

As soon as They had gone, the Livingstons plied us with questions concerning Beloved Saint Germain and His wonderful Work. They were the happiest people I have ever seen when they found He was ready to give them Instruction. They were so intensely interested that it was four o'clock in the morning before we knew it. It was truly the happiest Christmas of our lives.

The next day at one forty-five Saint Germain appeared and greeted us as usual. "I see you have all entered into the plan beautifully," He remarked, "and do you realize how all experiences are truly in Divine Order? Each person is a link in the Great Cosmic Chain of Perfection. I often marvel at the Perfection with which the 'Mighty I AM Presence' works.

"In the recent activity, our good brother Gaylord's experience led us to the Livingstons in order to give them protection, and through that We have found another set of Twin Rays—Zara and the one she is to meet. This will bring the Livingstons and another friend into the Everlasting Light. Is My Plan for this good brother Livingston agreeable to you all?"

"I am more than delighted with the arrangement, as it is a blessing to all concerned," Rayborn replied.

"Well then, with your cooperation, we shall enter into very intensive Training during the next three months. I am requested to do this by Those who are greater than I. We shall leave Washington on the seventh of April for the ranch. Bob, Nada, Pearl and Rex are to remain here until the tenth of January. They will return to school by the twelfth."

These glorious days passed all too quickly. Bob accompanied the others as far as the university, and from there went on alone to the mine. The rest of us settled down to intensive Training, and one of our greatest joys was to see the enthusiasm with which the Livingstons entered into Beloved Saint Germain's Instruction. To all of us, He truly is "The Light of God that never fails."

CHAPTER IX

The Ascension of Daniel Rayborn

OUR intensive training under Saint Germain continued for three months. During that time our happiness was very great; for the Joy and Blessing of actually seeing, knowing, and conversing with the "Mighty I AM Presence" was unspeakable—and can only be known through having the actual experience.

We received weekly reports from the children, whose progress at the university was splendid. Bob's letters told us that all was moving in good order at the mine and that the men were actually singing at their work. *Saint Germain said at this time that justice and loving service could and would bring about that same activity everywhere in the business world when those same principles were applied.*

Saint Germain promised to meet us at the ranch later, and then went to the Far East. We left Washington on the seventh of April. We reached Denver on the eleventh and drove to the ranch early the next morning when everything seemed to breathe the joy, peace, and freedom of the wonderful mountains.

As time for graduation drew near, we received a

wonderful letter from Nada and Rex describing an experience which they surmised was given them by Saint Germain, and that brought them all great happiness. They sat up late one evening discussing a graduation suit for Rex and gowns for Nada and Pearl. The next morning Rex found a beautiful new suit of clothes lying upon the table in his room, and attached was a slip of paper with this message: "Please accept this from those who love you." It was made of a most wonderful blue material and fitted him perfectly.

In the rooms of Nada and Pearl were complete ensembles for each with similar slips attached. Their gowns were of soft white material embroidered in exquisite design. Rex insisted that his father, Bob, Gaylord, and I attend their graduation exercises and was so determined there seemed no way of refusing, so we returned for that event. This university had a benefactor whom the public did not know, but we began to suspect Him to be Saint Germain. Later He told us that its president was a member of the Great White Brotherhood.

Rayborn had invited the president and his sister to have dinner with him before his return west. The affair was one not soon forgotten, for when they arrived, Saint Germain was with them, to everyone's surprise and joy. He spoke to us at length concerning the new era of university training.

"In all fields of education," He said, "a certain demand is asserting itself throughout the race to compel recognition of the 'Mighty I AM Presence.' This is the *Only Foundation* upon which Permanent Happiness, Freedom and Perfection can ever be built.

"It is only through the 'I AM' that humanity can find release from its selfishness and its greed. Then all will come into the full use of the eternal abundance that is waiting to serve mankind. Each individual is an open doorway to all Perfection, but that Perfection can only express itself on Earth when the outer self keeps its channel clear and harmonious by adoring and accepting the 'Mighty I AM Presence.' By accepting and keeping the attention on the 'I AM Presence,' the individual can at any moment draw all good into the outer use of the personality. Thus he can call forth into his Being and world all the good he desires. *But the Greatest Power that this Truth places at the command of the personal self is the use of Divine Love as a 'Presence' which goes before it and adjusts all outer activities, solves all human problems, and reveals the Perfection that must come forth upon Earth.*

"Divine Love, being the Heart of Infinity and of the individual, is an ever-flowing, *Intelligent* Flame that releases Energy, Wisdom, Power, and Substance without limit. It will release boundless

Blessings to all who will harmonize their own personalities enough to let It come through.

"Divine Love is the Reservoir of Life and the Treasure-chest of the Universe. It automatically draws to the personal self every good thing. When the outer activity of the mind acknowledges the 'I AM Presence' and keeps attuned to Divine Love, then all achievement is accomplished without struggle or strain, and all creative activity becomes the continual expansion and enjoyment of Perfection.

"The more one studies Life and contemplates Perfection, the less he struggles with people and things, and the more he adores the 'God Presence'; for one who worships Perfection must of necessity become *That* upon which his attention rests. When mankind fills the outer activity of the mind with thoughts and feelings of Perfection, the bodies and affairs of humanity will bring into the outer that order and Perfection also. The more we understand Life and Perfection, the simpler all becomes, until we have to do only one thing and do it all the time: fill our thought and feeling with Divine Love always.

"Life never struggles, for that which struggles is the consciousness which attempts to limit Life, and is but the interference with the Perfection which is forever trying to come through. If the personal or outer self will just *let* Life flow and keep at peace, the manifested result will be Perfection—the Divine Way of Life fulfilled. Many who start earnestly to attain this Understanding become discouraged and discontinue their search because they are looking for things instead of enjoying God—by adoring the Beauty and Power of the Great Light for Itself only. If we seek the Light because we love to adore the Light, results are absolutely certain to follow; and we are then putting God first, which must be. if the personal self is to be kept in its right relation to Life."

Late the following afternoon we bade our friends good-by, exchanged good wishes, and boarded the train for the West. The attendants whom Saint Germain had provided for Nada, Pearl, and Rex in their apartment while at the university disappeared as silently as they had come. Their entire association was an example of what it means *"To know! to dare! to do! to serve! and to be silent!"*

Our train reached Denver at four o'clock of the third day after graduation; and early the next morning, Nada, Pearl, Zara, Bob, Rex, and I left on horseback for the Cave of Symbols. We reached the summit of the mountain about eleven o'clock, and Zara was happy in the extreme. She excused herself, saying she wanted to be alone for awhile. In the meantime, the rest of us prepared lunch. Later she returned, and the Light in her eyes was brilliant.

"I have had a strange experience," she remarked. "I have seen the God of this mountain. He is a wonderful Being. Such Majesty, Wisdom and Power I have never imagined before in anyone! He is at least eight feet tall and is Guard of this Sacred Mountain, as He calls it. He is known as the God Tabor. He told me He would have much to do in helping us all in the near future.

"Everything around here seems so familiar—as if I had been here before. He said I had been here in very ancient times. I do not fully understand what He means, but I feel as though I were just about to remember something important in the past. He explained that one day I would enter the Heart of this mountain and receive of its Eternal Life and Wisdom, but not until after two years had passed. He asked me to be at peace, that all might come about in Divine Order, and said that I had entered the Great Stream of Life which would carry me on to Eternal Perfection."

"My Dear Sister, you are indeed blest," said Nada, going up and embracing her fondly. "Just trust the 'Mighty I AM Presence' within you, and all will be revealed at the right time. Now come and have lunch."

"I shall be glad to eat with you, but I feel a strength within which I have never experienced before!" she replied. "I am so grateful that you brought me here today—you are so wonderful to me. I deeply admire the scenic beauty, but this Inner Glory surpasses everything in my Life. God bless you, my Beloved Friends."

Then all understood why we had been impelled to come to Table Mountain. Lunch finished, Rex suggested we go down the opposite side of the mountain that Zara might see the amazing color effects of the more rugged scenery and pass the entrance to the Cave of Symbols. As we came to the entrance of the Cave, Rex stopped his horse.

"Come," he said, "let's go in."

"No, no!" cautioned Zara, her face turning white. "We may not enter now. Please, let us return home." We realized she was being directed from within and did not press things further, but turned our horses homeward. When we reached the ranch, Rayborn told us he had received a message from Beloved Saint Germain for us all to meet Him in the Tower Room at eight o'clock that same evening.

The hour arrived, and as we approached the door, it opened wide revealing Saint Germain. He welcomed us with His usual Grace, and we took our places in the chairs forming a circle. The Livingstons were surprised and admired the beauty of the room with great enthusiasm. When all had stilled themselves, Saint Germain said: "I have called this meeting especially for Zara, and secondly, for Daniel Rayborn." He gave a short but beautiful Tribute of Praise and Gratitude to the "I AM Presence"; and as He spoke, the Light blazed forth with great intensity and illumined the room brilliantly.

He stepped in front of Zara and touched her forehead. Immediately a circle of gold, rose, and blue Light surrounded us, and we were enabled to see into the next Octave of Light beyond the one in which humanity generally functions. The Light began to focus around Zara, and her Inner sight became opened, the experiences of many lives passing before her. In one of these she had been under the Instruction of Saint Germain, and at that time she had reached great enlightenment. In another life she had been a priestess in the cave of a great mountain, and it was then she had first met the God Tabor.

While this Revelation of past lives was shown, the former memory of these activities was established, and Saint Germain explained it would be of very great benefit a few years later. As He finished the Work with her, the beautiful Circle of Light slowly disappeared.

"My Brother," He said, addressing Rayborn, "it is My Desire that you be at the Cave of Symbols on the twentieth of July, that you may prepare for the Final Work We desire to do. This Brother," He continued, indicating me, "will accompany you. Nada, Pearl, Rex, and Bob will be there at eight o'clock on the morning of the twenty-sixth. Gaylord is to leave tomorrow morning on work for the Great White Brotherhood in South America.

"This Preparatory Work is invaluable to all, for as yet you have not the slightest conception of what it is doing for you. The Radiance which will be given in the Cave of Symbols will bring the earthly pilgrimage to a close for Brother Rayborn, but the exact day and hour may not be revealed to anyone who is unascended, because his own 'Mighty I AM Presence' alone knows the chosen instant in which the Great Work of centuries will be consummated.

"I trust all the outer affairs of business are in readiness for this Supreme Event. If not fully completed, they can be finished within the next ten days.

"Zara, your meeting with the God Tabor today is very significant; it means a great deal to you. Be patient, that the natural unfoldment of the Light within you may be as rapid as possible. That which you have seen of the past tonight is but a small part of your former experiences, but it is all that is essential for you at this time.

"Rex, to you, Bob, and this Brother" (meaning me), "I wish to say there is another great ore-body not half a mile from the Master Discovery, as you call it—which I will reveal during your next trip to the mine three days hence. As the claims are all patented and the deeds in your hands, they will be safe until your return from the East in two years.

"By the time the rest return from the Himalayas, our beloved Livingstons will be ready to meet you again and take certain steps that will lead to their Complete Freedom. I wish each one to follow the Directions you have been given, *and remember always, that nothing in Life is as important as loving, adoring, and reaching up to the 'Mighty I AM Presence' within you and in the Universe.* Never lose the joy and enthusiasm of the Quest for one moment!

"At intervals I will be present while you are at the mine, but not visibly. When you return, Bob will come with you, prepared to go to the Far East. I may not appear again to the Livingstons in visible, tangible form before our journey, but Zara, I wish to remind you that Dave Southerland, whom you shall meet at the mine, is your Twin Ray. You will remember and recognize his face and radiation, for his features are similar to those of the embodiment in which you were last together. Beloved Students, My Blessings enfold each of you in the Divine Embrace of the 'Mighty I AM Presence.'" As He spoke these last Words, His Body disappeared almost instantly.

We made the trip to the mine with the

Livingstons on the morning of July seventh; and when we arrived, Bob told us Saint Germain had left a note saying we were to arrive at eight o'clock that evening. When the Livingstons were shown to the bungalow, their joy was very great, and justly so; for Rayborn had spared no expense to provide every comfort. It was large and cheerful with every modern convenience provided, furnished handsomely, even with a beautiful baby grand piano. I have never seen greater or more sincere appreciation; and when we met at dinner, Zara threw her arms around Rayborn and kissed him—expressing her gratitude again and again for the wonderful blessings he in his great Love had bestowed upon them.

After dinner that evening Bob excused himself, and half an hour later returned with Dave Southerland. He was presented to all but Zara, who had momentarily left the room. She returned, and suddenly came face to face with Dave as Bob was about to present him. We were all watching intently without appearing to do so. As their eyes met, neither moved for a moment. "I have seen you often in my dreams," was Dave's comment, "and yet it always seemed so much more real than a dream."

"Yes," said Zara, "it is true, just as our Beloved Saint Germain told me. I do remember you. I too have seen you often while my body slept. When I was very ill and there seemed no hope of recovery, you came to me, and each time I felt much stronger and more encouraged. Then Saint Germain came and I was fully restored in a few hours. I will tell you all about that later."

Every eye in the room was wet with tears as the reunion of these Twin Rays occurred. We were grateful to Beloved Saint Germain for the Perfection He was constantly bringing about for each of us and the world. Truly there is no deeper tie of Love in the Universe than that between an Ascended Master and His students.

"My congratulations and blessings are ever with you both great souls of Light," said Livingston as he put one arm around Dave and the other around Zara.

"My cup of happiness is complete," said Mrs. Livingston as she kissed them both. Nada, Pearl, Bob, and Rex each congratulated them, for they above all others could truly understand and realize what this Union of Twin Rays meant.

Presently a Voice from the ethers began singing in clear, wonderful tones, "Love is the Fulfilling of the Law," with a beautiful accompaniment on stringed instruments. Dave was almost motionless with surprise, for it was the first time he had ever witnessed any Manifestation of the Ascended Host. The Music was Their Acknowledgment and Blessing upon the Eternal Union of the three sets of

Twin Rays, and Dave was like a flower just ready to open its petals to the Full Radiance of the Sun. We explained as much as we were permitted concerning Saint Germain and His Marvelous Work.

"It is all so amazing," said Dave, "but I feel something within that makes me know it is real and true. I want to know more about it and to meet Him face to face!"

The next day Livingston was made superintendent of the mine and shown the Master Discovery. He never tired of talking about it and was very happy about the entire arrangement. When we finished inspecting the workings, Bob turned everything over to his care. As each shift came off duty, Rayborn called the men together and introduced them to Livingston, explaining that he and Dave Southerland were to be in charge of everything during the next two years. He made them realize that he deeply appreciated their loyalty and service —their service to him being rendered through his assistants—and that those he left in charge were at all times to be considerate of their welfare. The quartet entertained the men again royally, to everyone's deep enjoyment.

That night, just as I was retiring, a slip of paper floated to the floor at my feet. I picked it up, and on it was a message from Saint Germain for Bob, Rex and myself. He asked that we come to a certain place on the Rayborn mining property at seven o'clock the next morning. We obeyed, and on our arrival the Electronic Current charged me from head to foot. All heard distinctly spoken audibly the words: "All calmly sit down in triangular form. Focus the attention of your minds upon the 'Mighty I AM Presence' within, and hold it there firmly."

In a few moments I stepped out of my body and, as I did so, passed through the Cosmic Veil. There stood Saint Germain in Glorious, Dazzling Radiance. He greeted me in His Loving, Gracious Way.

"Come!" He said, "We shall now enter the Earth, where I shall not only reveal the great deposit of Gold of which I told you, but the way the God of Nature and the God of Gold work together in Perfect Harmony to produce the precious metal that mankind intuitively loves to use for service and adornment.

"When I speak of the God of Gold and the God of Nature, I mean the Pure and Perfect Intelligent Beings that handle the forces in these realms and direct them consciously. The God of Nature draws and directs the magnetic currents of the Earth, and through intelligent manipulation, produces certain definite results in and upon our planet. This Activity is real, exact, and is performed according to law as accurately as a chemist works in his laboratory.

"The God of Gold draws, manipulates, and

directs the Electronic Currents from our Physical Sun. These Currents are drawn within the Earth's crust to a certain depth, as ribbons are sometimes drawn through lace. This tremendously concentrated electronic energy, by being combined with the magnetic force from within the crust of the Earth, reacts upon it in such a way as to slow down the rate of vibration. The radiation from Gold is absorbed by both plants and human beings and utilized for many purposes.

"As I mentioned to you once before during your experiences in *Unveiled Mysteries,* the emanation from Gold has a powerful purifying and energizing action within the human body and in Nature. In all Golden Ages, the metallic form of Gold was in common use by the mass of mankind, and during these periods its spiritual development reached a very high point of attainment.

"One reason for the chaos of the present time is because the Gold in the commercial world is being hoarded instead of being allowed to flow freely among mankind and carry its balancing, purifying, energizing activity into the commercial life of the race.

"The hoarding of gold in great quantities means an accumulation of Inner Force which, if not released within a certain time, will release itself by the overcharge of its own tremendous Inner Power."

Saint Germain drew me closer into His Radiance, and the Inner Activity of Earth was revealed. Before us stood two transcendentally Radiant Beings, one drawing and directing the magnetic currents of the Earth, and the other those of the Gold which had been formed within the Earth's crust.

The one whom He called the God of Nature was a Being of glorious beauty and power. His Body was fully six feet in height and clothed in garments of green, gold, and pink. They looked as if they were made of a Self-luminous Substance. An Aura of intense blue surrounded His head, and Rays of Light poured forth from the Heart, head, and hands. The Ray from the right hand was green, and that from his left, pink—those from the head and Heart being white and gold respectively.

The Being whom Saint Germain called the God of Gold was enveloped by such a Dazzling Golden Light that it took several seconds before I could look at It steadily enough to see further detail. His Garments too were of Light Substance, but the Rays that extended from the head and hands were of fiery gold, the Rays from the Heart blazing white, and the Aura—which extended fully a foot around the head—looked as if made of single Rays of white lightning.

"The existence of Gold," Saint Germain continued, "in white quartz, is its purest formation within the Earth at the present time—the white quartz being the residue, so to speak, from the magnetic currents, and the metallic gold being the lowered rate of the Electronic Substance from the Sun. This is the reason for its being spoken of occasionally as a Precipitated Sun Ray. That phrase is nearer the truth of what actually takes place than men dream.

"Now watch!" Here the two Beings directed the Rays of Light through Their hands to a cavity in the rocks into which a small quantity of Gold had run through a connecting fissure when in the molten state, evidently caused through volcanic action. The intense heat had sealed the fissure with molten granite, thus hiding the entire vein leading into the cavity.

"This particular ore-body," He continued, "at its highest point, is about two hundred feet below the surface. From a geological standpoint, it could not and would not have been discovered. After your return from the Far East, it will be opened; and one day the ore will be used for a special purpose so that mankind may be blest and enlightened."

We continued to watch these two Beings as Their Projection of the Light Rays caused the Gold within the cavity to expand and glow as plants do in sunlight.

"We have been here about thirty minutes," remarked Saint Germain as He turned away and we came back again to my physical body. Rex and Bob looked as though in a deep sleep. A few moments later when they opened their eyes, I explained to them what had happened. Their mission being different from mine, the Revelation and Instruction they received was of a more individual nature, yet they had retained full consciousness during the experience and had been shown part of the same activity I had been observing.

We returned to the bungalow at eight o'clock for breakfast and described our experiences to Nada, Pearl, and Rayborn. It was then he told us we were to return to the ranch on the tenth. The evening of the ninth was full of music and joy in which the Livingstons joined—for we were not to be with them again for two years.

Our drive home was uneventful, and the next ten days Rayborn spent in closing his business activities, giving everything to Nada and Rex. His holdings were very large, and his great fortune placed his two children among the wealthiest of our western country. Surely no two people were ever more worthy to be custodians of God's riches.

On the evening of the nineteenth, we all assembled in the Tower Room where a surprise awaited us, for as we opened the door, it was already illumined by a soft White Light. When we had become very still, Rayborn rose to his feet and poured forth a prayer of praise and thanksgiving in deep gratitude for the good that had been his, ending with a farewell blessing to all his earthly possessions for their great service to him. We then entered into deep meditation and received great Assistance and Illumination.

After our meditation we returned to the music room where the quartet sang for about an hour. Then Rayborn embraced each of his loved ones and went to his room, as he and I were to leave early the next morning for the Cave of Symbols. We left at six o'clock, Rex driving us to the nearest point. The walk to the entrance in the invigorating morning air was very exhilarating, and as we approached, we heard the sound of throbbing machinery. When we arrived at the second entrance, Saint Germain waited there for us. He seemed more Godlike, more Marvelous than I had ever seen Him.

We stepped to the white arch and it opened before us without anyone touching it. Where the blue and red arches had been on our previous visits, we now saw dazzling white ones instead. These symbolized a Cosmic Recognition of the raising of one of Earth's Children which was about to take place.

We entered the radio chamber, and I can still recall the feeling of Peace I enjoyed while there. Unless one has experienced the great happiness of being once again within the Radiance of those marvelous chambers, such feeling of exaltation can scarcely be conveyed to others. These halls have been charged for hundreds of centuries with the glorious Presence of the Mighty Ascended Masters of Love, Light and Wisdom, the Legion of Light, and the Great White Brotherhood.

Our meditation here was a vastly different activity from that in any other environment, and the value of such an Outpouring is beyond human conception. Saint Germain asked us to be seated while He gave the necessary Instructions as to what He desired us to do. I marvel at it to this day how clearly the memory of a student retains that Instruction, for it is never repeated, except by the Master Himself, yet it is as clear as though recorded in letters of Light upon my memory.

When He had finished the Instruction, we went to the sleeping apartments which we had occupied before, our Seamless Robes remaining there for our use. We entered into deep meditation, holding our attention on the "Mighty I AM Presence," the Master Christ within our own Hearts. At the end of three hours our consciousness was lifted to Great Heights, and Revelations that astonished us both were shown. We had entered Realms of which we had heard but never retained conscious memory of having been there. Presently we heard the sweet tones of a bell announcing the Master's approach. His face was radiantly happy.

"I am very pleased with your first real meditation," He said. "Keep this always a sacred hour every day." He extended both hands to us, and in each was a crystal goblet filled with a heavy Golden Liquid that looked like honey, yet sparkled as if made of diamonds.

"This," He said, "will be your principal sustenance during the ensuing days, for it is the very Essence of Life. The culmination of our Brother Rayborn's experience is the most vital of the soul's entire pilgrimage on Earth and the *summum bonum* of all human existence. Now come with me to the Chamber of Light, and do not be alarmed at what you either see or experience."

We passed through the audience chamber, and at its far end, a space about the size of a door opened before us, where an instant previous we had seen only a solid wall. The aperture closed quickly behind us, and we found ourselves in the center of a perfect sphere. There were three chairs of solid Gold placed so as to form a triangle in the middle of the floor.

"Please be seated," said Saint Germain, He occupying the third chair. The chamber was filled with a soft glowing Light, and this began to steadily increase in both intensity and movement until we became conscious of Its amazing velocity. Tongues of Flame began to dart forth from the surrounding Light penetrating our bodies with an astonishing effect in which we felt electrons entering and charging our minds and bodies with their tremendous energy—yet the sensation was one of delightful coolness.

As this continued we felt and saw the Light within us rise and expand, until in a few moments a most delightful fragrance of roses filled the entire sphere. It grew stronger, and then we became aware that it emanated from the Light within ourselves. Suddenly the essence of the roses condensed and we lay upon couches of roses of very exquisite colors. Our experience brought an exaltation to our consciousness that no words can describe and produced a feeling of Deep Peace. There was nothing imaginary about this whole experience, for the Perfection that exists within Pure Electronic Light is without limit, and by the proper understanding of Its manifestation, It can and will take any form and quality that an Ascended Master chooses to impose upon It.

The glorious feeling of Peace, Happiness and Bliss we experienced obliterated all idea of time, for the Inner and the outer activity had become *One Complete Unit of Harmony,* focused for the time being by Saint Germain into the Absolute Purity and

Perfection of the One Great Light—the "Mighty I AM Presence." Gradually the velocity of the Light changed, growing less and less, until It shone with the soft radiance of moonlight on a placid sea.

To our astonishment, we found the roses real. Although they had come out of the Light, they did not disappear with It. After this experience I could easily understand why the rose has been used throughout the ages as the symbol of the soul, and why the Radiation from an Ascended Master so often has the fragrance of a rose.

"You shall come here, My Brother," said Saint Germain, addressing Rayborn, "every day at this hour; but the remainder of the time you are to be alone." When we returned to the audience chamber, I realized we had been in the Chamber of Light for more than three hours—yet it had seemed only a few moments. Saint Germain gave us another cup of the Golden Liquid as nourishment for the body.

"Now go to your chambers and sleep," He instructed, "until I call you." Wherever we moved, the wonderful fragrance of roses enveloped us, and scarcely had we lain down until we were sound asleep.

Each day this Marvelous Work went on until the arrival of Nada, Pearl, Rex, and Bob on the twenty-sixth of July. When greetings had been exchanged, they commented upon the soft radiance and

fragrance of roses that surrounded my body continuously and were very happy about this part of my
attainment. During the twenty-seventh, many of
the Ascended Masters came, singly and in groups,
until all who were to take part in the Work had arrived.

At eleven o'clock that night, we were escorted
into the Electrical Chamber, where the marvelous
Atomic Accelerator was waiting to receive another
of God's children and send him forth into his
Eternal Freedom—a Son of Light—*a True Image and
Likeness of the "Mighty I AM Presence."*

As we entered the chamber, the Light within it
was intense, yet it held tiny points of more Dazzling
Light that darted to and fro in the atmosphere
continually. Rayborn seated himself in the Chair,
and the twenty-four present formed a circle about
the Accelerator, Saint Germain standing directly
behind him, and I just in front. Nada, his Twin Ray,
stood within the circle. When all were ready, Saint
Germain commanded the individual attention of
each one to be held steady upon the Presence and
Supremacy of the "I AM," and that of the Master
Jesus.

Suddenly, like a flash of lightning, a Circle of the
most intense Dazzling White Light surrounded us,
drawing steadily toward the Chair until it was only
about ten feet across. The Light within Daniel

Rayborn expanded and met the Circle of Light without. As they touched, he began to rise slowly to a distance of about his own height above the Accelerator, the Light within him continuing to increase.

Nada, his own Twin Ray, rose also and drew toward him, passing within the smaller Circle of Light. They met in divine embrace for a moment. The next instant the face of the Master Jesus shone out in an Aura of gold, pink and blue above them. Inclining their heads toward us and smiling radiantly, they looked upward as a Great Ray of intense White Light descended, enveloping them both in Its Protecting Radiance, blessing their Glorious Union, and hiding them from our sight while they passed beyond all care and limitation into their Eternal Perfection of Being—clothed in Bodies of Everlasting Light, the Robe of Immortality that shines brighter than the Sun at noonday.

Thus did another "Mighty Master Presence" of the "Great I AM" enter into Cosmic Service—as the Celestial Chorus sang Its Anthem of Eternal Praise and Victory unto "The Light of God that never fails."

CHAPTER X

Closing Experiences and Our Journey to Arabia

"**O**UR Work here is finished for the present," said Saint Germain as the singing came to a close. "Let us now go to the Great Chamber and dine." We had just become seated at the table when Daphne appeared at the great organ and Arion stood beside Her with a most wonderful violin.

They began to play, and a soft globe of Iridescent Light formed near the ceiling, out of which came a most Glorious Tenor Voice singing, "In the Name of Christ We Reign," whose melody and lyrics were tremendously inspiring. Saint Germain felt the question in our minds as to who the Singer was, and in answer to our thoughts, replied, "You shall one day see this Cosmic Singer face to face."

Daphne greeted the children rapturously and asked the quartet to sing to the accompaniment of the organ and violin. We enjoyed a glorious hour after the music by renewing our acquaintance with those present, some of whom we were to meet again in the Far East.

It was nearly daybreak by the time the other Guests had gone and we five were alone with Saint Germain. "Retire now," He said, "and get your needed rest so you may return home tomorrow afternoon." The next day the bell awakened us at eleven o'clock, for we were to meet with our Beloved Master in the Great Chamber. As we came near we noticed the great doors were already open and the interior was lighted as brilliantly as the noonday Sun. We had never experienced this effect of Interior Sunlight before.

"Why are you still astonished at these things?" asked Saint Germain, aware of surprise. "You know every conceivable thing can be accomplished in the Ascended State of Consciousness. These things are always possible and are produced with absolute certainty and perfect ease. I know you are not yet accustomed to what seems unusual, but to the Master Christ, the 'I AM Presence' within you, there cannot be anything unusual. Try to realize this fully, so you too can live in the Ascended Master Consciousness and come into the Knowledge and the use of this same Transcendent Freedom. Now let us be seated." Immediately a most delicious luncheon appeared before us, and while we ate, Saint Germain gave Directions for the journey to the Far East.

"I would suggest," He remarked, "that you travel as lightly as possible. Follow your Inner impulse always, for you will be perfectly directed at all times. You are surely aware by now that clothing or anything else you may require is always available. You need not be encumbered unnecessarily with luggage on this journey. I will meet with you in the Tower Room on the tenth of August at eight o'clock in the evening, when the date of your departure will be decided." Saint Germain went with us to the auto, and after bidding us a loving good-by, returned to the Retreat. We entered the car and drove back to the ranch. The next two weeks were busy ones indeed as we completed arrangements for our journey to the East. Upon Rex devolved the duty of giving some explanation to the foreman about Daniel Rayborn's continued absence.

"My father," he explained to him one morning, "has been called to the Far East, where he will remain indefinitely. I will be in charge of things here, although Nada and I will be traveling abroad for about two years. Can we depend upon you to look after the ranch during our absences?"

"I will do the best to take care of everything as you desire," he replied. "My assistant is quite dependable and capable of taking charge, should anything happen to me."

Time passed on wings, and the tenth arrived filled with joyous anticipation of our evening with Saint Germain. Until one has had some such experience as was our privilege of association with Him, it is impossible to convey the great happiness we felt in the contemplation of still greater enlightenment. Our recent Instruction during the Ascension of Daniel Rayborn and my contact with the white-haired, elderly gentleman who sought so long for the man with the Crystal Cup were a tremendous encouragement and sufficient inducement for us to reach to the Light with all the intensity of our Beings—to make the Ascension also.

At eight o'clock as we approached the Tower Room, the door opened, and Saint German stood before us with extended arms, Radiant and Resplendent. We exchanged loving greetings, took our places, and He conveyed the Love and Blessings from the Mother and Father of Rex and Nada.

"The time of your departure," He began, "is set for the twentieth of August. I think it would be well if Rex, Bob, and this Brother," nodding to me, "make one more trip to the mine before leaving for the East in order to give strength and encouragement to the Livingstons. I had not intended this when you left the mine, but I think it the part of wisdom to see them once more. Gaylord will meet you in Paris near the end of October as soon as he finishes his work in South America.

"Now I have something else to tell you. The outer entrance to the Cave of Symbols has been closed, and unless one had been there, it would not be possible to locate it again. Certain individuals did discover it and were planning to take a research party there. It has been necessary to prevent that. You see, Beloved Ones, We have all Power and limitless means within Our Control by which to guard and protect whatever needs Our Protection. I will give you certain Instructions for your immediate use, and then I must leave to meet with the South American branch of the Great White Brotherhood." After indicating what was needed, He raised His hand in Blessing, and with a Radiant Smile, was gone.

Bob's enthusiasm kept pace with his advancement. It was one of the most wonderful things I have ever experienced to observe how his intense longing for the Full Ascension focused his attention upon the "Light" with uninterrupted joy and determination. Nada and Pearl were expressing the Great Wisdom of the "Mighty I AM Presence" as the Expansion of the Light increased within them. It was most apparent in their eyes.

We drove to the mine on the twelfth and arrived there at six in the evening. All were surprised, except Zara, who said she knew we would visit them again before leaving for abroad.

We left early the next morning and returned to the ranch, knowing our visit would be a sustaining strength to the Livingstons. I shall never forget our last night in that wonderful ranch home where so much happiness had come to all of us and where events of such paramount importance had occurred that affected the Life of each one so vitally. I felt a strong impulse to go to the Tower Room for a farewell meditation. It grew so strong that I asked the rest to join me. As we approached the door, it opened to admit us, and within there was the same soft, Beautiful Radiance that hallowed it with a Sacred Presence—a Peace unspeakable. The door closed behind us, and involuntarily I dropped to my knees in the greatest praise and gratitude I had ever known.

Suddenly my feeling found expression and the Words poured forth from my "I AM Presence" giving voice to the deepest Outpourings of my soul in phrases far beyond my outer ability. As I finished, Bob uttered a prayer of such beauty that it thrilled everyone. The others felt the same impulse and expressed their feelings from the depths of their Hearts. Surely that Outpouring of our Love and Gratitude must have reached into the very Heart Center of Creation, it was so intense and sincere. As we finished, the Light in the room became perfectly Dazzling. Suddenly, a Strong, Masterful Voice spoke from the ethers, saying:

"All is well. In following your prompting to give expression to that Inner feeling of Praise, you have contacted great Heights—as well as Great Ascended Beings. This will bring you Blessings untold. The Peace of the Cosmic Christ enfolds you and carries you forth on Wings of Light until you have reached Eternal Perfection."

Slowly the Light diminished until only a soft Radiance remained. We silently left the room, knowing we were under the Loving, Watchful Care of Mighty Powers of Light of which as yet we had very little conception. A deep, unspeakable Radiation of Love and Heavenly Joy went from each one to the others, and we retired to our rooms.

We left by train early the next morning and arrived in New York a few days before we sailed. While enjoying many things of interest there, we felt a tremendous Inner appreciation for the Statue of Liberty.

"What a wonderful symbol that is," said Nada, "and how few ever stop to realize what it means. It is really a Focus of Spiritual Power guarding the shores of America. The Torch held high represents the Light of the 'Mighty I AM Presence'—which reveals the way and sends Its Rays of Love and Peace unto all mankind. The majesty and power of the Figure itself is a marvelous expression of the Great Presence which carries the Light, and not only guards and sustains America, but all of mankind who truly seek the Light.

"It is as though the Spirit of America held the Light high in silent greeting to the Figure of the Christ that stands high on the towering Andes in South America. Little is known of the Mighty

Power that caused the Statue of Liberty to be placed where it is, and why the Figure of Jesus occupies its high pinnacle in the southern hemisphere. These are not accidents or the results of blind chance, for there is no such thing anywhere in the Universe. What seems so to the intellect is but the lack of understanding of the Law of the Universe. You may be sure that these Figures placed at these particular points give indication of the service which both continents will give to the rest of the world!"

At four o'clock in the afternoon of the twenty-eighth, we boarded the *S. S. Majestic*—truly a floating palace. The tugboat towed her out towards the open sea, and as she began to plow her way through the mighty deep, we stood watching our Goddess of Liberty fade from view. We went down to the dining room at the first call for dinner, where we had reserved a table for six, expecting of course that our party would be alone. We had just finished ordering when the steward brought a Beautiful Young Lady to our table. As I looked up, imagine my astonishment when before us stood the Pupil of the Head of the Council in France—at whose home we had spent a week before returning to America with the Livingstons. It was She whom I had first contacted as the "Veiled Sister," and who was Gaylord's Twin Ray. She greeted me cordially, and as I turned to present the others, said: "You may call me

Leto." After greeting Her, they expressed their great joy and delight for Her Presence.

"I have come," She explained, "to take you to our home in Paris, which my Master wishes you to make your home while abroad. It will make Him very happy to extend His hospitality to you all."

We joyously accepted His Invitation, knowing it to be part of the Divine Plan Saint Germain had arranged for us. To add to our happiness, we found Her suite next to that of Nada and Pearl. When opportunity offered, I explained to the others that this little Lady, who looked not more than seventeen, had used Her present body over three hundred years. I almost strained the credulity of my friends in spite of all Saint Germain had said and done, that they might become accustomed to the Great Truth and Reality of the Ascended Masters and Their Work.

The first evening we sat on deck completely at one with the great peace of the deep, for it was calm as a mirror, silvered by the beauty of a full moon. The next evening we spent in our suite listening to the Instruction given by Leto. She explained how to lay the body down, leaving it consciously and at will. It was the simplicity and clearness of Her Explanation that made all comprehend everything so clearly and realize something of the possibilities of the attainment before us.

"This Training I am giving you," She said, "is

most efficient, and I will show you proof of it tomorrow evening." In Leto's Radiation everything seemed simple, clear, and easy of accomplishment; for all imperfection or human creation was instantly consumed on entering Her Presence. Our joy and gratitude were very great when we heard that She was to instruct us during the entire journey. Again we marveled at the way all was prepared ahead for us by the "Mighty I AM Presence" working through the Glorious Ascended Masters. This is Their Activity for and to the student when he enters sufficiently into the Light—the Great Ascending Stream of Life—where his Eternal Freedom always exists.

As each of us said good-night to Leto, it seemed as though a Gossamer Garment of Light enfolded us, and the fragrance of heather which had filled the room all evening clung to us while we retired. We met at breakfast and the Radiance was even greater than the night before. During the course of our conversation, I asked Her why we had been conscious of the fragrance of heather during Her Instruction.

"In the eleventh century," She explained, "I lived in Scotland, and during an experience of that Life, the memory of heather became very dear. Ever since then, at most unexpected moments, the fragrance of heather radiates very strongly—so much so that many times it is noticed by those about me."

I observed that Leto wore a simple white garment, yet it gave the effect of having a glint of many colors shining through. She answered my thought about it immediately by saying: "This garment I am wearing is a Seamless One, not made with hands, but precipitated direct from Pure Light Substance— hence, the glint and Radiance you see. It will never soil nor show wear. It will not be long until each of you will be wearing the same kind of Garment. In the fully awakened, or what you call the Ascended Master Consciousness, we never encumber ourselves with luggage of any kind, for in the ethers all about us is the Pure Substance from which we form everything as we desire to use it.

"All we need to do is to bring it into form through holding the conscious attention upon our mental picture, or visualized form. This creates a focus for the concentration and condensation of the Electronic Light in the ether which fills all space everywhere. Our feeling, united with the mental picture, sets up a drawing activity—a magnetic pull— upon the Pure Electronic Substance. With this feeling there must enter a certain knowledge of how to raise or lower the vibratory rate in the aura around the electron; for the vibratory rate of the aura determines the quality and material of the precipitated article.

"When I use the term electron, I mean an Eternally Pure Heart Center of Immortal Fire—a Perfect Balance of Light, Substance and Intelligence around which is an aura of lesser Light that the scientific world calls a force field. The electron is forever changelessly Perfect, but the force field, or aura around it, is subject to expansion and contraction; and this is the determining factor in bringing substance into form from the invisible into the visible.

"Because of the *inherent intelligence* within the electron, it becomes an obedient servant and is subject to the manipulation of the individual who acknowledges his Source of Life by his awareness of the 'Mighty I AM Presence' within himself. From this Height of Consciousness, such an individual, by a direct command to the Intelligence within the electron, can release a wave of its Fire to flow out, and cause the force field to expand or contract at his will.

"This is the raising or lowering of the vibratory rate and is the activity that causes the force field to register, or become the quality of the material which he brings into physical form. For illustration, iron has a much lower vibratory rate than Gold, and if one be precipitating Gold, the force field around the electron would naturally be much larger in extent, and hence contain more of the Immortal

Fire than would that of iron.

"In bringing about this sort of manifestation, the vision and feeling must be held steady to produce quick results. It is the work of the student to master himself and maintain the Conscious Control and direction of the energy within his own mind and body. Then he is able to govern the flow of its power—through the channels of sight and feeling —to a definite objective, and hold it there until the receptacle, which is his mental picture, is filled full of the Living, Luminous Substance from the Universal Fire of Life.

"This Instruction is for your use, and you must apply it if you wish to attain any degree of Mastery; for only by use of the knowledge we already have can we utilize that which is still greater. No one can ever attain any degree of Mastery except through the operation of the Great Inner Law of the 'I AM.'

"The greatest of all fundamentals is to remember—*forever*—that from the lowest to the Highest Being in the Universe, the *only* Presence and Power which can move or do anything constructive is that Conscious Intelligence which acknowledges its own Being and Manifestation by decreeing 'I AM,' followed by whatever quality that Being desires to bring into outer existence. It is the Word of God through which all Creation takes place, and without It, Creation does not take place. Remember, there is only One Power that can move through Creation, and that is the Mighty Electronic Light existing everywhere and interpenetrating all manifestation.

"The individual who can say 'I AM,' by that Acknowledgment of his own existence, must accept the responsibility of his own Decrees. The Great Creative Principle is everywhere present, the same as the use of the multiplication table, but it takes the individual's Acknowledgment of his 'I AM Presence' to set it into action and fulfill his plan of Life— which is Perfection, or Perfect Balance.

"The personality, or outer activity of the individual, is but one focus through which 'The Magic Presence' of the 'I AM' acts. If the energy of the 'Mighty I AM' is qualified by thoughts and feelings that consider only the appetites of the flesh body, the Perfect Balance of the individual's vehicle is not maintained and is like a wheel off center; hence imperfection and discord is expressed. But if the individual considers the *Perfect Balance* and makes his Decree include the whole instead of only a part of his universe, he will only follow his Acknowledgment of the 'I AM Presence' and the release of Its Power by Decrees that maintain the Perfect Balance. Any decree of Life that accepts less than Limitless Perfection is not the Plan of God and will continue to destroy the forms in which it is focused until the Decree of Full Perfection is expressed. When the student understands this, he will keep joyously radiant and firmly conscious of only his 'Mighty I AM Presence,' *never allowing his spoken word to go forth decreeing anything less than the Perfection of Life.*

"From Our Height of Consciousness, after having watched mankind for centuries in the struggle through self-created misery and discord, it is amazing how humanity refuses to understand why the minds and bodies of the race continue to grow old, decay and disintegrate, when some of the most materialistic scientists acknowledge that the cell of which the physical bodies are made up is eternally Immortal. The cell contains within it the power to eternally renew and sustain itself because there is Perfect Balance in all its parts. If left to its own activity and sphere, it will continue to maintain that Perfection. The wonder to Us is that the race is content to go through the experience of death, while all the time clinging to youth, beauty and Life, and yet refusing to keep harmonious enough to let it be maintained. The student who will stand at one with his 'I AM Presence,' accepting and decreeing only Its Perfection and Great Inner Power, will release Its Flow through the outer activity of mind and body and produce whatsoever he decrees.

"To be able to come and go from the body at will is a necessary step in the student's Freedom that will lead to many greater Attainments. A part of my

Service to humanity is in teaching individuals how to do this—a work for which I have a deep Love and natural ability. I am able to convey this idea to others so they too are able to go forth and comprehend Life in a greater measure.

"Within two months you will be able to come and go from your bodies consciously as easily as you now come and go from your home. At first I will assist you until you understand and fix the operation in your consciousness; then you will be able to accomplish what you desire entirely by your own effort. We rarely find several individuals ready for this Instruction at the same time, but because you four are two sets of Twin Rays working together, is this unusual condition explained.

"Let us enjoy the sea breeze, the beauty of the night, and the perfect weather which we shall have while crossing; for there are never storms or disturbances where there is a Focus of the Great White Brotherhood. Each Member is a Definite Focus. I have work to do now at a distance, so must leave you until four this afternoon when I will return and be with you at dinner."

I have always enjoyed travel at sea, but this voyage was more than enjoyable, for our association and work with Leto kept us constantly aware of the God Presence. Later in the day I had occasion to chat for a few minutes with the Captain, and he said during his entire fifteen years on the sea he had never had a more marvelous voyage. I could have told him why, but it was the part of wisdom to remain silent.

As we were taking our places at the table for dinner, Leto returned and joined us, saying: "I have joyous information! Splendid things have just been accomplished for the Blessing of humanity. I tell you this much that you may rejoice with me, but later you shall know the full details of it, probably when we arrive in Arabia. It pleases me that you have been able to keep your consciousness so well focused upon 'The Magic Presence' of the 'I AM.' Tonight before our work begins, I want you to enjoy the sunset with me; for you shall not have another such opportunity for fifty years due to certain Cosmic Activities which as yet you do not understand."

Leto had chairs placed on the top deck where we would be undisturbed. When we were all comfortably seated, She continued: "You remember that Beloved Saint Germain said to you, the Sun of this system is to the whole system what the Heart is to the human body, Its Currents of Energy being the blood stream of this system of worlds; the ether belt around this Earth, being the lungs through which the currents of energy, constantly pouring forth, are ever purifying the body of the Earth. The Sun is also the head, or Father of this system, through which this Mighty Energy is constantly generated by the Mighty Intelligence focused there—from Glorious Ascended Beings who have charge of and govern that Activity.

"The Sun is not hot as scientists think. It is as cool and a thousand times more refreshing than the gentle zephyrs of the most delightful summer evening. It is only as the Sun's Currents of Energy pass through the ether belt of the Earth that they become heat. The Sun is the electronic pole, and the Earth is the magnetic pole. The ether belt is the element through which the currents are diversified.

"The Christ Mind is embodied in Great Beings upon the Sun similar to the way It is here on Earth. Always keep this in mind: God sent forth His Rays individualizing Himself in order to govern, regulate and direct His Activity through Self-conscious Beings. That is why we, as the Sons of God, are given Free Will—choice.

"By recognizing and accepting fully this Mighty God Power, Love, and Intelligence anchored in us, we become able to express more and more of the Full Power of God in conscious action. Only the most advanced students realize there are Mighty Beings as much beyond the Lord of the Earth as the Lord of the Earth is beyond the ordinary mortal.

"Now, each of you, withdraw the consciousness from your body and place it fully upon the Sun. Partly close your eyes and then wait." We sat very still for almost twenty minutes and then went forth as a group, Leto leading the way. She became Dazzling and Radiant. Deeper and deeper we entered into the Intense Light of that Great Focus of Cosmic Light, and presently became aware that we were approaching the Globe Itself. The Radiance which It emitted gave one a feeling of great exaltation with a glowing sensation of Peace and Power. The nearer Leto drew, the brighter became Her Radiance.

We then approached a magnificent City called the "City of the Sun." Within it were wonderful, Perfected Beings—like ourselves, except Their Bodies were slightly larger than those of our humanity— but Their Radiance and Beauty were transcendent beyond words. Presently we found ourselves receding. The Glorious City began to fade from view, the Indescribable Light grew less, and then we heard Leto speaking, commanding us to return with Her. With a sudden shock, we were conscious again of our physical bodies.

"A grand success," She said smilingly. "I have brought this about that each may bear witness to the others of what you have seen, for in this is tremendous strength. The concept which mankind has that the Sun is a focus of great heat is absurd and infantile. The Truth is that the tremendous Rays of Energy which it sends forth to its system of planets are not heat rays at all, but Rays of Electronic Energy which only become heat as they contact and penetrate the atmosphere of the Earth. The atmosphere surrounding our planet is a force field produced by the rays of magnetic force sent forth from the center of this planet, and when the Rays of Electronic Energy from the Sun touch these, we have the phenomena in our atmosphere that we call heat and Light from the Sun."

We enjoyed the twilight on deck until seven-thirty and then went to Leto's stateroom. We took our places in five reclining chairs which She had provided for our use—in which the body was perfectly poised and at ease. Then Leto began Her Instruction.

"Focus your attention on the Heart for a moment," She explained. "Then raise it to the top of the head. Keep it there without change and let the following be your only thought: *'Mighty I AM Presence which I AM,' now take charge in Full Mastery of this body. See that I go and come from it consciously and at will. Never again can it bind me or limit my Freedom.''*

It could not have been more than three minutes until we stood before our bodies, free—consciously free—in bodies of substance, but finer than that of the physical body. In these we were more clearly alert and free than we had ever been in the physical.

"Come with me," said Leto, and instantly we passed out of the room over placid waters and went direct to Her home in Paris. We saw and greeted Her Master. Then we continued our journey to the

Home of the Brotherhood in Arabia which we visited later. When we returned near our bodies, She spoke again: "Wait—we are going to do this consciously," She directed. She went to each body as it lay in the chair and touched the forehead. Immediately the body stood up, yet looked as if asleep. Then She gave the necessary direction, which I may not give here, and we were again fully conscious in our bodies. The whole experience was different from anything we had ever lived through before, and it left us with a certain indescribable confidence that we could do it again. We tried to thank Her, but She raised Her hand for silence.

"Love serves, because it is the nature of Love to give, and it is not concerned with nor does it expect acknowledgment of its Gifts. However, your gratitude is beautiful and well known to me. Just try to become the Love that does not wish to possess, for then Love is truly Divine."

The following days were filled with joy, beauty, repose and peace as we watched the sunlit waters by day, and at night the wonderful moonlight, until one's very being breathed praise and gratitude for the happiness of just being alive.

The boat docked at Cherbourg, and following Leto as She led the way, we went to the waiting autos and were driven to Paris, Pearl and Nada riding in Her car, and Bob, Rex, and I in the second one. When we arrived at Her home in Paris, Her

Master greeted us in His Gracious, Courtly Manner:

"It is Our Great Joy," He said, "to have you make this your home as long as you wish, and We want you to feel just as free to come and go as if you were in your own home in America."

The next few days we spent with these Blessed Masters learning many wonderful things and receiving some insight into the Marvelous Work of the Great White Brotherhood. Its Stupendous Power, Inner Working and Accomplishment simply stagger the intellect of one unaccustomed to this kind of Knowledge.

We were placed under definite training, and Leto, after finishing our Instruction for the day, showed us the places of interest in the afternoon. Not a moment was wasted, as She said we were to leave soon for Arabia and that She expected the call within a week.

While visiting the Louvre, Leto showed us a painting by a young artist who had painted a picture called "The Union of Two Souls." It was intended to portray the Union of the Twin Rays and was a marvelous conception, a wonderful work of art.

"We are watching," She said, "for an opportunity to see if this artist can be awakened to the Inner Wisdom after having received such an interpretation of his idea. In the midst of his work he unknowingly shut the door to the inspiration he had received at the beginning, and My Master, seeing the need, gave the necessary Assistance which reestablished his contact with his Divine Inspiration and enabled him to complete the picture. It was unknown, of course, to him, but the marvelous painting you see before you was the result.

"Often an artist, musician, writer, inventor, and many other individuals doing creative work are given such Assistance from the Ascended Masters —of which those receiving the Help know nothing. This sort of Activity is one way in which We work impersonally."

We attended one Meeting of the Great White Brotherhood to which Members came from all over the world, among them being Gaylord's Friend whom I had met when Gaylord was abducted to Paris. It was a never-ending source of joy to know of the important Work being accomplished by the Members of the Great White Brotherhood, entirely unknown to the outer world. Many sincere people who wish to live the constructive way of Life are Members of this Brotherhood at the Inner Levels long before they become aware of it in the outer senses.

The time arrived for our departure, and Leto was to conduct us to the East. We said good-by to Her Blessed Master and drove to Marseilles by car. We went direct to the steamship office of the

Messageries Maritimes Line. As we entered, a tall, fine-looking man in Arabian dress came out and bowed before Leto.

"Your Highness," he said, "reservations are on the steamship *Mariette Pache*. This envelope contains the necessary papers. Your accommodations at the usual place are in readiness. Can I be of further service?"

He touched his Heart and forehead, and Leto, returning the Salutation, gave him a Sign which we recognized as belonging to the Great White Brotherhood. We knew by that he was one of the Brothers. We returned to the auto and were taken to what proved to be a private old hostelry—quaint, but spotlessly clean, and the accommodation good. Leto told the driver to call for us at nine the next morning, and I must confess, I was greatly interested to know why She was addressed as "Your Highness."

Promptly at nine we entered the autos and were driven to the pier, Leto telling the drivers to return to Paris. As we boarded the ship, our entire party was shown great deference, and our accommodations were truly palatial.

We had a delightful trip on the deep blue waters of the Mediterranean and finally docked at Alexandria. Leto again led the way to waiting autos, and after driving for about twenty minutes, we entered a walled enclosure and stopped before a beautiful home built in the Moorish type of architecture. A youth in Arabian dress admitted us and led the way to a circular room. A tall, beautiful woman who looked not more than twenty, yet whose eyes held deep Wisdom, came forward and greeted us graciously. Leto presented Her to us as Electra.

"Beloved Sisters and Brothers," She said, "I have been expecting you, and you are most welcome. Please accept my humble hospitality, now and at any time that you are in Alexandria. You will honor me to make this your home. Your Beloved Master was here yesterday and asked that you remain for two days. At the end of that time a boat will take you to a place on the coast of Arabia, from which you will drive to your destination." She then touched a set of exquisite chimes. The youth returned and showed us to our separate suites.

During our conversation at dinner we learned something of Electra's family. Her father was an Englishman, and Her mother was a French woman. Someone asked how long it had been since they had passed on, and She replied:

"One hundred and twenty-five years ago. You see," She continued, "I am not as far advanced as your wonderful Escort, but I have attained enough dominion to eliminate time and space."

"Electra," said Leto, "is far advanced and is doing beautiful work, as you will see later. While we are in Alexandria you shall see the places of interest, and we shall spend the next two days enjoying ourselves."

We were very much interested the next morning in sight-seeing. When we stopped at a certain jeweler's stall, admiring the beautiful jewels and the exquisite workmanship of their settings, the old jeweler made a deep bow, and in salutation touched his Heart and head, asking to see Rex and Bob's rings. He was very silent for a few moments, and then looking steadily at them both, remarked:

"My Brothers, you have done me a great honor; only once before have I ever seen such jewels. They are Condensed Light. They are 'Living Gems.' You are blest indeed." As we thanked him and turned to go, he asked the Blessing of the Most High God upon us.

The second evening after visiting the old jeweler, we were listening to Electra describing Her Experiences, when a sealed envelope dropped out of the atmosphere directly at the feet of Rex. He opened it anxiously and found a Message from our Beloved Saint Germain.

"In the morning," it read, "a yacht belonging to one of the Brothers will take you to a certain port from which you will proceed by auto to your destination in Arabia. Your Mother and Father send Greetings and Love to all." The next morning Electra accompanied us to the yacht, a beautiful, graceful boat as trim as a greyhound.

"I shall expect you on your return before you go to India," She said as She bade us good-by. When we went aboard the yacht, we had another surprise, for its owner was none other than Gaylord's Friend —the Brother who met me at the boat when I arrived in Cherbourg while Gaylord was being held captive.

Our entire journey was well prepared at every point with much comfort and convenience. One can scarcely realize the joy of these activities unless he has experienced something of this sort. As soon as we were well out at sea, our Host gave us His undivided attention.

"I have just received a letter," He said, "from Gaylord—who is still in South America. He is completing certain work there and asked to be remembered to everyone. He says he hopes to see you before many more weeks have passed, and until then his Love is ever enfolding you." We thanked our host for the message from our friend—for whose welfare we felt deeply concerned.

Our trip through the Suez Canal was delightful, and there was so much of divine tradition attached to the Red Sea that we expected to feel a thrill in passing through it. We had repeatedly experienced such wonderful things that we half anticipated the waters to divide and the scenes of long ago to appear in the ether. As we recalled the miracles of that time, our Host instructed:

"Miracles," He explained, "are but the result of a Mighty, Omnipresent Cosmic Law set into action— consciously—by one who accepts his Divine Authority and understands Its Use. The Laws governing any kind of manifestation which the human mind considers supernatural are as natural and unerring as the motion of a planet. All activity, from the electron to the greatest Suns in space, is under the control and exact operation of Law set into operation by Self-conscious, Individualized Intelligence. When an individual understands and applies the Great Law governing manifestation in form, he can and does produce exact results. So truthfully speaking, there are no miracles.

"Miracles are but the effect of the application of Law by an individual to bring about a specific result. All may learn to do this—if they desire it strongly enough and will discipline the outer activity of thought and feeling."

We reached our port, and two autos were waiting to take us the rest of the way. Our Host accompanied us to the Arabian Retreat and gave directions for His yacht to remain until we returned. We had dined before leaving the yacht, as it was late in the afternoon when we reached port. Leto explained that we were to travel during the night in order to be unobserved through this part of the country. We traveled through many strange places and arrived at our destination just before daybreak.

We came to a stop before the little hut that Gaylord had described to us near the foot of a hill. How we were able to reach it by auto instead of camels, we did not know; nor was it our business to inquire at this time. We knew we were guests of a Mighty Presence and Power, and our duty was to remain silent until information was volunteered. Curiosity on the part of a student is inexcusable in spiritual training and must be completely eliminated from the consciousness before certain understanding, power, and experiences are permitted to be given him along the path to Mastery. Unless it is completely consumed within the personality, it is a wide-open door through which the sinister force can act at any moment and cut off the further progress of the advancing student. Whenever it was necessary, all that we needed to know was explained without our asking.

Dawn was just breaking as we reached the hut, and immediately a Tall Man in an Indigo Cape came out to bid us welcome. He greeted each one cordially and requested us to return to our autos. Then had a cataclysm occurred, we could scarcely have been more surprised; for directly in front of us the earth opened, revealing a sort of jaw-like entrance made of metal, large enough to admit our cars.

This led onto a well-paved road with a downward incline. The jaw was controlled by powerful machinery, and when it closed after us a few moments later, it was to all appearances simply the floor of the Arabian Desert.

As our cars entered the roadway leading down, the surrounding walls became flooded with that Soft White Light which we knew so well and which the Ascended Masters always use for illuminating tunnels, caves, and all subterranean passageways. We traveled along slowly for about twenty minutes and then entered a circular room nearly two hundred feet in diameter. In this place all equipment was kept for the automobiles, and attendants provided, ready to render any service required.

The Brother in the Indigo Cape alighted and led the way to what proved to be an elevator. We entered, descended for about three hundred seventy feet, and came to a stop, entering an enormous chamber with huge columns, almost three hundred feet high.

These great columns were heavily covered with hieroglyphics, inlaid in marvelously beautiful colors. We found later that it had been the foyer to a large government building. Our guide led us through this chamber to a great arched doorway that opened at His Command, admitting us into another chamber that was beautifully decorated. Its ceiling was arched and very ornate, supported by a single colossal column in the center. This second room must have been at least two hundred feet each way. The Brother of the Indigo Cape broke the silence:

"This is one of our principal council chambers," He explained, "which we often use as a banquet hall. Beloved Sisters and Brothers, you who are not yet formally admitted Members of our Order are the first students ever admitted to this very ancient Retreat without having been fully accepted into the outer activities of this branch of the Great White Brotherhood; but I assure you, your credentials are quite sufficient." With these words He threw back the cowl of His Cape, and our Blessed Master Saint Germain stood before us. We were thrilled, and felt immediately quite at home.

"You will now be shown to your quarters, and after having refreshed yourselves and donned your Seamless Robes, come to me here." A youth and maiden appeared and showed us the way to our rooms. Later when we returned to the council hall, a number of the Brothers had already arrived and were talking to Beloved Saint Germain.

"In seven days," He explained, "an International Council of the Great White Brotherhood is to be held in this Retreat. The Greatest of our Members will be here, as this kind of Council is only called every seven years. On this occasion you will be made Members of the outer body as well as the 'Inner.' Please be seated, for I wish to give you information concerning the city you are now in." He then gave us another wonderful Discourse, and it made us marvel at what a place of wonders this Earth is—let alone the rest of the Universe.

"At one time," He explained, "this city was at the surface of the Earth. Certain of the Ascended Masters knew a cataclysm was threatening and sealed a portion of it for future use. In the catastrophe that followed, it sank deep below the original level and was filled in and covered over by the sand from the surrounding land, which had become a desert.

"The tops of the highest buildings are in some places fully one hundred and twenty-five feet beneath the surface. Air passages have been kept open and always give perfect ventilation. Within this subterranean city have been perfected some of the most wonderful achievements in chemistry and invention the outer world has been privileged to receive. Whenever this has occurred, some worthy man or woman has been found through whom the world has been privileged to receive these Blessings.

"There is here much of vital importance ready to be brought forth for the use of humanity when it is the part of Wisdom in the Judgment of the Ascended Masters to give it out. Again there will be another great cataclysm that will rend the surface of the Earth, removing from further self-created destruction those human beings who have the ignorance and presumption to say there is no God. Those who are so bound by their self-created darkness that they destroy the very symbols on Earth of what is good, true, uplifting and enlightening, must —because of the very darkness of their own minds— be prevented from creating any further discord upon this planet and from influencing others by their own mistaken concepts of Life.

"Whatever and whoever denies God—the Source of all Life and Light—can only exist as long as the energy which they have already received can sustain them; because the moment an individual, group, or nation denies the very Source of Life, that instant the Inflowing Stream of Life Energy is cut off, and it can only continue to function until the force which has already been accumulated becomes exhausted. The collapse and self-annihilation of these is inevitable.

"Denial of Life and Light cuts off the sustaining energy, while Acknowledgment of Life and Light releases it and lets it flow through the body and mind that makes the Acknowledgment.

"The Great Law governing all form, or the *Law of*

Cause and Effect, tolerates man's iniquity to man only so long. When that iniquity is directed to the Godhead, or Source of Life, retribution is swift and certain. There is *an automatic purifying and balancing process* within all Life, and when any outer activity opposes itself to the Cosmic Law of forward motion and ever-expanding Perfection—which is always pressing from within outward—then the hour arrives when all opposition is swept aside and annihilated by the onward moving impulse within Life Itself. When those ruling a nation turn from God, destroying all that calls attention to the Light of Christ, it means the end of that government and group is close at hand; because it causes a certain Cosmic Activity to be released upon the planet which sweeps them out of existence.

"The human intellect acquires many peculiar kinks in its thinking, and one of the most disastrous of these is the activity of human consciousness that refuses or forgets to love and thank Life, the 'Mighty I AM Presence,' for the Blessings Life is constantly bestowing upon mankind and this Earth.

"The average human being lives Life after Life without once loving or thanking his own 'Mighty I AM Presence' for the energy which flows ceaselessly through his mind and body; for the substance he uses in his body and world; or for the hundreds of good things by which he is constantly

surrounded which he uses and enjoys, and yet gives
nothing of himself in return.

"Many people carry a feeling of personal grudge
against Life, blaming It for their suffering and
failures, when even a very small amount of gratitude
and Love poured out to the 'I AM Presence' within
each human Heart would transmute every discord
into Peace and Love, releasing the Perfection of Life
into the outer activity of the individual.

"Human beings find plenty of time to love dogs,
cats, food, clothes, money, diamonds, people, and a
thousand and one things; but it is very rarely that an
individual takes even five minutes out of a lifetime to
love his own Divinity—yet he is using every second
Its Life and Energy by which to enjoy those things.
Even those who think they love God give almost no
Acknowledgment to the 'Mighty I AM Presence'
within themselves, and no gratitude goes up to It for
the good things that come to them in Life.

"It is not that we should not pour out Love to
things in the outer activity; but we should certainly
love the Divinity Within first—*and more*—than any
outer thing or personality. It is this very Life and
Consciousness by which we exist.

"*Happiness cannot exist except when Love is pouring
out.* This is Life's Law. When people are loving
something or somebody, they are happy. Even a
miser is happy when he is loving his Gold, because

he is pouring out a feeling of Love to the thing he tries to hold. What he is really trying to hold is happiness; but he does not realize that the feeling of happiness is not contained in the Gold, but is in the pouring out of Love from himself. In that outpouring he lets Life flow uninterruptedly and harmoniously.

"However, having received all good we ever used from the 'Mighty I AM Presence' which builds each physical body, the *first and greatest* Outpouring of our Love belongs always to our own Individualized Flame of God—the Mighty Consciousness of Life within us which enables us to acknowledge our own existence and Source of all Life when we say 'I AM.' In those Words is *All of God,* and nothing in human experience is really important but *All of God.* When the individual accepts, acknowledges, and feels *All of God,* he is happy, he has all good, and then he lives in the Father's Mansion. Is it possible for anything to be more important or greater than *All of God?* Only with the Understanding and Feeling of this can mankind break the chains of self-created limitations.

"Now you must rest, and then it will be my privilege to escort you through this underground city, where you will see the Brothers at work. I make but one request: that no detail of this Work be revealed without permission from the Highest Master in charge."

He bade us good-night, and we went to our quarters. These had been constructed similar to the Greek and Roman type of architecture, yet they were far older. The room assigned to me contained a built-in Roman bath, the most beautiful thing I have ever seen of this kind. Everywhere the atmosphere was laden with the fragrance of flowers, usually roses.

In the morning we were awakened by soft music played on instruments of a most unusual type, and the effect upon our bodies can hardly be described, for it gave one the feeling of ease and freedom—as if a pressure of some kind were being released. The sensation continued to increase, and while we were clearly conscious of some change going on within us, yet we did not realize to what extent our Inner Bodies were being attuned. The curious thing about the whole experience is that when we compared notes with each other, all had been affected in a similar manner.

As we entered the Council Chamber, Saint Germain and Gaylord's Friend greeted us. Saint Germain asked us to be seated, and breakfast was served immediately. The first thing that appeared was most delicious fruit. Then came what He called Sun-cereal, over which was a substance like honey and whipped cream. Several other dishes were served, and we finished the meal with a steaming hot drink that took the place of coffee, but was not like anything physical I have ever tasted.

Even after our many experiences, it always seemed so marvelous to me to have things appear at the Conscious Command of these Blessed Ascended Masters. Everything came directly from out the Universal Substance the instant They desired it: food, clothing, gold, anything and everything They wanted. They are all the word "Master" implies. It is the only description that does Them justice. They are glorious and majestic—always.

As we arose from the table, I heard Gaylord's Friend address Leto as "Your Highness," and again I wondered why that title was used in a Retreat. She turned to me and explained most graciously.

"My brother, whom you have met, inherited the title of Prince Rexford, and I that of Princess Louise. Mine has clung to me through the years for no particular reason. That is why I am often addressed as 'Your Highness.'

"Forgive my curiosity," I replied, as I realized how keenly aware of my every thought and feeling these Ascended Masters were.

"Come," said Saint Germain, "We shall go first to the television chamber." We followed Him and soon came to a great circular chamber. In the center of the room stood an enormous reflector surrounded by a maze of electrical apparatus, at one side of which was a large dial.

"This room," said Saint Germain, "is insulated in a special way which enables us to make observations of very great accuracy. By means of this instrument, through focusing the dial upon any given point on the surface of the Earth, we can see instantly any place or activity occurring at any distance. Notice! I shall direct it to New York."

He turned the dial, and we saw—as clearly as if we had been in Manhattan—the Grand Central Station, Fifth Avenue, and the Statue of Liberty. Then turning the dial to London, we were shown Trafalgar Square, the Houses of Parliament, the British Museum, the Bank of England, and the River Thames. He turned it again and we saw Melbourne and Yokohama, and we were able to observe everything as clearly as if physically present.

"This wonderful instrument," He continued, "has been in use in this Retreat for more than a hundred years. Come now into the adjoining room. It is the radio chamber. Notice the intense stillness! The walls, floor and ceiling are covered with a precipitated substance that makes it absolutely sound and vibration proof."

He stepped to the instrument that stood in the center of the room and directed it to New York. We immediately heard the sound of the traffic, and as we listened more closely, we could hear clearly and distinctly the conversation of individuals passing on the street. Distance made no difference.

"This instrument," He said, "will soon be in use everywhere. Now let us go to the chemical laboratory where some of the Brothers are at work upon many wonderful inventions. Here, ways have been discovered to counteract destructive gases, chemicals, and activities of various kinds that the sinister force and its unfortunate pawns might try to use against humanity; for it is positively known in certain quarters that feverish efforts are constantly being made to produce various substances that are of a very destructive kind. The Brothers in this Retreat work to neutralize all such activity.

"When misguided members of mankind discover a more than ordinarily destructive agent, the chemist making such experiments always loses his body when his diabolical work reaches a certain point, for the destructive quality he desires to use upon the body of mankind reacts upon his own."

Next we visited the Cosmic Ray Chamber. "This room," explained Saint Germain, "is lined with pure metallic Gold. The Brothers of certain advancement who work here are taught how to distinguish the difference between the various Rays and to direct and use them for stupendous Good. The Great Ascended Masters are constantly watching in the world for those students whose attainments will permit them to take up this Work." When Bob understood this phase of Their Activity, he became most enthusiastic.

"I would love to serve in this manner!" he exclaimed.

"We shall see," said Saint Germain as He smiled knowingly. "Among those who are working in this room, there are seven of the Brothers and three of the Sisters who are just completing their Training in the use of these Rays. At the coming Council they will be allotted their field of service in using this Activity for which Training in many lives has fitted them.

"Now we shall visit the Chamber of Art, where twenty of the Brothers and ten of the Sisters are being trained in a new kind of art which they will bring forth into the outer world. They are being instructed concerning the secret of imperishable colors and shown how to produce them. Within the next twenty years this form of art will find its way into the Life of humanity, and bring with it a tremendous uplift.

"From here we shall go to the Chamber of Music. It is a most beautiful place I assure you, and the Perfection of the instruments is truly remarkable." Saint Germain led the way, and we entered with great anticipation.

"This is a new metal for band instruments," He

continued, showing us certain alloys, "which gives an unbelievably delicate tone. Here are three new materials for making violins. As you will see, one looks like mother of pearl, one like frosted silver, and one like Roman gold. The musical instruments of the New Age will be made of materials like these."

One of the Brothers played these instruments for us, and human ears have never been blessed by more beautiful sounds. Each was distinctly different, but all were so beautiful there seemed hardly any choice between them.

In rooms adjoining the Chamber of Music, beautiful musical compositions were being written and prepared so the Brothers could project these magnificent harmonies into the consciousness of musicians working in the outer world.

"Some of these Brothers," said Saint Germain, "will come into the outer activity and work in the capacity of teachers, while others will serve from the invisible side of Life.

"We are now entering the Chamber of State. Here training is given in the higher forms of statecraft and national government. Some forty of the Brothers are being trained, as you see, in the right use of this Knowledge, and are also being shown how to project it to others who are already in official positions—that is, wherever the sincerity of the official will permit. Ten of these wonderful Brothers will go forth in person and serve by being elected to governmental positions in the usual way. Five of them will go to the United States of America."

During our visit to these various rooms and the explanation of the Work the Brothers were engaged in, we felt this the most wonderful education of our lives. It was such a relief to know that notwithstanding all the distressing outward appearance of the conditions in which humanity finds itself to day, the Power of the "Mighty I AM" is doing everything possible to bring enlightenment and relief to mankind. It lifted our Hearts and hopes to the height of expectation for great good to all mankind in the near future—at least for all who desire the constructive Plan of Life.

We were shown secret chambers of riches untold, others of records so old it seemed almost inconceivable. Some dated back to the advent of man upon this planet. When we returned to the Council Chamber, we found we had been gone eight hours. Not once in all this amazing subterranean city did we find the least particle of dust, dirt, or confusion of any kind. Everything was in a most wonderful state—perfect and spotless. We marveled at this, and Saint Germain again explained the Law concerning it.

"This Perfect Cleanliness is maintained by the conscious use of the Great Cosmic Rays, and within the next one hundred years, hundreds of housewives will be using the Violet Ray to keep private homes in the same wonderful state. Oh, that humanity might realize quickly what Glory, Freedom and Blessings stand ready for their use at every instant when they hold to wonderful Ideals unwaveringly, tenaciously rely upon the 'Mighty I AM Presence,' and know It is the *only real Power* of Permanent Accomplishment!"

Suddenly we felt a tremendous vibration, and looking around, saw five of the Ascended Masters had arrived from India—for the men wore turbans. These were two Ladies and three Gentlemen. As we were presented to Them, we were surprised indeed, for one Gentleman and one Lady were two of whom we had heard much. The Gentleman came up to Rex, Bob and myself; the Lady to Nada and Pearl, and extended a most gracious invitation to be Their guests as long as we were in India, and consider Their home ours at any time.

"Will you," said the Gentleman, turning to Gaylord's Friend, "come with these friends and bring them to us as our guests when they are ready to come to India?"

"I shall be most happy," He replied, "to accept your invitation and take them to Bombay in my yacht."

Saint Germain then asked us all to be seated, that we might enjoy another precipitated dinner. The entire meal seemed more delicious than ever. We listened attentively to the Work being planned and the reports of what had already been accomplished. For the first time in my Life I realized how very little the outside world knows of this True Inner Activity, and how puny human achievement becomes in relation to that which is accomplished by these Ascended Masters who are expressing Their Full Freedom as Sons of God. It is fortunate indeed that there are infinitely more magnificent ways of Life than our humanity is now experiencing. When one can look away from his own mental concepts long enough to get a perspective of his own intellect in relation to the rest of the Universe, he really begins to learn something of importance.

We all need to take mental journeys that will stretch our mental muscles, and realize that each human intellect is only one out of approximately three billion souls in incarnation upon this Earth. Our Earth is one of the smallest in our solar system. Our system is only an atom in the galaxy to which we belong, and there are galaxies of galaxies.

When the student thinks of this occasionally, he will no longer be able to accept the conceited theories and egotistical opinions of intellects that scoff at and doubt the existence and marvelous Manifestation of Perfection which these Ascended Masters constantly express.

The personality of anyone is only of as much importance in the magnificent scheme of Life as it is obedient to the "Mighty I AM Presence," by letting Perfection expand into the outer activity of the individual. Otherwise the personality is only a barnacle in the Universe, using substance and energy without building anything permanent.

Time sped by on wings under the intensive Training we were receiving from these Great Perfected Ones until the day came for the Great International Council. The Brothers and Sisters kept arriving at intervals from every part of the world; and when the meeting was called at seven o'clock, more than two hundred Guests were present, most of them being Chiefs of the various Councils. When all were in readiness, we bowed our heads in silence and awaited the arrival of the Great Presiding Master. Suddenly a Great Oval of Dazzling Light appeared at the head of the main table. As we watched It steadily for a moment, a man's form gradually became visible within It, growing more and more definite and tangible as He lowered the vibratory activity to manifest in our octave of consciousness, until His Body became clearly visible, perfectly tangible.

His face was truly magnificent, glorious and radiant to behold—the eyes dazzling—and His whole Being *luminous* from head to foot with the Majesty and Power of His "Mighty I AM Presence." The first tones of His Voice sent an Electrical Thrill through my body that I shall never forget throughout Eternity as He said, "Beloved Ones, be seated."

After listening to a brief report from certain of the Brothers, He commended Them, and then in a very brief manner gave directions for Their continued Work. When He had finished, He turned to us, saying:

"We can use many more who are at a point where they are ready to be trained in the Understanding and use of the Great Cosmic Rays of Light. It is My Privilege to inform you that We have ten with Us who are ready—if it be their desire to take up the Work." All was intense expectation as He asked those whose names He called to stand if they were present. Then He went on:

"Nada, Pearl, Leto, Rex, Bob, Electra, Gaylord and His Beloved Friend, Nada and Daniel Rayborn. Beloved Sisters and Brothers from America, this event brings very great joy and is of much importance to the Great White Brotherhood. You are to be congratulated, as well as the Brotherhood, that this has become possible. Within a short time you will go to India for a stay of ten months'

Training, and then return here to finish it. You will be instructed in the use of these Mighty Rays, and through Their Use, you have an opportunity to give a Transcendent Service.

"On the fourth day from today, you will return to Alexandria, and there Electra will join the party. From thence, journey at your convenience to Bombay. Your Beloved Host will conduct you to your destination. Is there the slightest objection on the part of anyone chosen for this Work? If so, speak now."

We all joyously accepted and expressed our gratitude for the opportunity to serve in this way to the best of our ability. There was a great deal more under consideration at that time which was of great importance, but I have not permission to record it here. The meeting finished, and we spent an hour meeting the other Members present. Our Friend from India presented us to the Presiding Master, and I shall never forget the Power that shot through my body as I shook hands with Him. It seemed as if I were lifted completely off the floor. One of the Brothers from South America brought us greetings from Gaylord, whom he had seen two days previous.

The entire Council was a Perfect Manifestation of Great Decision, Supreme Wisdom and Limitless Activity. Presently, beautiful strains of Music were heard in the atmosphere, and all turned involuntarily toward the Master. He raised His hands, giving His Blessing to all present; and as He did so, He rose from the floor, the Oval of Dazzling Light enfolded Him, and He disappeared.

Never in all Eternity will I ever forget that first visit to the Arabian Retreat of the Great White Brotherhood. Four days later we left this marvelous Haven of Peace, Light, and Wisdom, with the Love and Blessings from all Its Members whose Loving Service to the "Great I AM Presence" in themselves and in all humanity is the most wonderful Activity in Life's Experience. We made the trip back to the coast of Arabia by night, where the yacht awaited us; and a few moments after we went aboard, we were gliding swiftly through the Red Sea on the wings of the night.

The next morning we breakfasted on deck in order to watch the sunrise, for in that part of the world, it is truly a most glorious spectacle. The evening of the second day we arrived at Electra's home in Alexandria and found She was fully aware that She was to serve with us in using the Great Cosmic Rays of "The Light of God that never fails."

CHAPTER XI

The True Messenger of Divine Service

LATE one afternoon we were returning with Electra from a drive along the shore of the Mediterranean and had just entered the door of Her home when a Sealed Letter dropped at Rex's feet. He picked it up, and opening it, read:

> My Beloved Children:
> Leave tomorrow morning for India. All is in readiness, and we are happy to welcome you.
>
> Saint Germain

Our Host of the yacht had not been with us during our sight-seeing trip in Alexandria; but when we arrived at the pier, He greeted us joyously with the news that we had been assured of a calm, delightful voyage. We again passed through the Red Sea as we sped swiftly on our way to one of the Greatest Centers of Spiritual Light and Power on this planet.

Leto continued Her Instruction during the entire trip at Saint Germain's Request, that Bob and Rex might reach the point where they could come and go from the physical body consciously and at will. By the fifth day of our journey they had become quite proficient, and like most young people, wanted to experiment often in using their newly-evolved Powers. This Leto would not permit.

"There must be a very great sense of Spiritual Honor and Integrity," She explained, "in regard to the use of these Mighty Powers of the 'I AM Presence'; for the Great Law of Being does not permit them to be brought into our outer use except where it is for the accomplishment of permanent good. We must be aware at all times that whenever we use the Life, Substance and Power of this Universe for the mere gratification or pleasure of the senses, only misery and destruction can be the result.

"The 'Mighty I AM Presence' works ceaselessly to build, release, express, and constantly expand Perfection in all Its Creative Activity, and permanently maintain Love, Peace, and constant Service to all. If the sensations of the body and the outer activity of the mind are permitted to run riot and interfere with the Divine Life Plan of the individual, disaster and failure are the result. The True Student of Light never, never uses his powers for the amusement and gratification of the senses, for exploitation of anyone's personality or to make money by producing phenomena.

"The Ascended Masters' Way of Life is to give,

give, give! First, Love and Adoration to His own 'Mighty I AM Presence,' and then expand Love and Perfection by pouring It out to everybody and everything. To send out Divine Love without limit, all the time, is the whole of the Law applied. If mankind could only understand this, the individual would realize that he must pour out this Flame of Divine Love before the Perfection which he desires can flow into his world and release—things—into his use.

"Divine Love is a Feeling, an actual Ray of Light which flows out from the Flame within the Heart. It can be sent forth so powerfully that this Ray of Light Substance is both visible and tangible. It is the most Invincible Power of the Universe. Use It, Beloved Ones, without limit, and nothing is impossible to you."

By temperament and training, Leto was a calm, sweet, marvelously poised teacher; but we were amazed at the Power She could release when She wished to impress a certain Understanding of the Law upon our consciousness. She was not accustomed to the boyish pranks of Bob and Rex, but She soon made it unmistakably plain to us all that no boyish pranks played any part in the operation of these Great Cosmic Laws.

"The Cosmic Law acts," She continued, "wherever the thoughts and feelings direct and qualify the energy; and It is no respecter of persons, places, conditions, things, motives, ignorance, or knowledge, anymore than is a current of electricity running through a motor or dynamo. If you turn on the Power, it acts, according to the direction given it. This is a point that many students do not seem to comprehend, or for which they do not wish to take the responsibility; but the Truth of the Law is the only thing with which We are concerned.

"Our Work is to put the *exact Truth of the Law* before individuals. If they refuse to understand and obey it, then their suffering must increase—until the human side breaks its shell of obstinacy and selfishness and lets the 'Mighty Presence of the I AM' control all, according to the Perfection of Life.

"Therefore, never joke in thought, feeling or the spoken word about the Powers of the Godhead; for to do so—without exception—draws heartbreaking experiences into your world. Therefore, govern your outer moods with an *Inflexible Will* whenever you use the Powers of the 'MIGHTY I AM PRESENCE.'

"In order to manifest the greater Expressions of the 'I AM Presence,' the individual must become aware of and feel that 'Presence' within himself, and know that the very Life Energy which beats his Heart and breathes through his lungs is constantly flowing into his physical body from his Electronic Body. His Electronic Body is projected into space from the very Heart Center of the Cosmic Life of the Universe, which you have heard us refer to as the Great Central Sun.

"This Pure Life Energy flowing ceaselessly into the mind and body of the individual is the Triune Activity of the Supreme acting everywhere throughout Infinity. It is Intelligence, Substance and Energy —the *One Universal Light* out of which comes all manifestation.

"It is subject at all times to the conscious direction and use of the individual with Self-conscious, individualized Free Will. The minerals, plants and animals do not have the control of this activity; for only the Flame of the Godhead is endowed with Self-directing Free Will.

"The more attention one gives the 'Mighty I AM Presence,' the more he will learn of the Vast Realms of Wisdom that stretch before him. The more he realizes the immense responsibility and limitless opportunity that are his, the more should he ask the 'Mighty I AM Presence' within his own Heart to teach him all things.

"If one wants Wisdom, he must turn his attention to the only Source of Wisdom—the 'Mighty I AM Presence.' Only by acknowledging the 'I AM,' can the first impulse be given which releases Its Wisdom into the outer use of the individual. It is by Acknowledgment, that the first wave flows forth to release It into the physical activity. Otherwise It remains forever quiescent within the Consciousness of the 'I AM.' The Release of It can come only at the Command of the Self-Directing Will of the Flame of God.

"Learn to call forth these God Attributes and Activities from the very Heart of the Universe, and then use them in Love to bless all Life. If you will do this, there is no height you cannot attain and no gift you can ask of Life that Life will not release to you—when you understand what part of you says 'I AM' and you are willing to use all to bless Life everywhere with Love.

"Use, use, use, use the Understanding of the 'I AM Presence' that you now have, and persist in loving, in blessing Life everywhere; and you will open wide the Floodgates to Freedom—*the Realm and Activities of the Limitless*—the Natural World and Life of the Ascended Masters. Use the Wisdom you now have, and more will come as surely as your Heart beats and your mind thinks."

At dinner on the evening of the seventh day of the voyage, our Host announced that we were to reach Bombay late the next evening, but we were to remain aboard until the following morning. Bombay is one of the most beautiful harbors in the world; and as our yacht came alongside the pier, we were greeted by the Indian Master Chananda, to whom we were presented by our Host. We drove to the railroad station where we were conducted to a private car—every convenience being provided for us so very graciously until we reached our destination.

It was here only that the outline of our stay in India was given. First we were to go to Calcutta and remain there two days while certain Work would be given. The trip to Calcutta was delightful, and although the days were very warm outside, we were not aware of it in the train. We passed many places of great scenic beauty, and shortly after leaving Bombay, we missed Bob. We started a search for him and, as we entered his compartment, realized he had left his body. Leto warned us immediately:

"Do not touch his body," She said, "for he has gone with the Master Chananda." For a few moments Nada had a hard struggle to command herself and keep at peace, for this was the first time Bob had gone forth from his body without previous preparation. However, she soon controlled her feelings and became at ease. In about two hours Bob came walking into the observation car in which we had all gathered. He was as serene as could be, but the rest of us immediately asked concerning his experiences and of course wanted to know where he had been. We could get him to reveal nothing, and finally he said:

"Each of us is to keep his experience strictly within his own consciousness until the end of our destination, and then we are to compare notes."
That afternoon Nada and Pearl were gone about

two hours. The next morning Rex and I left our bodies. Each of us had experienced practically the same things, for we were being trained in accurate observation.

Shri Singh, the Brother who had taken Chananda's place, was delighted in every way, but very silent; yet when He did talk, it was always for some very definite purpose. The day we arrived in Calcutta, Chananda reappeared to us, and when we had become seated at dinner, with His magic, radiant smile, remarked:

"I congratulate each of you on the fearless way in which you are able to leave your bodies and go forth strong and free. It means great enlightenment for all, as well as the entering into a tremendous field of Service. Leto, My Sister, You are a most efficient Instructor, and Your Work with these students is remarkably well done. It is only in this Freedom, My Friends, that you are permitted to know, feel, and experience the Full Use of the Cosmic Rays. You are now in a position to receive the Full Benefit of your training with Us."

Electra and our Host of the yacht were silent but very careful observers of all that had taken place, and were no doubt being trained in the same way. We felt keenly the intensity and power of the Instruction, for everything we did had a definite objective and purpose. We arrived in Calcutta and drove rapidly for about half an hour, finally coming to a stop in front of a beautiful building situated upon a prominence in what was evidently the best residential section of the city.

Chananda led the way into the building—which He told us was secretly owned and maintained by the Great White Brotherhood. The interior was a perfect dream of beauty, typical of many of the marvels in India. It breathed the Wisdom, Light, and Purity of ages of Perfection. We went immediately to the Council Chamber on the second floor where we found the Brotherhood already assembled. We noticed seats had been left vacant at the head of the table of honor. Chananda led the way to these seats and took the head Himself. It was only then we learned that He was the Head of the Indian Council.

As soon as all had assembled, the business part of the meeting was called, and some of the Ascended Masters were asked to give Their Protection to certain Englishmen in India who were sincere in their desire to bring about greater good. They also arranged for Protection to be given a group of lesser Brothers whose desire to do right was sincere and who were giving good service—but who did not always use the greatest discrimination in the outer activity because their zeal exceeded their wisdom.

After the meeting we were presented to all the Members and spent a delightful social hour. We motored back to our private car and found it had been run out on a spur of track into surroundings that looked like a flower garden—with a beautiful fountain playing just outside the windows where we dined. We commented on the ability of Chananda to have the beautiful always expressed to us, and with one of His smiles that ever gave one the sense of sunshine, He replied:

"It is really much easier to express the beautiful, because it is natural and the true expression of the 'Mighty I AM Presence' within everyone. When anyone truly accepts this Glorious 'Presence' and feels It as the Godhead doing all things through and for him, the rest of his activity must conform to Its marvelous Beauty and Perfection. The Full Acceptance of the 'Mighty I AM Presence' by the individual always commands and governs all outer experience harmoniously. It is only when one *truly and fully* accepts this Glorious 'God Presence' within himself that he becomes a True Messenger for Divine Service.

"Then as the Perfection of the 'Mighty I AM Presence' begins to be released in a greater degree through the outer activity, all the courage and assurance comes through; for at last the personal self sees and feels the 'Mighty Inner Presence,' knowing Its Full Power, Majesty, and Mastery."

The next day we were taken to one of the ancient Temples in whose subterranean chambers is going on a Work undreamed of by the outer world. That night at dinner Chananda told us we were to leave for Darjeeling early in the morning, and that we were to eat breakfast en route. The scenery was gorgeous, and the sensation of watching the giant snow-capped mountains come closer and closer as we gradually climbed in altitude was fascinating; but we soon began to feel the change, for we had risen more than seven thousand feet.

We arrived at the top of our climb just in time to see a glorious sunset in a very clear atmosphere. In the distance we could see Mount Everest and the other famous peaks of that glorious range. The majesty—towering presence of these mountains— and the mystery of the ages that shrouded their past made us all feel a deeper longing than ever to reach to the inmost Heart of the Great Eternal Wisdom, to feel ourselves a part of It, and to be able to pour forth Its Blessings to all mankind, that it might be happy also.

"I want you to stay here tonight," said Chananda, "and see the sunrise from this particular spot, as it will be many years before we shall see it again—in cooperation with a certain Cosmic Activity that is taking place at this time. It is the first time in seventy years that these two activities occur simultaneously."

At three o'clock we arose and mounted our little ponies which took us still higher up the mountain to a point where we could see the sunrise to best advantage. We reached this place just as its Radiance began to grow brighter. In a few seconds Great Rays of Light of every conceivable color began to shoot into the sky and continued for fully ten minutes. It was as if Light Itself rejoiced in the Mighty Presence of Life.

Then as the Great Golden Disc came into view, a Quivering, Sparkling Radiance pierced our flesh and penetrated into the very centers of our bodies. Never before had we experienced any such sensation from sunlight. The vivifying effect lasted for hours, and the glorious feeling the beauty of the scene left with us still floods over me as I recall the experience. One knows after such an occurrence that the Mighty Master Intelligence of the Universe is still at the helm and guides the destinies of our Earth and humanity, notwithstanding all outer appearance of chaos to the contrary.

"You have felt within your bodies," said Chananda, "a slight Action of the Mighty Cosmic Rays which have been directed to Earth at the present time—by Great Cosmic Masters who are giving Transcendent Assistance in this cycle to humanity in its outer struggle. Their Outpouring is a Radiance of Love, Courage and Strength to the race which sustains the individual during this period of change and so illumines his Inner Bodies that It enables the 'Mighty I AM Presence' to release more of Its Perfection into and through the outer self.

"Those of you who are to receive Training in the use of these Rays will be enabled to focus Great Streams of Light Essence and consciously direct them—pouring forth Blessings to mankind through Great Currents of Healing Power and Harmonizing Streams of Love. Few are ready to be taught how to control and use these Mighty Rays, but all for whom it is possible are being prepared now. These Great Streams of Condensed Light and Pure Substance can be drawn, qualified, and sent forth again to produce a definite result as easily as a searchlight reveals the scenes it passes over.

"Come now, we must return and go to the home of the Chief of the Council at Darjeeling." We went back to our ponies which took us to Darjeeling, and thence were driven by auto to a beautiful home built upon one of the lovely hills surrounding the city. The grounds were filled with stately trees, and the view over the country that lay below us was one of the most beautiful on Earth. We were ushered in and presented to the Head of this Branch of the Great White Brotherhood.

He was a tall, handsome man with piercing dark eyes that seemed to look clear through one; but when there was no intense feeling being expressed, they were as soft as those of a fawn. To our surprise,

He did not wear a turban, but His soft, beautiful, dark brown hair waved slightly and fell to his shoulders. He was very gracious and gave us a most loving welcome. A Glorious Peace clothed Him and His surroundings filling the entire place with His Wonderful Radiance.

He inquired about our trip, asked if we had enjoyed the sunrise from the mountain, and invited us to dine with Him that evening. He talked very freely and told us many wonderful things about India. He repeated for our enjoyment many legends about the Himalayan Mountains, and one in particular about the Holy Caves within the Heart of this Mighty Range. His Discourse was fascinating and instructive beyond words.

"Some of these caves," He said, "you shall see while you are in India, for I know you are interested in the ancient records of mankind; and in one of them the most ancient records upon this Earth are still held in safekeeping. These records are not brought forth into the use of the outer world at the present time because of the lack of spiritual growth and understanding of the people. The race has a restlessness and critical feeling that is a very destructive activity, and these feelings find vent through fanatics of various kinds whose understanding of Life and this magnificent universe is so narrow and childish that they seek to destroy whatever does not agree with their own petty notions of what has been—or ought to be—the Infinite Plan of Creation.

"It is this misguided, selfish ignorance in mankind which has been responsible for all inharmony down the ages for the destruction of records that would throw Light upon humanity's many problems. It was this unbridled vicious feeling that destroyed the wonderful library at Alexandria and the marvelous records of the Incan civilization.

"Yet notwithstanding these former losses, the Ascended Masters of the Great White Brotherhood have always foreseen such destructive impulses and have withdrawn all important records of every civilization and preserved them, then left the less important to be destroyed by the vicious impulse of the vandals.

"One day, when humanity is prepared for it and it is positively safe for these records to be given to the outer world, there will appear in a central location a marvelous library—not made by hands—where these records will be available, and those in the outer world who have received the necessary credentials may see them.

"When mankind becomes enlightened enough to cease generating the vicious destruction it has been expressing up to the present time, this will be done. Mankind, through its irritated, destructive feeling and powerful thought force, has peopled the visible and invisible with thought-forms of intense passion, hatred, fear, and destruction. These fasten themselves upon the human beings who generated them, and also upon others who, because they have a similar feeling, open themselves to this malignant force.

"Humanity has almost no understanding of what happens when the personal self sends out a feeling of irritation, anger, hate, envy, jealousy, criticism or condemnation. The feeling side of human nature is the feminine activity of consciousness within every individual. The thought is the masculine activity of the mind. A thought never becomes dynamic in the outer life until it passes through the feeling body. The feeling condenses upon the thought pattern the atomic substance of the outer activity of Life. In thus passing through the feeling body, the thought becomes clothed, and thereafter exists as a separate living thing outside of the individual's mind.

"There have been platitudes by the million written and preached about Divine Love being the Law of Life. But who knows how to generate the Feeling of Divine Love consciously and at will to a limitless degree—and put It in the place of irritation, hate, *et cetera,* as a wave of actual force and substance in one's own emotional body? Such a thing is not only possible, but must be done if human beings are to stop suffering and express Perfection. The personality cannot be permanently harmonious except it be kept filled with Divine Love—consciously generated.

"If mental statements of the Law of Life and prayers were the way to Perfection, Happiness and Freedom, the number of sermons preached on this Earth should have perfected and illumined a hundred planets long before this. If prayers—which, by the way, are generally a series of 'I wants,' or 'O Lord give us'—were the way to Freedom from limitation, the prayers that have been uttered in this world should have perfected a dozen humanities.

"I do not say that prayers have not brought good; they have. But prayer should be a quieting of the intellect and a stilling of the feeling, that the personality might *feel* the Outpouring of the 'Mighty I AM Presence' and receive the Response from within. Prayer should be an Outpouring of Love and Gratitude to the 'Presence' for the limitless opportunities and good contained within Life.

"The outer world likes to flatter its vanity by the feeling that it has the ability to accomplish great things; but so far as the control and Perfection of the feeling is concerned, the outer world is still in a savage state. Human beings sting others as well as themselves through vicious feelings just as surely as does the scorpion. The predominant feeling in our modern world is terrifically vicious when personalities are opposing and criticizing those who disagree with them. So-called civilized people commit murder every day of the week through sending out angry and irritated feelings that kill the higher impulses in others.

"It is the feeling of the race that needs to be redeemed and saved from its own self-generated destruction. Until the individual understands the need of Self-control in regard to his *feeling*—in the waking consciousness—it is impossible to maintain any permanent forward movement of a constructive nature. All accomplishment that is not attained through the Feeling of Divine Love is but temporary, for Divine Love alone is the way to Permanent Perfection.

"It is pitiful to see how for centuries the human race has occupied its time and used its energy to build up things through thought, and at the same time tear its creation to pieces by inharmonious feelings. It is childish and is a stubborn refusal to fulfill the Eternal Plan of Perfection.

"The hour is at hand when the Great Cosmic Law which governs this system of worlds is releasing a tremendous Expansion of the Light of the 'Mighty I AM Presence' throughout our group of planets, and whatever cannot accept the Power of that Light is consumed thereby. So mankind need no longer fool itself with the idea that it can continue to generate destructive feeling and survive. The end of the former dispensation has come, and all things are made new. Let him who runs, read—that he may learn the Way of Light while there is yet time.

"There is no evil anywhere on this Earth or any other except that which human beings have generated themselves sometime, somewhere. Most of it has been done through ignorance, but a great deal has been done willfully by those who ought to know better and who are fully aware of their wrongdoing. The individual who uses his intellect to foster destructive activities in the New Cycle into which we have recently entered must face his own destruction, for its recoil is inevitable. It will be swift and definite, for the present activity is expressing such speed that the recoil is many times only a matter of hours, weeks, or months at most, where heretofore it has been a matter of years.

"The Ascended Masters work ceaselessly to have humanity understand and see this; and the work of Our Messengers is to get this Truth into the consciousness of mankind as clearly as possible.

"It is now nearly dinner time. Attendants will show you to your quarters. After refreshing yourselves, return here, and we shall dine." Later, dinner was announced by beautiful chimes. Our Host offered His arm to Nada and led the way into a magnificent banquet hall, which must have seated fully five hundred people.

"This is really our Council Chamber," He explained. "Later this evening all the members of the Darjeeling Council will assemble here." We enjoyed a most delicious dinner while our Host entertained us with an endless fund of information. As we were leaving, He asked to be excused as He had work to do before the Council met.

"Our Host," said Chananda, in whose care He had left us, "is a Brother of Great Wisdom and Power, but the very embodiment of gentleness and kindness."

At nine o'clock He returned, and offering His arm to Leto, led the way into the Council Chamber where two hundred Members of the Great White Brotherhood had already assembled. He took His place at the head of the main table, and seated half of our group on His right and the other half on His left. He called the meeting to order, and Their Work began. We were thrilled again and again as we listened to the solution of many important world problems—especially some of those which were holding the attention of Europe at the moment. He then assigned certain duties to many of the Brothers.

The meeting adjourned and we were presented individually to many of the members. We had been enjoying the social activities for some few moments when I noticed that Rex was laboring under the strain of some intense excitement. He watched one of the members closely for some time, and then went quickly and boldly up to our Host. He informed Him there was a spy in the room and pointed out the individual. For an instant it seemed as if the power within the Chief would crush him, but Rex was clothed in a Divine Dignity that never flinched.

"That is a grave charge," said the Chief. "It will require proof."

At that moment the man in question came up to Pearl and realized instantly that he was being watched. He reached into the folds of his robe, drew something forth and raised it to his mouth. Pearl seized it as quick as a flash; and Bob, who stood near, with one leap pinned the man's hands behind him in a grasp of steel.

"Search him!" said Pearl, as our Host stepped forward; and Rex, without waiting for authority from anyone, went through the spy's clothing like lightning. He found all the proof they needed of his activities as a spy. As the Chief came forward and saw the name on the papers Rex handed him, he was surprised indeed; for the spy, who was an educated Afghan, had been sent into India by a government that breeds only destruction and had ferreted his way into the outer ranks of this Council to obtain information which he had been using against them. At a signal, one of the Brothers stepped forward and led the spy from the room.

"Brother Rex," said our Host with a gracious smile, "you have served the Cause of Light well and rendered our Brotherhood a Blessing of tremendous import. There has been a leak in some of our activities recently. Tell me, how did you become aware of his operations? He has been deceiving us very cleverly."

"My attention," replied Rex, "was drawn to him by the Inner Power of my 'I AM Presence,' and as I watched his eyes, I knew he was practicing some kind of deception. It all happened so quickly I hardly knew in the outer activity of my mind what was occurring. If it had not been for Pearl, my Twin Ray, we would have been too late."

"Outwardly, you three may not have known what it was all about, but the 'Mighty Presence of the I AM' has acted with unerring Decision. You see, My Beloved Ones, how the Twin Rays can act with the speed of lightning in perfect unison when the Great Inner 'Presence' is allowed to have Full Control.

"My Sister and Brother," He continued, as He extended His left hand to Pearl and His right one to Rex, "you will be able to do splendid work for the 'Mighty I AM Presence,' the Great White Brotherhood, and humanity. I bless you for that Service."

"What is to be done with the spy?" asked Pearl.

"The man knows what he must do," replied the

Chief. "Let us forget it ever happened. We shall always remember your Service to the Brotherhood." By this time most of the guests had left, so we bade our Host good-by, for we were leaving Darjeeling in the morning. We did not stop again at Calcutta but went directly through to Benares, the Sacred City of the Hindus, and one of the oldest cities in India. As our private coach drew into the railway station, we became keenly aware of a sincere devotion in the very atmosphere of the place.

Imagine our joy when almost the very first person we saw was our beloved friend Alexander Gaylord, who had arrived in Benares only a few hours before. Rex, Bob and I made a dash for him as soon as the train stopped. When his Friend, the owner of the yacht, came up to greet him, they looked into each other's eyes with a deep Love and Understanding born of centuries of association. As Leto, Gaylord's Twin Ray, approached, he extended his arms and held Her close to his Heart. Chananda then presented Electra.

"We are to be guests this evening of one of the oldest Councils in India," He said. "It is to be purely a spiritual feast—devoted entirely to the guests. All Members of the Order are to wear their Seamless Robes. I shall return for you at six o'clock." We returned to our compartment and prepared for the evening banquet. When Chananda returned He was accompanied by his sister, Najah, a beautiful young girl—or at least so She appeared—to whom we were presented. We were driven to a beautiful building on an elevation overlooking the city. As we approached the entrance, involuntarily we expressed our joy at the beauty and exquisite surroundings of the scene we gazed upon.

As we passed through the entrance we entered a rotunda of pink marble veined with soft green, in which there were seven white marble pillars. The effect was warm, delicate, and very beautiful. Najah led the way to the dressing rooms where we donned our Seamless Robes, and then conducted us toward a great arched doorway that opened at our approach, admitting us into a large magnificent council chamber made entirely of white marble and elaborately decorated in gold. There were no lighting fixtures in the place, yet it was filled by a soft White Light that was wonderful. This great hall seated fully five hundred people, some two hundred having already arrived.

"We are to be honored tonight by three Divine Guests," announced Chananda, as He presented us to those assembled and we took our seats. "Let us meditate upon the Great Principle of Life—the 'Mighty I AM Presence'—until music shall signal the close of our meditation." Presently the soft tones of great bells stole gently upon the air, and as we raised our heads and looked toward the head of the table where the three vacant chairs had been, we could scarcely repress our exclamation of joy and surprise as we saw our beloved Saint Germain at the head of the table—on His left Nada Rayborn, and on his right, Daniel.

Everyone in the room rose in honor of these Blessed Beings, as the guests of honor. Our impulse was to rush to Them in greeting, so great was our joy, but something in each of us controlled all outer activity, and we bowed low in quiet dignity and loving respect.

"I present to you our Beloved Brother of Light, Saint Germain," said Chananda, addressing those assembled, "and His two Guests, Nada and Daniel Rayborn, who raised their bodies as His Students in America. Our Sister raised Her body after what to the outer world seemed death. Our Brother Daniel accomplished His Victory without coming to that point." At the close of this Explanation, the Light within and about Chananda blazed forth in a Dazzling Radiance as He continued:

"Our Blessed Brother and Honored Guest Saint Germain will have full charge of the evening and will conduct the rest of the work." Saint Germain, in His usual Loving Dignity, bowed in Acknowledgment of the greeting and replied:

"We shall have a banquet tonight served from the cosmic kitchen. Many of you have heard of these

Activities but have not seen or experienced the substance from which is produced everything the Heart Desires.

The beautiful banquet tables had jade tops, so no linen was supplied to cover their magnificence. Saint Germain asked all to bow their heads in loving acceptance of the great Abundance and Outpouring from the "Mighty I AM Presence." As He finished His Acknowledgment to the Source of all Life, the service for the meal began to appear. The plates, cups, and saucers were made of pink china decorated with delicate moss roses. The silver knives, forks, and spoons had carved jade handles; and tumblers of carved jade filled with a golden sparkling nectar appeared at the right hand of each guest. Then followed a tiny loaf of bread about two by two by four inches, appearing upon each plate. The food for each person came individually as if it had been ordered separately, for everyone received that which he most desired until all were served abundantly and were satisfied. Next came many kinds of luscious fruit in great golden containers, and for dessert a kind of fruit-whip appeared in crystal dishes. The entire banquet was served without the clatter of a single dish, and at the close Saint Germain arose and addressed the guests.

"The Great Ascended Masters," He began, "have wanted you to see, know, and partake of food which is produced direct from the Omnipresent Cosmic Substance. This Substance is what has been explained to you as the Pure Electronic Substance which fills Infinity, and out of which all forms are created and all manifestation produced. This Limitless Substance about you everywhere is yours to manipulate, to mold into form without any limit whatsoever when you hold close enough and sincerely enough without interruption to the 'Mighty I AM Presence' in you. This Glorious Angelic Being and Power which is the *Real You*—who is constantly pouring Its Energy into your physical brain and body, is *God Individualized* at your point in the Universe to mold this Cosmic Substance into whatever form you decree.

"To the human beings who do not or will not recognize the 'Mighty I AM Presence,' the Use, Joy, and Freedom of this great bounty by direct precipitation remains unused because their feeling of fear, doubt, hate, anger, selfishness, or lust builds an impassable wall around them, shutting out the Power and Perfection of the 'Light' which would otherwise come through.

"The Great, All-Wise Creator of Perfect Form everywhere throughout space builds those forms according to the Pattern of Perfection, which is another name for the Law of Divine Love. This always means the orderly, harmonious way of attraction. The feeling of fear, doubt, *et cetera,* is a rate of vibration which shatters form and scatters substance; hence, is diametrically opposed to Love, Harmony and Order.

"To the individual who acknowledges the 'Mighty I AM Presence'—takes a determined stand with It, and continually maintains a feeling of Divine Love in the personality—to him all that you have seen done tonight is possible of accomplishments right now in this lifetime. This banquet has been given for your encouragement, enlightenment, and strength.

"The power of precipitation used here tonight is within every individual; I assure you it is no myth. Turn to your own Mighty Master Within; this will enable you to acknowledge the 'I AM.' Continually turn to It, that Its Mighty Power may be released and the Ascended Master Wisdom come forth—directing your every activity. Break down the self-created barriers that have bound you and see what an avalanche of good the 'Mighty I AM Presence' stands always ready to pour out into your use at your conscious command when you charge your feeling with Divine Love and maintain order in the temple —your mind and body. Our good Brother Daniel Rayborn has something which He wishes to tell you."

As Rayborn arose, we felt a thrill pass through

the whole room; and for more than thirty minutes, He poured forth Marvelous Wisdom with a Force that seemed to burn the very Words into the consciousness of everyone. He spoke with a conviction that could only come from One who had more than human power. Chananda said a few words in praise and gratitude to our wonderful Guests, asking Them to be with us again soon. Saint Germain then arose and continued:

"Most Gracious Host and Friends," He began, "I wish to present the entire service used at this banquet to your Council for future use. Observe!" Instantly all the used service began reappearing on the table as clean and fresh as if it had never been used. In the midst of this joyous experience a beautiful vase of carved jade filled with wonderful pink roses appeared on each table.

"This comes to you, Our Beloved Friends," He continued, "with the Love and Blessings of the Ascended Host. May it ever be a fond memory to you all." Then with one word—"Dismissed"—the banquet was over. As quickly as our dignity permitted, we hurried to greet our Beloved Saint Germain, Nada, and Daniel Rayborn. The parents held Their children long in Their Loving Embrace —Nada the mother holding Bob in Her arms, and as She released him, said:

"My Blessed Children, I congratulate you for

your Love and Devotion to the Light. Your Reward will be very great, for at the end of the two year period of your probation, a Glorious Surprise will await you. Until then We shall see you often at your destination in India. We have Work to do now so I must say good-night and God bless you." Then bowing to Chananda and Najah, They disappeared with Saint Germain.

We thanked our Host for the wonderful evening, and it was then that He told us we were to leave early the next morning for our destination, as we had remained as long as the work permitted. We returned at once to our private car, and as Chananda bade us good-night, gave directions to breakfast en route, saying that He would return before we reached Simla.

We left at seven o'clock the next morning, hoping to stop at Benares, Lucknow, Delhi, and Simla. We received direction to lose no time but to go direct to our destination in the Himalayas where we were to make our home for many months—and nothing else was really of importance but obedience to that Command. *Unless one is seeking the Release of the Light within himself, no one can fully understand and appreciate the feeling that nothing is really important but "All of God" and those experiences by which the Light is released.*

Gaylord was to meet us at Benares on our way

north and remain with us during the rest of our stay in India. The country we passed through was very beautiful. We discussed what modern equipment could do for India, and through it she could become the garden spot of the world. Her countless rivers could make it into a Perfect Paradise; for India is beginning to feel her wings again, and her industries will rise once more. She will return to that majestic glory she has reached several times in her past, and regardless of the crushing influences that have preyed upon her in the last two or three hundred years, *India's great problem will yet be solved —in Perfect Divine Order.* Her teeming millions will be given the opportunity to express the Light and God Presence that is within them.

There is a Great Cosmic Wheel of Progress which affects our entire Earth. It governs the Expansion of the Light in the entire system to which this planet belongs. When that Wheel turns to a certain point— and it is nearer than mankind realizes—it will focus certain Rays of Energy upon the Earth. Then the resistance to greater good that is set up by puny, selfish personalities and unawakened mentalities will be as chaff before a mighty wind. The efforts of those human beings will be useless, and they will be compelled to obey a Power far greater than their own selfish cravings.

The day passed quickly, and after dinner we

gathered in Gaylord's compartment, asking him to tell us something of his own experiences. After considerable coaxing and a promise on our part not to divulge what he revealed, he described briefly one of his embodiments in South America during the time of the Incan civilization. We listened spellbound for more than three hours to the experiences of that Life, during which Leto was also in incarnation. In one part we were so fascinated by his portrayal and had so entered into the activities with him that we were all in tears before we realized it. His narrative was one of the most thrilling to which I ever listened, and at the end he told us he had in his possession the ancient records in the Incan characters to prove the principal experiences of that Life. These were of such an heroic nature, and because of the stand Leto and he had taken for the Right in that Life, the Release of the Light within both of them was revealing Its Freedom now.

The next morning Chananda greeted us and explained that He had made arrangements to take us from the train to the end of our journey at once.

"You must arrive at your destination," He announced, "before the Cosmic Cycle reaches a certain point." As we left the train at Simla, Chananda led the way to a compound some distance farther. It was surrounded by a high wall, and as we entered the gates, a caravan stood waiting for us, ready to leave immediately. The attendants brought our luggage, and we mounted small mountain ponies. Chananda gave the command to depart at once; and due to His mysterious influence, no one paid the slightest attention to us as we passed out of the city.

We soon entered the mountain fastness and for quite a while followed a beautiful stream. We kept on ascending for some distance and then suddenly, passing behind a great wall of rock extending from the side of the cliff, we came to an opening leading directly into the side of the mountain. Chananda led the way without a moment's hesitation, and soon the entire place became illumined by a Soft White Light. From all appearances, we must have followed the bed of an underground watercourse.

We entered this underground tunnel at noon and continued until four-thirty in the afternoon. As we emerged we found ourselves in a beautiful sunlit valley about four miles long and perhaps two miles at the widest point, with a lovely stream running through the center of the entire length. The climate was semi-tropical, and as the valley ran from east to west, it was filled with sunshine the greater part of the day. The north wall was a sheer cliff hundreds of feet high, and at the west end played a waterfall that looked like a bridal veil. The most rare, luscious fruits and vegetables grew in lavish abundance. I was wondering whether this was the place that Gaylord had described in telling us of his former experiences in India, when he answered my thought.

"No, this is not the place I mentioned," he said. "We are far from there." As we came nearer a great building, I called out involuntarily to the others, "This is the Palace of Light!" And much to my surprise, Gaylord replied, "Yes, that is true. It is so known by all who enter this Retreat."

As we came to the entrance of the grounds, the beauty and grandeur of the entire setting sent a thrill through us of Love and admiration for the place. We dismounted, and attendants took charge of the caravan, leading the animals to a group of smaller buildings half a mile away across the stream. Chananda led the way to the entrance, and as we came nearer, the beauty of the building held us spellbound, so magnificent was its architecture and workmanship. It was built of pure white onyx, four stories high, having a great dome in the center. As we came up the steps, the tones of a beautiful bell announced our arrival and welcomed us as guests of the Retreat. In a moment, the great door opened, and Najah stood there to greet us. Chananda gave us one of His magic radiant smiles in enjoyment of our surprise.

"This is Our Home," He commented happily. "We welcome each one of you; for it is your home as long as you desire to stay and whenever you wish to come. You will find silk Robes and undergarments in your rooms," He continued, "which you are to wear while here. They will not soil nor wear out, so have no fear in wearing them.

We were shown to our quarters on the second floor, overlooking the valley. They were a dream of beauty—exquisite, comfortable, and provided with every possible convenience and luxury. We refreshed ourselves for dinner and put on our Robes as requested. We could not refrain from comparing them with the ones in which we had been traveling. The fabric of our wonderful new Garments was a precipitated material of such quality as has never been produced by any physical means of manufacture. The fabric was unlike anything in the outside world. It was shimmering with a Dazzling Radiance, thick and soft as down inside. Each Robe was worn with a girdle of the same material, heavily jeweled, and Sandals of beautiful design were also provided to match each Robe.

The moment we placed these Robes upon our bodies a thrill of lightness passed through us making us feel as if we were about to float into the air. The effect was amazing and instantaneous. We were happy beyond words as we contemplated the wonder of the whole experience and the marvelous Power of these Blessed Ascended Masters—who are so Transcendent in Their Power and yet so humble and so natural in Their Loving Association and Friendship. While we were admiring our wonderful Garments, the chimes sounded to announce dinner. We went at once to the reception room on the first floor where the ladies of our group awaited us in similar Robes. Chananda offered His arm to Pearl and led the way to what He said was Their private dining room. It was large enough to seat at least forty people in great comfort and was magnificently decorated in white and violet. To our amazement we noticed that the chairs were similar to those in the Diamond K Ranch in America, except that they were upholstered in violet silk velvet instead of blue.

Toward one end of the room stood an enormous teakwood table, seating at least twenty people, heavily inlaid with a substance that looked like gold but was in reality a precipitated material. Toward the other end of the room was a white onyx table of the same size, the top of which was inlaid in violet and gold—it too being a precipitated substance. Just inside the position where each plate would rest was a white rose with a delicate pink center—also inlaid on the violet part—and in the center of the table were two clasped hands of most beautiful gold inlay. It is utterly impossible to put into words the beauty and Perfection of these things which are precipitated; for it is easy to produce effects entirely impossible in any other type of substance.

We took our places around the table, and Chananda poured forth an Adoration from the depths of His Heart to the Supreme Presence of Life. We in the outer world have no concept of the Adoration these Great Ascended Masters constantly pour out to the Great Giver of all Good.

Presently two dark-skinned attendants appeared with the service, following with a dinner of wonderful nut-loaf, luscious salad, hot rolls, and for dessert, the most delicious fruit pudding I have ever tasted. The drink served with the meal was what Chananda called a golden wine. It was not intoxicating, but wonderfully invigorating.

"We shall breakfast at nine and have dinner at half-past five, except on special occasions. All are to retire not later than eleven and arise at six o'clock in the morning. There will be containers filled with fresh fruit and honey cakes in your rooms every day, if at any time you should feel hungry.

"You are here to enter upon Definite Attunement and Work that will fill your Hearts with great joy; but at times it will demand your utmost strength. Tomorrow I shall show you the palace. I have received a communication announcing that tomorrow evening we shall be honored by the Presence of the Ascended Master Council, and as the Guest of Honor we shall have the Great Divine Director.

He is seldom seen, I assure you, even by those who are far advanced. I feel some *Tremendous Special Dispensation* is at hand—so tonight retire early, and you will know for the first time what it means to rest in the *Embrace of Light,* a Light which is rarely seen. Come now, and we shall go to the Chamber of Music, for Najah has heard of your splendid voices and would enjoy hearing you sing."

When we entered the music room, we saw that their organ and piano were exact duplicates of those used in Saint Germain's Retreat at the Cave of Symbols in America, and there were also several small musical instruments and a beautiful harp. Najah seated herself at the piano and ran Her fingers lightly over the keys, the instrument responding like a living thing to the magic of Her touch. Nada and Rex sang their "Arab Love Song," and the quartet followed with several numbers which we all greatly enjoyed.

"Beloved Friends," said Chananda, "you are wonderfully blest with God's Marvelous Gifts, and through them you will be able to reach and bless many in your service to mankind."

We asked if They would play for us, and They assented graciously. A glance passed between Them, and Chananda stepped to the organ, seating Himself at the instrument. They sat in meditation a few moments, perfectly motionless, and then began.

The vibrations in the atmosphere around us commenced to increase. Then the Music surged forth like an ocean of sound, as if a Great Soul were entering the Ecstasy of Eternal Freedom and the Legions of Light from out Infinity were welcoming the Ascending One as a New Sun rising within space.

They modulated from one number to another until They had played four pieces, and by the time They finished, it seemed impossible to move, so great was our attunement and happiness. We tried to express our appreciation, gratitude and joy but it was impossible to put our feeling into words. Najah understood and said humbly:

"The 'Mighty I AM Presence' does all things when there is no longer any obstruction between the human and the Master Self; for the outer is raised into the same vibratory action as the Inner Light."

With a joyous good-night and blessing to each other, we went to our rooms. I wondered if I should be able to sleep at all, so raised was the vibratory action of my body, but I dropped off before I knew it. I awakened in the morning with a very vivid consciousness of having gone forth in my Finer Body, and in doing so, entered the mountain back of the Palace of Light through a secret, massive door. I then entered a series of caves where there was evidence of a very ancient civilization—very, very ancient—beyond anything of which we had ever known in the outer world. When we met at breakfast, I asked Chananda the meaning of my experience. His face lighted up with that wonderful smile.

"My Good Friend," He explained, "you have seen a Great Truth, and I assure you it is very Real. At the appointed time you shall see with your own eyes what you have seen in that experience with the Inner Sight. Your experience convinces me of the great importance of the visit from Our Guest of Honor tonight. Truly, My Beloved Friends from America, you are ready for the full Light. I only await the Command of My Superior to unfold to you many real wonders.

"Each one of you has gone through innumerable experiences, the full memory of which is about to be revealed. You are ready to leap forward in a way that will astound you. Come now, if you are ready, and I shall show you many of the marvels that we have in this Retreat."

We went first to the dome in the center of the building; and instead of it being an ordinary observatory, we found it to be what Chananda called a Cosmic Observatory. It was filled with many instruments of which the scientists of the outer world know nothing. One of these was an Absorption

Reflector which drew the image of the desired object through the Etheric Rays and then reflected it to the observer. It was a simple thing in its construction, but not in the quality of the substance of which the instrument was composed. Chananda explained at this point that the Etheric Rays and those which are being called the Cosmic Rays by the scientists of the outer world are not the same.

There was another piece of mechanism called a Light Projector, by means of which it was possible to send either a Life-giving or a disintegrating ray to an incredible distance. There was a radio-television so Perfect that it is the marvel of all ages.

After observing several other inventions in this room we went downstairs to the next floor where we saw a great council chamber seating seven hundred people. The walls of this room were of a beautiful milk-white onyx, with the most marvelous blue trimmings. On the floor was a thick carpet of the same wonderful blue. There were no windows, and the room occupied almost the entire floor of the palace. Here again were beautiful chairs like those we had seen in the dining room, but upholstered in the soft rich blue that trimmed the rest of the room. At the side was a dais on which stood an Altar and a Golden Chair. It was the most perfect thing one could imagine. The main part of the Altar was Precipitated Gold, but the top was made of another precipitated substance, the shade of blue that borders onto violet—the substance itself emitting a Silver Radiance because of its luminosity. Around the edge was a border of Gold about two inches wide. The Chair carried out the same designs as that on the Altar; the seat was upholstered in blue and had a high back extending well above the head.

We then proceeded to the rooms on the ground level which were devoted to electrical and chemical laboratories for experimental purposes. We were passing about the central point of the west wall on this floor when I stopped suddenly.

"Here is the place where I entered the caves last night," I said to Chananda, "while I was in my Finer Body"; and with a very intense, serious expression on His face, He asked:

"Do you see any door or entrance?"

"No," I replied, "but it is there, and I know it."

Then with a smile, He looked at me rather quizzically. "You are right," He remarked. "It is there, and I am glad you are certain in your convictions. Be patient, and you shall see all."

We then returned to the great reception hall. "How is it," I asked, "that other students and people do not see the entrance to this place and find their way into such a paradise?"

"If you were to go to the entrance," He replied,

"you would not find an opening of any kind. Yesterday after we entered, it was sealed again so that it looks now like solid wall, and so far as Protection is concerned, it is as impenetrable as the wall of the mountain itself. For more than twenty centuries this valley has remained just as you see it today.

"Man can, by the use of the Light Rays, or Cosmic Currents of Light through the 'Mighty I AM Presence,' forever annihilate time, space, age, inharmony and limitation of any kind. Discord is really the first wave, or starting place of limitation. With Perfect Harmony maintained in the individual's consciousness, the Door to God's Kingdom of Perfection—the Activity of Life without any limitation—stands wide open forever."

"Now come with me," He continued. "I shall probably strain your credulity considerably, but you shall learn much if you so desire. All of you have heard about the *Arabian Nights Tale* of the Magic Carpet. I shall show you that the legend is true."

He led the way out of the palace onto a beautiful lawn in front where we saw what looked like a copper plate about fourteen feet square. The two youthful attendants brought out a gorgeous Persian silk rug of a most wonderful golden yellow. They covered the plate with it at Chananda's direction, and then He inquired:

"Is anyone afraid to come with me?" No one

answered, so we stepped upon it and gathered around Him near the center. He immediately engaged us in a very animated conversation—which was quite unusual for him—and in a moment we all began to feel lighter and lighter. We glanced down, saw that we were leaving the Earth, having risen about twenty feet in the air, and were floating smoothly along in the atmosphere. We continued to rise until we were about fifty feet above the ground, and then floated near the waterfall—which was glistening and glorious in its beauty. We continued on drifting out over the valley and enjoying its enchanting loveliness.

"Now if you are ready," continued our Host, "we shall view the mountains." We continued to rise until we were fully eleven thousand feet above the palace. The scenery that lay below us was perfectly entrancing, and the peaks of the snowcapped mountains glistened in the sunlight like diamonds.

We became absorbed in the view and Chananda's conversation; we were not aware of temperature or transportation, yet we were comfortable and did not feel any change of either altitude nor climate, our Host holding us all in His Aura, which controlled everything within it, thus causing all to experience only His own Glorious Perfection.

We circled around, returned to the palace grounds, and descended. As we stepped off the plate, our Beloved Host laughed heartily at our comments and surprise, enjoying greatly our exclamations of happiness.

"My Beloved Friends," He explained, "I assure you there is nothing mysterious or unnatural in what you have just experienced. It is all according to simple immutable, Eternal Law which every individual may set into action without any limit—if he but will."

"Why did we not feel the altitude?" someone asked.

"In God's Perfect Kingdom, which means the 'I AM Presence,' wherein there is *only Perfection*— the Feeling of Harmony—there is no awareness of change either in altitude or temperature. Thoughts of Perfection and the Feeling of Harmony are simply rates of vibration that consciousness decrees into substance, which give to energy those qualities that manifest as Perfection. Perfection cannot exist without Love, for It is the highest rate of vibration in the Universe. It is the highest and most powerful Activity and controls forever all that is less than Itself.

"Although you still have your physical bodies, while you were on the rug and in My Aura, you could only have the conscious awareness of that Perfection which My Aura is at all times; for all Ascended Masters send out only the Vibration that is the Tone of Divine Love. Hence all else must become obedient to Our Consciousness and the Perfection of Our Love.

"The next step for you will be to learn how to turn the Cosmic Key and light your way wherever you wish to go. The Key is within you. The Light is within, and also all about you. Now return to your rooms and meditate upon the Dazzling, Fathomless Mind of God—the 'Mighty I AM Presence' which is within you." We obeyed, and never have we found meditation so easy and so wonderful.

At half-past five, beautiful chimes sounded throughout the building announcing dinner. Chananda sat at the head of the table and Najah at the opposite end. We became perfectly still for about two minutes. Then an Oval of Golden Light with a shade of pink became visible and encircled the table, enveloping our heads through the entire meal. It produced the most wonderful feeling, and as we finished dinner, Chananda gave certain Directions for us to follow.

"Now return to your rooms," He said. "Lie flat on your backs with arms outstretched, and for an hour do not move a muscle. Then bathe, anoint your bodies with the Liquid Light which you will find provided for your use, and put on your Precipitated Garments."

We obeyed, and when the Liquid Light touched

our bodies, no words can ever tell the thrill of Energy and the Peace we experienced. As we finished and robed ourselves in the marvelous Garments, we could see the Soft White Light radiate from our bodies for fully three feet, from which emanated a most wonderful rose fragrance, yet each one was distinctly individual in the particular quality of the rose fragrance poured forth. Just as we finished the chimes sounded calling us to the reception room. As we entered the room we noticed the Light about the ladies was similar to our own, except that around Leto, Electra, Gaylord, and his Friend, the Radiance was much brighter and extended farther than ours.

"At seven o'clock," said Chananda, "we shall go to the Great Council Chamber." He led the way and seated us facing the Altar, placing Leto and Gaylord in the center and the rest of us on each side of them. Chananda took the end seat on the right and Najah the last one on the left. Seated directly behind us were our Beloved Master Saint Germain, Nada and Daniel Rayborn, surrounded by two hundred of the Ascended Host.

In a few moments, a Soft White Light with a touch of pink illumined the entire hall, and Chananda asked us to enter the deepest meditation of which we were capable, adoring the "Mighty I AM Presence" within our own Hearts. We became very still, and into the Stillness entered deeper and deeper. We remained in this Silence for some time, and then we heard the tones of a most wonderful Voice that thrilled every atom of our minds and bodies.

We opened our eyes and saw standing before us a Marvelous Being. This "Great Glorious Presence" was the embodiment in Perfect Balance of all Transcendent Qualities both masculine and feminine, and held focused forever under His Conscious Command the Wisdom and Power of Eternity. This Majestic Being stood fully six feet four inches in height, with wavy hair falling to the shoulders that looked like sunshine on Gold. His Robes glittered with Points of Light like great jewels that flashed continually with the tremendous Radiance of the Power held under His Control and obedient to His Conscious Direction. The Girdle encircling the waist was a mass of sapphires and diamonds, and from it hung a panel to a few inches below the knees. This also was a mass of jewels.

These Jewels, as we afterward learned, were a Condensation of Light, and one can imagine the Rays that blazed forth—constantly pouring out the Tremendous Power focused within them. This Glorious Majestic Being has become known to us as the "Great Divine Director." He is the Great Cosmic Master under whom Beloved Jesus, Saint Germain, and the Master Kuthumi Lal Singh were trained; and His Great Love and far-reaching Care often enfold many of Their students now. No words in any language can do justice to this Majestic Being, and when His Students speak of Him, they are as humble before His Mighty Light as we feel before Them. Oh! that the people of America and the world might know more of these Great Blessed Beings and share the joy that lifts me beyond the outer self! As He began speaking, He gave the Cosmic Sign of the Ascended Master, saying:

"Beloved Children of Eternal Light, great is the rejoicing of the Ascended Host at the call of this Meeting. These Blessed Ones before Me are ready for Our Assistance; for their bodies can now be raised, and they shall enter their True Freedom.

"Beloved Saint Germain, You have patiently, lovingly guided and instructed these Children of Light through the centuries, and Your Work shall bring Its Reward, for it is most nobly done.

"Is there another willing to bear witness that they are ready to enter the Light?" Chananda immediately arose as our Sponsor and replied:

"Most High Master, I bear witness as to their readiness." And the Great Divine Director continued:

"Then We shall give them Bodies such as have not been manifest before upon Earth, that they may stand before the world a Living Example—revealing the Fulfillment of the Law of Love and Light. These shall be similar to the Bodies of the Ascended Beings; yet they shall retain the appearance and some of the outer activities of the highest type of mankind.

"Under their control shall come the Unlimited Use of the Cosmic Energy and the Direction of the Mighty Light Rays. They shall minister unto humanity side by side with their Beloved Master who has so lovingly brought them to this point. Henceforth, I receive you all into My Eternal Embrace of Light. The two year period that is usually required, I now set aside. In two days you shall acquire what, under the former Activity, would have taken two years to accomplish.

"Remember, in the 'I AM Presence,' there is no time nor space. It is All-wise and All-powerful, and through It We shall remove the atomic obstruction forever.

"Brother Chananda, take them to the Cave of Light. They are to remain there for two days. You are to anoint the masculine bodies three times a day with Liquid Light, and our Sister Najah will do the same for the feminine bodies."

As the Great Divine Director finished speaking, a Ray of Dazzling Crystal White Light streamed out from His Forehead and swept the head of each one of the students; then It withdrew into His Body. Instantly this was followed by a very intense Soft Golden Ray that poured out from His Heart, sweeping the Heart area of those before Him, and again returning into His own Body. He paused for a moment and seemed to record the strength of each one. From that He knew the intensity of their own Light.

The next instant a Dazzling White Light blazed forth from His entire Being, spreading into a fan-shaped Radiance and encompassing all our bodies. Within this Mighty Stream were Currents of Energy flowing in at the feet and out at the top of the head of each student. Shadow after shadow passed off like sheaths, and the moment they left our bodies, were consumed. The color of the Light became a delicate pink, changing again into a soft gold, gradually blending into violet of a shade never seen in the outer world. Our Inner Sight and Hearing were forever cleared and made our permanent servants. Then the Light became such a Dazzling White that we were compelled to close our eyes. Presently, by an Inner Command of the "Presence," we opened them.

The Great Being before us was almost terrifying in the Majesty and Power that poured out from Him. The Ascended Guests had disappeared and we were left alone with this Dazzling Celestial Envoy of the Godhead. Then in a Voice as gentle as a mother caressing her child, He said:

"You are all—now and forever—a part of My Love, Light and Wisdom. I shall meet you in the Cave of Light in an hour." Then He drew the Stream of Light into Himself and disappeared.

"Come," said Chananda, and as we rose to our feet, we had no consciousness of weight and could have floated as easily as walked. We went to the lower floor where I had passed through the door in my experience while in my finer body. In front of us was the door, just as I had seen it. Chananda placed His hand upon it. Slowly and steadily it opened, a massive, ponderous thing weighing many tons.

We went into a narrow passage which suddenly became illumined by a Soft White Light that shone upon walls as smooth as though polished. We must have walked for nearly half a mile when we came to another door, less massive, but wonderfully carved in very ancient writing. It opened at Chananda's touch, and we entered a Cave of Wondrous Beauty, similar to the second chamber in the Cave of Symbols in America, only much larger. This Cave also contained those same symbols encrusted with that dazzling crystalline substance. Going still farther, we came to Doors of Solid Gold.

"Who seeks entrance here?" suddenly spoke a Voice from the ethers, and Chananda answered instantly: "Children of the Light—seeking more Light—Thy Light and Its Perfect Use."

"Speak the Name!" again commanded the Voice. Together we spoke the "Word." Then the Doors of Gold slowly began to open. Inside it looked like the white heat of a great furnace, and again the Voice spoke.

"All who enter here leave—forever—their earthly garments behind. Who dares to enter first?"

"I will," Bob answered instantly, and the rest followed.

Two days and two nights later, we emerged from the Eternal Flame wearing our New Bodies of Immortal Endurance. The inharmony of Earth can never register within These permanently. As we came back into the reception hall of the Palace, the Great Divine Director with our Beloved Saint Germain, Nada and Daniel Rayborn were there to greet us. The Great Being addressed us:

"Now your Real Service will begin. All but this Brother," indicating me, "are to remain here in the Palace of Light for one year. You are now True Messengers of the Great White Brotherhood. Regarding your earthly affairs, your Beloved Master Saint Germain will direct you." Making the Ascended Masters' Sign and Salutation to the Heart of the Great Central Sun, He gave us His Blessing:

"Children of the Diamond Heart!
I enfold you in the Golden Flame of My Love,
I protect you by the Armor of My Power,
I Raise you by the Hand of Your Own Divinity,
I bless you with the Fullness of My Light,
I give you the Scepter of Your Own Dominion,
I seal you in the Eternal Freedom of your Ascension,
In that Ecstasy Supreme, The Presence of the
Diamond Heart, 'I AM.'"

A Flash of Blazing Glory filled the room, quivered a moment, and He was gone. Saint Germain then turned to us and said:

"Remember, Beloved Ones, you are the Grail, the Cup of Light from which all who are athirst may drink of the Radiance of your Being; for you are now the Victory of Love. The Glory of Love sings throughout Infinity its Paean of Praise in continual adoration to Life. Obey, My Blessed Children, Its Timeless Fiat. Make the Salutation of Light to the Heart of Creation, and ever Stand True to the Immortal Decree of Love:

"O Children of the Light! O Flames of the Morning!
call unto the Secret Love Star.
Let Its Rays weave for you an Eternal Garment of
Transcendent Loveliness,

*And wear upon your Heart the Jewel of the Sacred
Fire.*

*Let Its Glory pour through you, that yours may be
the Scepter of Power Supreme.*

*Speak only the Decree of Love, that Perfection may
be everywhere.*

*Listen to the Sound of Its Voice, that all may hear
the Song of Joy,*

*Gaze only upon Its Light, that the Flame from the
Seven Elohim may rest upon your forehead.*

*Hold the Cup of Liquid Light, and forever pour
forth Its Life-giving Essence.*

*Then the Rays from the Diamond Heart shall illu-
mine your pathway, and*

*When the Knight Commander raises His Sword of
Flame, you shall pass through,*

*And stand face to face with Your Own Divinity upon
the very Altar of Life;*

*For within That Holy of Holies is the One—Omni-
potent in Blazing Glory—*

*Your Own Beloved Self, The Magic Presence—
'I AM.'*

*In the Crown of your Everlasting Victory shines a
double rainbow,*

The Result of Love's Attainment, encircled by All
  Wisdom;
Your Royal Robes of Authority are the Deeds of
  Love,
The Rays of Light from The Magic Presence—
  'I AM.'
These forever clothe all Beings with their Radiance,
And are the Fountain of Eternal Youth and Beauty;
Through them, your Scepter draws unto Love Its
  Own—
The Fullness of The Magic Presence—'I AM.'
The Rays from the Seven Builders reach up—
And pour out Their Glistening Streams of Love's
  Lightning,
Weaving Great Rivers of Force into an Imperishable
  Garment,
In Blazing Glory and Dazzling Beauty—the Gift of
  The Magic Presence—'I AM.'
O Children of the Flame! sing the Anthem of Cre-
  ation,
It is the Song of Love that makes the Music of the
  Spheres
Ring throughout space in an Adoration and Hymn
  of Praise, which is The very Worship of Life,

The Magic Presence—'I AM.'

Let It flow through you in Ever-expanding Perfection:

Be the Ecstasy and Glory of Light unto all!

Know the Secret of the One! Waft the Love-Breath of Joy everywhere: and

Feel the Great Heartbeat within the Flame, The Magic Presence—'I AM.'"

FINIS

SERIES